To Dr Finlay,

with the compliments of

the author,

Rosalind K. Marshall.

MARY OF GUISE

Rosalind K. Marshall

MARY OF GUISE

COLLINS
St James's Place, London
1977

William Collins Sons & Co Ltd
London · Glasgow · Sydney · Auckland
Toronto · Johannesburg

First published 1977
© Rosalind K. Marshall 1977
ISBN 0 00 216508 2
Set in Monotype Caslon
Made and Printed in Great Britain by
William Collins Sons & Co. Ltd, Glasgow

For Colonel Constantin of Verteillac

Contents

Tables and Maps

Illustrations

Foreword

The story of Mary of Guise is a fascinating one. She has for many years remained an enigmatic figure, now portrayed as a devious daughter of the House of Guise, now as a pious, placid woman of agreeable disposition but small talent. These two views hardly accord and, in the end, the truth is rather more interesting than either. A woman of high intellectual ability and of well-nigh irresistible charm, Mary lived her life at the centre of political events, and she influenced these events to a significant degree. Known to history primarily as the mother of Mary, Queen of Scots, she deserves recognition for her own indisputable qualities of courage and determination.

In writing her biography I have had valuable assistance from a number of people and I would particularly thank Professor Gordon Donaldson of the University of Edinburgh for reading the entire text for me and making many illuminating comments. Miss Maureen Richardson, RGN, RFN, gave me her expert analysis of the symptoms of the Queen Regent's illnesses and in so doing has afforded me a deeper understanding of Mary's last days.

Others have helped in a variety of ways, and I am especially grateful to: Monsieur J. Ciepka of the Musée de Cluny; Father Mark Dilworth, OSB; Monsieur G. Dumas of the Departmental Archives of Aisne; Monsieur Pierre Gérard of the Archives of Meurthe-et-Moselle; Dr John Imrie, Keeper of the Records of Scotland; Monsieur G. Leglaye and Monsieur Pierre Gasnault of the Bibliothèque Nationale, Paris; Mrs Betty Lowson; Dr Emily Lyle; Mr Michael Lynch of the University College of North Wales; Mrs Pauline Maclean of the Scottish Record Office; Mr A. F. Marshall; Mrs Nan

Marshall; Madame Pierre Noailles of the Société Archéologique de Vervins; Dr E. F. D. Roberts, Librarian, and Dr T. I. Rae of the National Library of Scotland; Mr R. N. Smart of St Andrews University Library; and the staff of the Archives of the Ministère des Affaires Etrangères, Paris.

In my search for illustrations I have had the kind assistance of Mr Robin Hutchison, Keeper, and my other colleagues in the Scottish National Portrait Gallery; Mr James Holloway of the Department of Prints and Drawings, the National Gallery of Scotland; Mr P. Cameron of the Department of the Environment Photographic Library, Edinburgh; and Mrs Caroline Pilkington of the Courtauld Institute, London.

The following owners have allowed me to reproduce pictures and objects in their collections: His Grace the Duke of Hamilton; the Marquess of Bath; the Abbot of Fort Augustus; the Bibliothèque Nationale, Paris; the Trustees of the British Museum; the Department of the Environment; the Departmental Archives of Haut-Marne; the Trustees of the National Galleries of Scotland; the Trustees of the National Museum of Antiquities of Scotland; the National Trust; and the anonymous owner of a private collection.

For permission to quote extracts from printed books and from original manuscripts, I would thank the Trustees of the National Library of Scotland; and the Council of the Scottish History Society. Quotations from Crown-copyright records in the Scottish Record Office appear by permission of the Controller of HM Stationery Office.

Mrs Ann Munro produced a meticulous typescript of the entire text of this book, and it is with pleasure that I take this opportunity of thanking her for the excellence of her work.

The publishers acknowledge the financial assistance of the Scottish Arts Council in the publication of this volume.

R.K.M.

Edinburgh,
June 1976

NOTE

I have modernized the spelling in all quotations and, where necessary, have translated
quotations in sixteenth-century French and
Latin into modern English, following the
original documents rather than the printed
text where any divergences between the two
occurred.

1

The House of Guise

On 20 November 1515 in the Castle of Bar-le-Duc, perched
high on its rock above the River Ornain, the young Countess
of Guise gave birth to a daughter. The baby was her first, and
as she lay in her great bed watching her women bustling around
the child, Antoinette was well content. The dangers of the last
few months were now past. Not only had she come safely
through childbirth, but her husband had miraculously survived
near-mortal wounds in battle. In this tranquil interlude she
could plan happily for her daughter's future and she could
reflect on recent events with a deep feeling of gratitude, her
mind dwelling thankfully on the husband she had so nearly
lost.

Claud, Count of Guise, was nineteen, a younger son with an
interesting heritage. His father René had possessed the vast
territories of Lorraine, an independent duchy on the German
borders of France, and he had also inherited extensive lands
in France itself. In addition, René laid claim to the kingdoms
of Naples and Jerusalem, and it was his custom to style himself
by yet another of his titles, King of Sicily. He married twice.
When his first wife, Jeanne d'Harcourt, failed to produce any
children he divorced her and married Philippa of Gueldres, a
lady of great beauty. Philippa succeeded where Jeanne had
failed, and bore her husband eleven children. Unfortunately,
René's previous marriage complicated matters. The papal bull
confirming his divorce did not come through for several
years, by which time his eldest surviving son, Antony, had
been born. Jeanne was still alive, which meant that, in future,
doubts might be cast on Antony's legitimacy. There was no
such shadow over the birth of the next son, Claud, for by then

Jeanne was dead. It therefore seemed possible that one day Claud might contest his brother's right to inherit the family honours and estates.

Fearing some such difficulty, René decided to divide his possessions between his two elder sons. Antony would inherit the dukedom of Lorraine, both estates and titles, along with the claims to the foreign kingdoms. Claud would become a naturalized Frenchman and would receive the lands in France.[1]

Two years after he made his Will, René died. It was 1508, and from this time onwards Claud was to be a figure of growing significance at the French Court. In accordance with his father's wishes he settled there, and it was not long before he became the favoured companion of the heir to the throne, the future Francis I. He was, indeed, closely connected with Francis, for their mothers were cousins. Claud was soon popular with everyone – the royal family, the nobles, the Court officials, the merchants and the townspeople of Paris itself. It has been said that on his arrival at Court he set out to make a deliberate study of his new companions, noting their temperaments and their tastes, cultivating their friendship by careful forethought.[2] This is to put too cold-blooded an interpretation on events. From the beginning Claud possessed that powerful charm which was to be a characteristic of the Guise family throughout several generations. He and they had what is often called 'the common touch', the ability to be at ease with all sections of society and to win the affection and support of ordinary men and women as well as of high-born friends. Nor was there anything calculated or contrived about the Guise charm: it was entirely natural, an innate quality which was to prove of immense value to those who possessed it.

Part of Claud's success may be attributed to his sheer physical impressiveness. He was very tall, well-built yet elegant, and he had considerable presence. A drawing of him made when he was in his prime shows handsome, resolute features. His face is broad, with high cheekbones. The eyes are keen and intelligent, and the neat, square-cut beard enhances the impression of determination given by the firm mouth and chin.[3]*

Needless to say, Claud's personal magnetism did not go unnoticed among the ladies of the Court. By the time he was seventeen it was rumoured that he would marry Louis XII's daughter, but it was not a royal princess who became his bride shortly afterwards. On 9 June 1513 he signed a contract promising to marry Antoinette of Bourbon, sister of the Count of Vendôme.[4] Antoinette was two years older than Claud, a smallish, auburn-haired girl with strong, aquiline features. She brought with her only a modest dowry, but her lineage was impeccable. She was a descendant of an earlier French King, St Louis, and she was already distantly related to the Guise family. She was highly intelligent, she was warm-hearted, and her organizing abilities were to be a great asset to her husband in the future. She had met Claud for the first time a few months before, and Court gossip now declared that this was a love match, hinting that the Count had refused the offer of the royal princess in order to marry Antoinette. Their wedding took place with much magnificence in the Church of St Paul, in Paris.

Because of his close friendship with the King's son Francis, it was only to be expected that Claud would remain at Court. Not for Antoinette, however, the idle, pleasure-filled days there: she required a more active role in life and she expressed the desire to live on her husband's estates, where she could take a personal interest in the activities and welfare of his tenants. This was a normal enough procedure, but it did present something of a problem. There was no obvious residence for Antoinette, for her mother-in-law, Philippa of Gueldres, retained possession of the principal castle at Joinville, which had been settled on her when she married René. Since she had been widowed she had stayed there, running Claud's estates for him. Obviously she could not be displaced, so Duke Antony came to his brother's rescue and offered him his castle of Bar-le-Duc.

There Antoinette made her first married home. Claud still

*See Plate opposite p. 32

spent much of his time with the King, but he joined her whenever he could and she went to Court herself for important ceremonial occasions. When she had been married for almost two years, Antoinette discovered to her joy that she was expecting a child. That summer, Claud had to explain to her that he could not be with her in the final stages of her pregnancy as they had both hoped: he had to march south with the French King. Louis XII had died, Francis I was now on the throne and he was determined to renew yet again his country's claims to the duchy of Milan. He intended to invade Italy in the autumn. A practical woman, Antoinette understood and she bore their parting bravely. Her subsequent anxiety was inevitable, but she occupied her mind with day-to-day affairs. Time passed, and it was only a month before her child was due that they brought her desperate news. Claud had been wounded and was lying critically ill. The doctors despaired of his life.

Accompanied by his two brothers, Duke Antony and young Ferry, the Count had marched south with the royal army. Shortly after entering Italy, on 13 September 1515, they were attacked at Marignano by Swiss mercenaries in the employ of the Duke of Milan. The ensuing struggle lasted from eleven in the morning until darkness fell. The soldiers rested that night in their armour, French and Swiss lying side by side in the confusion. When dawn came, fighting resumed and it was not until afternoon that the Swiss were finally driven back on the arrival of French reinforcements.

By that time, both sides had suffered heavy losses and among the wounded and the dying lay Claud of Guise. They told Antoinette afterwards that he had received twenty-one wounds. His right arm was shattered, his thigh pierced by a ball from an arquebus and his horse had been killed under him, pinning him to the ground as they fell. While the battle raged around them, his German esquire Adam Fouvert lay down and covered Claud's body with his own. The enemy surged forward and Adam died beneath the horses' hoofs.

As soon as the fighting ceased Duke Antony sent out his men to search the battlefield for his brothers, and the King himself told members of his own retinue that they must help.

According to tradition it was a Scottish gentleman of the royal household by the name of James Scott who found them at last, lying together. Ferry was dead and it seemed at first that Claud was also beyond help. However, the anxious searchers discovered that he was breathing faintly still. They carried him carefully to Duke Antony's tent, and the royal doctors were hastily summoned. They shook their heads over the gravity of his condition, but they did all they could for him. As they struggled for his life messengers were sent to Bar-le-Duc to tell his Countess what had happened.[5]

Antoinette was a strong woman and a devout one. She sought consolation in prayer and it seemed to her that her prayers were answered. Contrary to all expectations, Claud recovered consciousness and began to recuperate with a rapidity which surprised everyone. By the beginning of November he was able to leave his bed and a month after the battle he took part in the royal procession when the French entered Milan. Claud rode proudly at the side of Francis I, splendidly arrayed in white velvet and cloth of gold, his heroic aspect emphasized by the fact that his arm was in a sling and his leg heavily bandaged.[6]

For Antoinette, the birth of her daughter therefore brought a double measure of rejoicing, nor was Claud's survival at Marignano merely a matter of personal relief for his wife. Perhaps from that day dates the real fame of the House of Guise. Later centuries have coloured and exaggerated the reputation of the family. For Catholics, Claud was to become the Christian hero, the protector of the Faith, the soldier of God, appearing at the head of his army in a nimbus of light, a flaming sword in his hand. For Protestants he was to be the Great Butcher, the savage murderer of the innocent, the rapacious, Machiavellian leader of a group of treacherous schemers. Religious controversy has shaped and distorted posterity's view of this family more than most, so it is all the more important to discard preconceptions and to remember that in the winter of 1515 the name of Guise had none of the sinister overtones which it was later to acquire.

Rather, Claud was the handsome and popular hero of the

day, on the threshold of a brilliant military career and establishing a family of his own. He could not, of course, get back to Bar-le-Duc in time for his daughter's christening, but the knowledge of his restoration to health mitigated for Antoinette the pain of his absence. After all, she had the company of other members of the family. Her own mother, Mary of Luxemburg, had come to Bar for the birth and so had Claud's mother, Philippa of Gueldres. These two formidable ladies would stay on to act as godmothers. Claud's brother John, the Bishop of Metz, would be godfather and the ceremony would be performed by a cousin of Antoinette's who was Bishop of Châlons.

So it was that when she was just twelve days old, the baby daughter of the Count of Guise was christened in the castle church at Bar-le-Duc. She was called Mary, from the Virgin Mary and after her grandmother, Mary of Luxemburg, and she was to be known to history as Mary of Guise or Mary of Lorraine.[7]

Several months were to elapse before Claud had his first sight of his daughter. After the triumphal entry into Milan, Francis I visited the Pope, then he made a leisurely progress northwards. Pageants and celebrations accompanied him all the way, but when they arrived at Lyons Claud sought permission to return to his estates. Antoinette had gone to the castle at Joinville, presumably taking her daughter with her, and it was there that the family were reunited. Claud spent two days with them, recounting his experiences, before setting out on a pilgrimage to the Church of St Nicholas, 25 leagues from Joinville. As he had lain wounded in Italy, he had sworn that if he ever saw his own country again he would walk to St Nicholas, wearing his full armour. In thanksgiving for his recovery, he kept his promise.[8]

The pilgrimage accomplished, Claud spent some further time with his wife, then he returned to Court and Antoinette went back to Bar-le-Duc. The previous pattern of their life was resumed, but now Antoinette had her little daughter to occupy her attention. Far from consigning the child to the care of nurses, Antoinette took a deep personal interest in all she did, and this probably accounts to some extent for the particularly close relationship which mother and daughter were always to enjoy.

For the next four years, Mary of Guise was her parents' only child. Most of this time she spent with her mother at Bar-le-Duc, but in the winter of 1519 when Antoinette was pregnant again the family's domestic circumstances underwent a considerable alteration. In December of that year, Claud's mother made a decision which astonished her family, although it was not really so surprising in itself. She made up her mind to enter a convent.

Throughout her life, Philippa had been an upright, devout woman and more than a hint of her character is found in the device she adopted and in the motto she chose for herself. Her emblem was the leaf of a thistle, and above it were placed the words 'Do not touch me, or I will prick'. No details of her own early life are known, but it can be assumed that, like her cousin Louise of Savoy, she was a well-educated, well-read woman. Her children were still very young when she was widowed, so she was appointed their guardian and she ran their estates with vigour and determination. Increasingly, however, her health began to fail. She suffered from dropsy, she had severe headaches and she experienced bouts of giddiness. This probably influenced her decision to retire to a convent.

Telling her family that she needed a change of air, she went to Pont-au-Mousson, twenty-five kilometres north of Nancy, to stay with the Poor Clares. A few days after her arrival there, she announced to the nuns that she wished to spend the rest of her life with them, as a member of their community. She then returned to Nancy, where Duke Antony lived, to put her affairs in order. On reaching home she summoned all her sons, and when they had gathered together she told them of her decision. They were astounded. Certainly the Church provided a fine career for an intelligent girl who could become an abbess, but Philippa's circumstances and her ambitions were very different. She was already fifty-eight, and she had chosen a cloistered Order devoted to poverty. The Poor Clares had been founded by St Clare, the friend of St Francis, who had given them their Rule. They renounced all their possessions and lived under the strictest conditions. They received visitors only under special circumstances, they slept on straw mattresses on top of bare boards, their clothes were of the coarsest and their food was of the plainest.

Philippa's sons did their best to dissuade her. They pointed out that her fragile health would never stand up to the rigours of the convent. They urged her to choose a less ascetic way of life, to live in a much less strict convent as an honoured guest, not as a novice. They pleaded that she was needed still at the head of the family's affairs.

Philippa remained adamant and on 15 December 1519 she was formally received into the Order. Her family all attended the service. Her youngest son was only twelve, and he wept bitterly throughout. Philippa gave her sons and their wives her blessing, then she retired to her cell. She was to spend the next twenty-seven years in the convent at Pont-au-Mousson.[9]

Shocked as Claud seems to have been at his mother's decision, he must have welcomed the attendant alteration in his own circumstances. The castle at Joinville with all its revenues now belonged to him outright. Bar-le-Duc reverted to Duke Antony, and Antoinette could now move to Joinville.

Mary of Guise was four when she went to live at Joinville, and to her it was always home. Bar-le-Duc had been an impressive fortress, but Joinville was a civilized, domestic place in pleasant surroundings. The elegant, turreted castle stood on a low hill above the River Marne. With its graceful towers, its tapering spires and its steeply pitched roofs it seemed almost to float above the little town of Joinville. In the centre was a massive round tower of obvious antiquity. 'Jovin's Tower', the local people called it, believing that it dated from Roman times when a Roman consul named Jovin had been connected with the district. According to some accounts the castle had been founded in the ninth century, but it is probable that the building known to Mary of Guise dated rather from the eleventh century. The lord of Joinville of that time had certainly felt the attraction of his castle there and, riding away to the Crusades, he had declared to his companions that he dared not look back lest his resolution melt away at the sight of his beloved home.

That same lord, John of Joinville, founded the castle chapel. This was, in fact, a small church with a tapering, hexagonal spire. It was rededicated to St Louis, and later generations of the family added to the splendours of its interior decoration, bestowing on it precious relics and jewelled images. Claud was passionately fond of church music, so when he and Antoinette moved to Joinville they installed nine canons and five choristers to sing the daily services.

By that time, of course, the castle had been considerably enlarged since the days of John of Joinville. The old tower was surrounded by attractive, two-storey buildings with narrow, round towers at almost every angle. The principal chambers were in a wing of the building which looked out towards the east, and a covered passageway led from it to the chapel. Behind the chapel was a small cemetery, and surrounding it and the main buildings were the gardens. There were flower gardens, vegetable gardens and orchards, nor were there merely apple and plum trees. Oranges, lemons and pomegranates grew in profusion at Joinville.

Beyond the protective perimeter wall, the ground sloped gently downwards to the river. The upper slopes, immediately outside the wall, were covered with vineyards, but on the lower slopes stood the town of Joinville. Three main streets ran parallel to the river, with a network of narrow lanes connecting them at right angles. The imposing parish church of Our Lady, founded by the Guise family, dominated the entire town with its lofty, Gothic tower. Beside the church was the market place. At the foot of the slope, the river flowed along, dividing into two broad streams and thus creating an island where there were more houses and gardens. On the far side of the river were further vineyards, then the rolling, wooded countryside of north-east France.[10]

In these pleasant surroundings, Mary of Guise spent her childhood, in the midst of a large and loving family. When she was four, Antoinette gave birth to a son. The heir to the Guise

THE HOUSE OF GUISE

(1) Jeanne d'Harcourt, = René, King of Sicily = (2) Philippa of Gueldres
Countess of Tancarville   and Duke of Lorraine
(marriage dissolved)

Antony,   Claud, Count and later   John, Bishop of Metz   Ferry
Duke of Lorraine   Duke of Guise   and later Cardinal of Lorraine
                         =
                  Antoinette of Bourbon

MARY   Francis,   Charles,   Louis,   Francis,   Renée,
OF GUISE   Duke of   Archbishop of   Bishop of Troyes   Grand Prior   Abbess of
(b. 1515)   Aumale   Rheims and later   and later   General of   St. Peter,
              and later   Cardinal of Guise Cardinal of Guise the Galleys   Rheims
              of Guise   then Lorraine   (b. 1527)   (b. 1534)   (b. 1538)
              (b. 1519)   (b. 1524)

        Louise   Claud,   Antoinette,   René,   Peter
        (b. 1520)   Duke of Aumale   Abbess of   Marquis of Elboeuf died young
                        (b. 1526)   Faremoutiers   (b. 1536)
                                         (b. 1531)

estates, he was named Francis, in honour of the King. The following year Antoinette had another daughter, the first of her children to be born at Joinville. On 22 January 1521 this baby was baptized Louise in the castle chapel. As at the christening of Mary of Guise, Antoinette's mother was to act as godmother but this time, of course, the other grand-mother could not be present. Philippa was in her convent and so the second godmother was 'Mademoiselle de Guyse' – the five-year-old Mary of Guise. In the years which followed, Antoinette had two more daughters, Renée and Antoinette, as well as seven more sons. Peter and Philip died in childhood, but Charles, Claud, Louis, Francis and René survived to adult life.[11]

Happily established in her castle, Antoinette brought up this large family with energy and affection. She talked to her children, played with them, scolded them, nursed them when they were ill and in all this she was helped by her capable eldest daughter. Antoinette's family was spread out, often with three years between the births of her various children. The result was that Mary was eleven by the time her third brother was born, twenty-one when her youngest brother appeared and twenty-three when the last child, Renée, arrived. She was always very much the elder sister, having an almost maternal relationship with the smallest members of her family.

Apart from the numerous children, the household at Joinville was an extensive one, consisting as it did of over a hundred servants. There were cooks and butlers, grooms and footmen, Three secretaries helped the Count and Countess with their correspondence and with estate business, two doctors, a surgeon and an apothecary were at hand when anyone fell sick, and there were ushers and choristers, pantry-men and pages.[12] Antoinette made sure that this large establish-ment was run with the maximum efficiency, but even this did not occupy all her time. She was very much concerned with the administration of her husband's estates, for his career at Court and in the royal army was exceedingly expensive and had to be financed from his private revenues.

Antoinette performed this task with great success. In

sixteenth-century France as in sixteenth-century Scotland it was customary for a nobleman to spend a good deal of time at Court. In his absence someone had to run his affairs for him. Sometimes it was a trusted steward or agent who acted in this capacity, but more often the nobleman would leave everything in the hands of his wife or mother. In this way, any number of vigorous, intelligent women set about the administration of farms and property, protecting their husbands' interests and at the same time enjoying a satisfying outlet for their energies. Some ladies may have sat at home sewing until their husbands returned, but many would have found such an idea absurd, and Antoinette was one of them. In 1520 Claud therefore drew up a document appointing his wife to act as his representative in all his business, and a few months later he had their marriage contract altered, making over to her the castle and the lands of Joinville.[13]

So successfully indeed did Antoinette manage their affairs that she not only raised enough money to finance her husband's career at Court and run her own household, but even had enough left over to think of making improvements at Joinville. She laid out fine new gardens below the castle and added a new eastern façade to the main wing, with an elegant gallery looking out over the vineyards and the town below.

From her earliest days, Mary of Guise therefore saw as a normal state of affairs a woman managing all manner of important financial, legal and household matters. It would only be natural if she grew up with the expectation that one day she herself would fulfil a similar role as the wife of a great French nobleman.

That lay in the future, however, and as a child she was happy with the varied and secure life in her mother's household. The busy routine at Joinville was further enlivened by visits from her parents' relatives. Mary of Luxemburg often came to stay, while Duke Antony and his family were fairly close by at Nancy. The greatest pleasure of all, though, was when Claud came home. These occasions were less frequent than they would have wished, for after his triumphant return from Marignano the Count had resumed his life in the King's immediate circle, accompanying him on his constant progresses through the realm. Francis, the great Renaissance prince, was the centre of a glittering Court. He lived magnificently and he gathered around him writers, artists and scholars. He collected the finest paintings of the Italian school and his agents scoured Europe for sculpture, pictures and manuscripts. He combined with his passion for the arts a love of gaiety and enjoyment.[14] He was devoted to hunting, to music and to women. He was married, of course, and he had a young family, but he also sought the company of a long series of mistresses, procured for him, it was said, by Claud's brother John. A Bishop at four and a Cardinal by the time he was twenty, John shared to the full the King's love of luxury and sophistication. He lived in splendour in the Hôtel de Cluny in Paris, patronizing the arts, distributing his wealth with a lavish hand and forming a variety of liaisons on his own account.[15]

Claud was rather different in temperament. Certainly he played a leading part in the hunting, the masques and the entertainments of Court, and he had his share of mistresses, but he was discreet. His attachments were not with the ladies of the Court but with girls from ordinary families whose names have been lost to history. Only one illegitimate son is recorded, Claud, named after himself.

For all that he might enjoy the attractions of the Court, he was his mother's son. He had a deeply religious nature and his pilgrimage after Marignano was only one of many evidences of his piety. In later life he was to wear an iron band round his upper arm as a reminder of the sins of his youth, but when he died his eulogist spoke at length of his temperate way of life. Whenever he could, he escaped to Joinville and the simple, domestic pleasures of his family.[16]

His enemies, of course, were quick to point out that self-indulgence was of less interest to him than personal advancement. He was undeniably proud of his position, and he was ambitious. His wife and children regretted his absences, but they watched with pride the development of his military career. The campaign culminating in Marignano was but the first of many in which he took part, although he never again fought in Italy. With the death of the Holy Roman Emperor, Maximilian I, in 1517 Francis I began his struggle with his great rival, Charles V. At first they competed for the imperial crown, then, when Charles succeeded in having himself elected Emperor, Francis had to fight against complete encirclement by his enemy. By 1521 war was raging on all the country's frontiers, and Claud marched with an army into Spain. His courage on that occasion was praised by the Queen Mother herself, and brought him financial rewards along with military honours.

The following year found him waging war against the English in the north of France, then against the Imperial armies in the east. The King granted him vice-regal powers in his own area and when Francis invaded Italy in 1525 and was taken prisoner, it was Claud who acted as the principal adviser to the Queen Regent. During that time, a new threat arose from a rather different quarter. For several years past the doctrines of Martin Luther had been finding increasing support in Germany and now the peasants actually rose in revolt against the Emperor, turning at the same time to invade Lorraine. As soon as Duke Antony alerted him to the danger, Claud felt that he must hurry home to defend his family's lands. The Council of Regency saw things rather differently and forbade him to use the nation's forces to defend an independent duchy. This placed him in a difficult position, so he resolved to seek the opinion of his oldest and most trusted adviser, his mother. Even in the seclusion of her convent Philippa was not proof against the demands of her affectionate, importunate family. Claud and Duke Antony rode at once to Pont-au-Mousson and explained the situation to her. Should he obey the Council of Regency, Claud asked, or should he defend Lorraine against the Lutherans? Philippa did not hesitate. Some illnesses could be cured by gentle care, she told them, but others required more radical treatment. Heresy resembled a gangrene which must be destroyed with fire or with iron. She therefore urged them to march against the Lutherans.

From that moment, Claud seems to have adopted her attitude towards the Protestants as his own. Heresy was a disease to be rooted out. He was not a cruel man and he had no desire to persecute his enemies, but he firmly believed that the Protestants must be destroyed and that he was God's instrument for that destruction.

The short war which followed was a further triumph for him and in the mood of elation which greeted him on his return to Paris, all criticisms of his behaviour in leaving were for the time being forgotten. Parliament congratulated him, the Pope congratulated him and when Francis I returned from his captivity he rewarded his valour by creating him Duke, granting him additional revenues from the royal demesne itself so that he might live more easily in the style befitting his new dignity.[17]

Such then, was the background to Mary of Guise's childhood. Spending her days in the loving, protective circle of mother, brothers and sisters, there was nevertheless a constant awareness of the world beyond. There was continual anxiety when Claud was away on a campaign, and even the shadow of personal danger when war threatened the immediate neighbourhood. On one occasion Antoinette and her sister-in-law were able to look down from the Castle of Neufchâteau on a battle which took place beneath its very walls as Claud drove back the Imperial armies. Pride in their father's military achievements, pride in their family's position were natural sentiments for the Guise children, along with a firm belief in God and the knowledge that no one must value too highly the glories of the impermanent world here on earth.

Her parents' insistence on the spiritual values was at the forefront of their minds when they came to consider how to educate Mary of Guise. Some girls simply remained at home, learning from their mothers how to run a household and how to please their husbands. That was an old-fashioned way of doing things, though, and it was now important that a girl should be well-educated, even more so when she was as obviously intelligent as Mary was. There would probably come a time when she would marry and go to live at Court. Her best protection against the moral dangers there would be a sound Christian education. It was the custom for noblemen to send their daughters to be taught by nuns, and for Claud's eldest child this seemed to be the obvious course. He and Antoinette therefore resolved to send her to her grandmother at Pont-au-Mousson.

As Claud's visit to discuss the dangers of heresy had shown, Philippa remained a force to be reckoned with even though she had entered her cloistered order as a tired, sick woman. Her biographer was to note with pardonable satisfaction that after she went to the convent 'she became as a young girl'.[18] This was no doubt something of an exaggeration, but the strict regime obviously suited Philippa and her health improved enormously. She was now living the life she had longed for, in all its austerity. Her anxious sons had obtained from the Pope a special dispensation releasing her from the severities of the novitiate. This she ignored, and lived exactly as the other entrant nuns did.

One day her son John, the Cardinal, came to visit her at Pont-au-Mousson. Showing him over the convent buildings, Philippa pointed out a rough straw mattress on the plain wooden boards of the dormitory floor. That, she indicated, was where she slept. The Cardinal was shocked. He thought of his own beds with their fine feather mattresses, their linen sheets, their comfortable pillows and their embroidered hangings. He looked again at the straw mattress. The contrast was unbearable. Something must be done. Prince of the Church that he was, he hurried back to his luxurious Hôtel but he did not install a straw mattress in his bedchamber. Instead, he ordered a magnificent bed to be sent to his mother. When it arrived, Philippa smiled wryly but she was not surprised. She knew her son. She slept in the magnificent bed for one night so that she would not offend him, then she returned to her straw mattress on the bare boards.

Even when the Mother Superior felt impelled to urge her to have her garments made of less coarse cloth, Philippa refused and continued to dress in the poorest of materials. Apart from surprising her own family with her austerity, she gained something of a reputation as a visionary. She foresaw the death of her youngest son in battle and foretold various other momentous events. It was scarcely surprising that the King of France himself came to consult her in moments of crisis. She was a formidable woman.

Philippa of Gueldres was to play an important part in the upbringing of her granddaughter. 'In such a school . . . and from such a mistress,' Mary of Guise's eulogist was to declare, 'did she [Mary] learn from her youth the love and fear of God.'[19] How old Mary was when she went to Pont-au-Mousson is unknown, but whatever her age she found herself in a different world from the one she had known at Joinville. She probably missed her young brothers and sisters a good deal, but with her lively mind she was no doubt intrigued by the novelty of her surroundings. Certainly the girls who went to be educated in convents were not normally expected to share the nuns' conditions, but one could scarcely imagine Philippa permitting her charge much in the way of physical comfort.

A good deal of Mary's time would be spent in religious studies and in attending services, but the Poor Clares occupied themselves with practical tasks too. Philippa was often to be found doing the cooking, weeding the garden or helping with the laundry and a strong, healthy girl like Mary would no doubt be called upon to assist with all manner of domestic tasks.

It may be that when they sent her to the convent, Claud and Antoinette had thoughts of a career in the Church for their daughter. Like many a well-born girl before her, Antoinette's own sister had become an abbess and eventually two of Mary's sisters occupied similar positions. If any plans of this sort did cross their minds, they were destined to be unfulfilled, for Mary's time with the nuns ended abruptly.

One day, when she was about fourteen, Duke Antony and his wife decided to pay a visit to Pont-au-Mousson. They had not been there for some months, apparently, and as well as enjoying a reunion with Philippa, they met their niece once more. They were immediately impressed. Since they had last seen her, Mary had become a young woman. She had always been a large child: now she was a very tall, handsome girl nearly six feet in height. She had her father's reddish-gold hair and broad cheekbones, and her slightly tilted, blue-grey eyes added to her attraction. As they talked to her, both Antony and his wife noted her intelligence and her quick wit and they realized that she had inherited all Claud's irresistible charm. Husband and wife exchanged meaningful looks and were quick to express their opinion. It was ridiculous to keep a fine young woman like this hidden away in a convent. A promising future awaited a personable, high-born girl like Mary, who could be an immense asset to her family. Any man would be glad to have her for his wife so she could be most useful in making a matrimonial alliance with some powerful family.

Philippa, of course, was reluctant to agree to their plans but in the end she acquiesced. Perhaps Mary had added her own pleas to those of her uncle. Certainly, when Duke Antony and his Duchess rode back to Nancy, they took their niece with them. Henceforth, she would live at their Court and when the time came they would arrange a suitable marriage for her. Duke Antony lived in considerable state. His establishment was at once more formal and more opulent than the household at Joinville, but Mary now had the company of his six children and she probably enjoyed to the full a life which was infinitely more lively than the one she had known at Pont-au-Mousson.[20]

While she was at Nancy, her relatives prepared her carefully for the event which would launch her in the world – her first appearance at the royal Court. Early in 1531, when she was just fifteen, Duke Antony decided that the time was right. Francis I was about to marry for the second time. Two years earlier, the hostilities with the Emperor had temporarily ceased when he and Charles signed the Treaty of Madrid. Among the provisions of this treaty was a clause stating that Francis, now a widower, should marry the Emperor's sister, Eleanor of Austria. The marriage took place at the beginning

MONSEIGNEVR·DE·GVISE

Claude de lorraine
5.e fils de Rene II. né le 20. 8.bre 1469. mort le 12. avril 1550.

Claud, Duke of Guise, Mary's father, by an unknown artist

16.

Antoinette, Duchess of Guise, Mary's mother: a sixteenth century copy
of a drawing by an unknown artist

of 1531 in an abbey near Bordeaux and in February the Court travelled northwards for the coronation of the new Queen.

It would be the event of the year, and the ideal opportunity for Mary of Guise to make her first public appearance. All the nobility were flocking to St Denis for the ceremony, and the Guise family were no exceptions. Old Mary of Luxemburg set out for the Court, so did Antoinette; and when Duke Antony and his wife came they brought Mary of Guise with them. There was a joyous family reunion and on 5 March Mary excitedly took her place at St Denis to watch her father and her uncle play a leading part in the Queen's coronation. Afterwards she was presented to the King and Queen, and it was agreed that she would ride with the other ladies in the royal procession when the Queen made her formal entry into Paris.

To everyone's dismay, this event was delayed for several days. The weather was particularly bad that year. So torrential was the rain, in fact, that the procession had to be postponed not just once but three or four times. At last, however, conditions improved slightly and the royal officials decided that the entry could now take place. It was still very cold and wet, so Antoinette, who was pregnant, decided to remain in her lodgings. Her daughter was undeterred, and that morning her ladies helped her to put on a mantle of purple velvet under a surcoat of ermine, both heavily encrusted with jewels. Thus attired, Mary rode into Paris behind the Queen, and that evening she attended the royal banquet, one of her cousins acting as her escort.[21]

Her public life had begun. She now found herself at perhaps the most civilized and elegant Court in Europe. The splendour of the royal palaces in Paris, the magnificence of the King's favourite residence at Fontainebleau, the thronging crowds of fashionably-clad noblemen, the artists and poets and scholars who surrounded the King – all were a revelation to her. Joinville and Nancy were fine castles but the wonderful Renaissance palaces of Francis I surpassed all others. The walls were hung with tapestries threaded with gold; there were cabinets of jewels in the chambers; paintings by Raphael and

Leonardo in the galleries; fine, gilded leather-bound books in the libraries.

For the first time Mary was able to observe for herself the machinations, the intrigues and the pretences of fashionable, sophisticated people. She learned the value of discretion, of temporizing. At Joinville, she and her mother had always enjoyed an honest, open expression of their opinions. She saw now that frankness was not well-received by courtiers and she realized that there were occasions when it would be better to remain silent rather than to speak her mind. She learned how to smile and dissemble. People flattered her and fawned on her because she was the daughter of an important man, yet she was aware of undercurrents of jealousy and hostility. There were many who envied the good fortune of the Duke of Guise and his family and Mary was astute enough to recognize insincerity when she saw it.

Nevertheless, her own natural tact and warmth of character won her many friends. The King treated her almost as his own daughter, and the ladies of the Court were charmed by her wit and her high spirits. All in all, she was a great success. It is therefore surprising that Mary did not marry almost at once. Child marriages were still frequent and the general feeling was that once a girl had reached maturity there was no point in delaying further. Sometimes, of course, a loving family was unwilling to part with a beloved daughter, and this may have been the case where Mary was concerned. After all, her mother had not married until she was nineteen. Then again, there were financial considerations. For all his exalted position, Claud was not an outstandingly wealthy man, and he could not provide Mary with a large dowry. This may have restricted the offers made for her, and her parents would naturally be very selective when considering a possible husband.

Whatever the reason, Mary was to remain unmarried for the next two and a half years. It would be interesting to know how much of this time she spent at Court, but in the absence of evidence it can only be assumed that she divided her time between the royal circle and her own family. Francis I was as restless as ever, and some months after his second marriage he set off on a series of progresses throughout his realm. For the next three years the Court moved with him through Picardy, Normandy, Champagne and Provence. Mary probably accompanied the Queen when the royal household was in Paris or in the north-east of France, but the fragmentary accounts from Joinville which still survive show that she would often be at home with her mother. A brief glimpse of Mary is afforded by the family's account for 1532. On 1 June that year she, her parents and her brothers and sisters spent the day together at a little place called Roches, on their estates. None of their activities that day is recorded, but it is noted that they dined on cheese and eggs, trout pastries, figs and strawberries.[22] They were probably making a short tour of their estates as they had often done in previous summers when the children were younger.[23]

By the beginning of 1534, they must all have felt that the question of Mary's marriage could not be deferred for much longer. She was now eighteen and four years had passed since Duke Antony had decided to find her a husband as soon as possible. Because of her family's position, it was to be expected that the King would take a hand in the matter and might select an eligible bridegroom for her. Among those who had played a principal part in the Queen's coronation that day at St Denis had been Louis, Duke of Longueville. This young man was Grand Chamberlain of France and although he had no royal blood, he was a descendant of the heroic Count of Dunois who had driven the English out of the north of France in Joan of Arc's time. Louis was himself a younger son, but his elder brother had died fighting in Italy at the age of sixteen. Louis therefore came to inherit extensive estates in Normandy as well as the castles of Châteaudun, Amiens and Rouen, the family wealth, and an important position at Court.[24]

He was a year or two older than Mary, and they had probably known each other since childhood. His dukedom lay to the north of the Guise lands, and as neighbours the two families must have had frequent contact with each other. Louis was in every way a suitable husband and when she became his wife, Mary would be able to pay frequent visits to her old home. With her own approval and that of all her relatives, the marriage articles were signed some time before the summer of 1534. Louis settled on his future wife the castle and lands of Châteaudun while Mary brought with her a dowry of 80,000 livres together with an additional 40,000 livres presented to her by the King. Understanding Claud's reluctance to part with any of his lands, Francis had decided to augment the dowry so that Mary might have the husband chosen for her.[25]

They were married on 4 August 1534. The ceremony took place in the chapel of the royal Palace of the Louvre, and the entire Court was present. The King and Queen, the young princes and princesses, Cardinal John and all the other Guise relations thronged into the chapel for the Nuptial Mass and the celebrations afterwards lasted for more than a fortnight. One contemporary Parisian was sufficiently impressed to note in his journal that the wedding was followed by 'jousts and tournaments for sixteen days, in great triumph'.[26]

Louis, Duke of Longueville, remains for the historian a somewhat shadowy figure. No likeness of him survives, scarcely any documents relating to him have been preserved, and it is difficult to discover what sort of man he was. According to tradition, however, and to Mary's own funeral eulogy, she lived with her husband in real happiness, finding personal felicity in his companionship and satisfaction in her new life as Duchess of Longueville.

In some respects her circumstances were little changed. Louis and she were required to be in attendance at Court for much of the time, and Mary's position as a favoured member of the royal circle was consolidated. The King's sister Marguerite and the young princesses were her close friends and beyond this inner circle too she seems to have won universal popularity. Contemporaries were unanimous in praising her prudence, her wisdom and her chastity. She indulged in none of the dalliance so fashionable at Court, but behaved always with dignity and correctness. In some ways she was very much her mother's daughter.

In the summer months, she and Louis travelled round their

estates, making a ceremonial entry into each of the towns that lay along their route. Mary of course rode in these processions, but once arrived at one of her husband's residences, she occupied herself with simple things. She was particularly concerned with the welfare of their tenants and she made a point of going out with her ladies to visit local convents and hospitals. As soon as she arrived, she would make inquiries as to which of the local women had been widowed, whether there were any orphans in need of protection, which of the old people were living in poverty. Following the example of both Philippa and Antoinette, she went out personally to buy cloth which she had made up into garments for the needy. She took a special pleasure in providing dowries for poor girls who might not otherwise have found husbands and she paid for the education of local children with money from her own revenues. In all these activities Mary was carrying on the medieval tradition whereby the lady of the castle was the source of charity for the local people. For her, however, these activities were not merely duties to be performed: her concern for her tenants was entirely sincere and she found in her role as Duchess of Longueville fulfilment and a sense of purpose.[27]

Her happiness was increased when, after a few months of marriage, she discovered that she was pregnant. She went to her husband's castle at Amiens in the autumn of 1535 to prepare for her confinement and there, on 30 October, her son was born. He was christened Francis.[28]

The following year passed uneventfully for Mary and her husband and the winter of 1536 found them in Paris for an important royal occasion: the King's eldest daughter was to be married. Princess Madeleine was a tall, delicate girl whose health was a constant source of anxiety. She was tubercular, and doctors had warned her father that she should never marry and have children. With care, her life could be prolonged, but she should stay at home where she would have the constant attention she needed.

That winter, however, the King of Scotland arrived in Paris seeking a bride. James V was anxious to strengthen the traditional alliance between his country and France, and he had various possible ladies in mind. Naturally enough, he met the King's daughters, and as soon as she saw him Madeleine decided that she would marry him. Her parents were immediately alarmed. Her physicians said bluntly that she could never survive in the colder climate of Scotland, but when James V added his own persuasions to Madeleine's pleas, the French king gave way. On the last night of 1536 James lodged with Mary of Guise's uncle in his Hôtel de Cluny and the following morning he married Madeleine in the Cathedral of Notre Dame. Amongst the principal guests at the ceremony was Mary of Guise.[29]

During the celebrations which followed, French and Scots mingled together. James V had brought over with him an entourage of Scottish bishops, earls and barons, and they all stayed on in Paris until spring was well advanced. In May, they set out at last for home, but poor Madeleine's doctors had been all too accurate in their predictions. After only a few weeks in Scotland, she died.

Mary of Guise shared in the general sorrow when the news came. She herself was pregnant again, and as she waited peacefully for the birth of her second child, she may perhaps have been tempted to compare Madeleine's brief marriage with her own settled life. Like her mother, she would bear a large family. She would spend more time in the country bringing up her children and running her husband's estates. There would be visits to Court from time to time and her contacts with her own family would remain unbroken.

Of course, life was not idyllic, nor could it be. If Mary had any serious fault it was, perhaps, impatience. She liked things to be done at once and with her own outstanding energy and intelligence she demanded high standards from herself and from other people. She was proud too, and a little imperious, but these were small things. She would have the occasional disagreement with Louis, she would sometimes rebuke the members of her household, but she had the loyalty and affection of almost all who knew her. This was her chosen way of life, and she would have it no different.

The future Mary envisaged was not to be. On 9 June 1537

Louis, Duke of Longueville, died at Rouen.[30] That spring virulent fevers had swept northern France. People blamed the previous summer's drought for the incidence of epidemics and it seems probable that Louis contracted one of these highly contagious illnesses. Whatever the nature of his malady, it proved fatal and Mary found herself a widow at twenty-one, with one young child and another baby expected in a few weeks' time.

Her grief at the death of her husband was very real. None of the letters she or her family wrote at this time has survived, but there is one scrap of paper which hints at the affection she had for Louis. One summer, when they were apart, he had written her a hasty letter 'so that you will not worry about what keeps me from coming to see you,' he explained. He went on to tell her, 'I am anxious to let you know that I have had a headache for the past five or six days. Today, however, the doctors have diagnosed my illness as chicken pox. The rash is well out now and they assure me that I am almost better, for which I am very glad. I shall say no more, praying God to give you always whatever you desire. From Peronne, this day of Pentecost, your good husband and friend, Louis.'[31]

Mary kept his letter for the rest of her life. It may have been by chance that the pathetic scrap of paper has survived, but it is tempting to speculate that she kept it deliberately as a touching token of the happy companionship her first marriage had brought her.

2

The Reluctant Bride

For the first few weeks after her husband's death, Mary gave herself up to the ritual of grief. Mourning had its own elaborate conventions, there were complicated funeral arrangements to be made, and masses had to be endowed for the soul of the dead Duke. In the forefront of everyone's mind, of course, was Mary's own pregnancy. It was feared that the shock of her husband's death might bring on a premature confinement, but she carried her child to full term and on 4 August 1537 her second son was born. He was christened Louis, after his father.

At a low physical and spiritual ebb, Mary sought comfort in familiar things. Her mother was with her at Châteaudun, and of course there were her two small sons to divert her. Gradually, her thoughts turned to the future as, ever practical, she began to plan her intended way of life. Henceforth she would live away from the Court, making her home at Châteaudun, a turreted castle set high above the valley of the Loire. From there she would run her little son's estates and bring up her two children personally.

In making these plans for her future, Mary had unfortunately overlooked one important factor. She was once more an eligible woman. Before her marriage she had been an attractive enough prospective bride, a charming young girl from an important family. Now, at twenty-one, she was a wealthy widow and as such she would be much sought after, all the more so since she had given proof that she could bear sons. Her tact and diplomacy were well known and she would be a fitting consort for any ambitious young man in search of a wife.

Such thoughts were far from Mary's mind as she played with her baby sons that September in Châteaudun. Of course, she was aware that at some time in the future there might be an offer for her hand, but she had no intention of accepting any such proposal. She would never marry again. It was therefore with a profound sense of shock that she received a letter from Francis I announcing that he had found her a husband. She should prepare at once for her wedding, he told her, for she was to marry the King of Scots as soon as all the necessary arrangements could be made.

Mary had, of course, met James already when he had come to France to marry Madeleine. From personal knowledge she could conjure up his image, recollecting the thick red hair, the narrow eyes, the long nose and the neatly trimmed beard. The Scottish King was handsome enough and his air of restless vitality made him attractive to many women.

There were, however, less attractive facets to his character. In the autumn of 1537 he was a highly-strung, neurotic young man of twenty-six. His upbringing had been unorthodox, to say the least. When he was only a year old his father had been killed fighting against the English at the battle of Flodden. He was thus left in the immediate care of his mother, Margaret Tudor, who was the sister of Henry VIII. Scotland had suffered from a long series of royal minorities, during which the widowed Queen of the time often assumed power as Regent. On this occasion, the situation was rather different. The Scots had just suffered a humiliating defeat at the hands of the English and they were hardly likely to accept the rule of the English King's sister. In any case, Margaret's matrimonial adventures complicated matters. A year after her husband's death, she married again. Her new husband was the Earl of Angus and, in becoming his wife, she reduced her own status and ended her legal rights as her son's guardian. Therefore the Scots chose a new Regent or governor – the Duke of Albany.

A cousin of the dead King, Albany was half-French by parentage and entirely French by upbringing. He came to Scotland reluctantly but he governed the country for the next ten years, until the tide of opposition to his policies became too strong and he retired to France. By this time Margaret Tudor had become bored with the Earl of Angus and was trying to divorce him. Fearing that she would seize power entirely and, to spite him, ally herself with the French, Angus kidnapped the young King.

James was now fourteen years old. His stepfather showered him with fine clothes, indulged his every whim, surrounded him with flatterers and introduced him to a series of highly unsuitable pleasures. At the same time, he made it plain that James was his prisoner. Angus took for himself the office of Chancellor of Scotland, and he made sure that members of his family occupied other important positions. His brother boasted openly that if anyone tried to rescue the young King, Angus and he would see James torn apart before they let him go.

In the end, after two years of captivity, the boy managed to escape. Making his way to Stirling Castle, he rallied his other nobles to his cause and he exiled the Douglases, including the head of their house, the Earl of Angus. Henceforth, he ruled Scotland for himself. His experiences would have had a traumatic effect on any young boy, and when that boy was also King the political repercussions were endless. For the rest of his life he loathed the Douglases with an implacable hatred. He disliked and distrusted his mother. Most of all, he hated the English and all who favoured that country. His enthusiasm for a French alliance was the logical outcome. With the support of France, he could protect his realm's independence.

From his clever, cultivated father James had inherited considerable intellectual gifts, but he was also possessed of his mother's instability and his upbringing had not helped. After his captivity he turned with feverish enthusiasm to the business of ruling the country. Constant warfare followed by Albany's extravagant way of life had depleted Scottish finances and James's attempts to augment his revenues bordered at times on rapacity. Similarly, in his desire to restore justice and the rule of law, he could be harsh and repressive. Alternating with his bouts of energy were periods of depression and melancholy, when he would seek relief from his own thoughts by turning to the pursuit of pleasure with an intensity which alarmed his friends. By the time he was twenty-six he had at least seven illegitimate sons and two illegitimate daughters. Sexually attractive he undoubtedly was, but he was hardly likely to make an ideal husband.[1]

His brief, first marriage ended, James was now mourning the death of his young French bride, but he did not allow grief to preoccupy him to the exclusion of all else. Madeleine was not long dead when he decided that, for the sake of the French alliance, he must seek another French wife. Encouraged by Cardinal David Beaton, his principal adviser, he determined to write at once to Francis I, asking him as politely as possible to supply an immediate replacement for Madeleine.

Francis had another daughter and James may well have entertained hopes in that direction. If so, he was disappointed. Having already lost one child to the cold Scottish climate, Francis had no intention of risking another. In casting around for an alternative, he suddenly thought of the young woman whom he had come to regard almost as another daughter – Mary of Guise. He was at once struck by the suitability of the match. James had lost his wife, Mary had lost her husband. They could console one another. The Guise family would be pleased with this singular honour accorded to their child and for his part James would be willing enough if Francis made sure that the dowry was sufficient. After all, Mary might not be a royal princess but she was tall, broad and the mother of sons. There would be none of the fears about her health that there had been with Madeleine.

Delighted with his inspiration, Francis wrote to James offering him 'Madame de Longueville'. Of course, he explained, Mary had been recently bereaved so there would be a little delay, but the marriage would be arranged as soon as possible. He then sent Mary the letter outlining his plans for her.[2]

Outrage and dismay were Mary's immediate emotions. She was not at that time much concerned with thoughts of James V himself. Most of the details of his character and career were probably known to her, for Court gossip was more liable to embroider a man's faults than to suppress them. For the moment, however, she did not stop to reflect on the bridegroom proposed for her, for she regarded the whole notion of the marriage as preposterous. Her husband had been dead barely two months and nothing was more repugnant to her than the thought of marrying again at all, let alone so soon. She discussed the matter indignantly with her mother, then she sat down in considerable agitation to compose her reply to the King. Monarch of France he might be, but surely Francis would not be so brutal as to force her into this unwanted match.

Her suitor's reaction was rather different. He received the French King's suggestion with apparent enthusiasm and dispatched his acceptance. This time, he would not go to France in person to seek his bride. After all, he was no longer an eager young bachelor and she was not the daughter of a King. Instead, he would send Cardinal Beaton, the wily diplomat who, after studying law in Paris, had often acted as Scotland's ambassador at the French Court and who, as James's leading adviser, was the principal architect of the French alliance.

Anxious to complete his mission, the Cardinal hurried to Fontainebleau. To his exasperation he discovered when he got there that he could not see the King, for the Court was about to move on. The very next day they left, and the Cardinal was forced to pursue Francis all the way to Lyons. Experienced diplomat that he was, Beaton nevertheless chafed at the delay and it was only after a good deal of trouble that he eventually obtained a royal audience and passed on his master's message. Francis was graciously pleased. He would give Mary to James as if she were his own daughter, he said, and he spoke 'many good words of her wisdom and guiding'.

Nothing could be done, of course, without the Duke of Guise, and a few days later Claud received a summons to Court. He was at home on his own estates but he had been fully apprised of the situation. Contrary to Francis's expectations, the Guise family had not received the news of the proposed marriage with unmixed delight. Certainly Claud appreciated the implications of such a match but he also shared the feelings of his wife and daughter. Another marriage again so soon would be most improper and there were other difficulties in the way. He and Antoinette could not bring themselves to think of their beloved daughter going so far away from them. Travel being what it was, they might never see her again. Moreover, what would become of her two baby sons? The King of Scots would hardly want his bride to bring her children with her, and in any case, Francis, the little Duke of Longueville, must remain in his own country. He was Grand Chamberlain of France as his father had been, and so he must be brought up at the French Court. The whole idea of the Scottish marriage was impossible.

Claud therefore did what he could to delay matters, trying desperately to find a way of changing the King's mind without offending him. He waited for as long as he could, talking it all over with Antoinette, who had returned from Châteaudun, but the time came when he could delay no longer and he was forced to set off for the south.

When he arrived at Lyons it was to find that Francis had now moved on to Grenoble. This accorded him little respite however, for Cardinal Beaton had elected to remain behind, waiting for him. Claud had no sooner arrived than the Cardinal accosted him and demanded to know what had kept him. Claud replied in a soothing manner that he had been busy sending letters to his daughter and to Duke Antony, the head of the family. The Cardinal was only slightly mollified, so Claud was forced to pretend great eagerness for the marriage. This had the desired effect and, amity restored, the two set off together for Grenoble.

Beaton was now more anxious than ever to do his business and be gone. He had wasted enough time in France and he wanted to go home. The weather that autumn was surprisingly good so, if it remained settled, he would make the voyage north that winter. After all, as he told James V, Mary of Guise was 'stark [i.e. strong] and well complexioned and may endure travel'.[3]

A royal marriage was not to be so speedily accomplished,

though, and at this point events took an extraordinary turn. To the astonishment of French and English alike, Henry VIII announced that he, too, was a contender for the hand of Mary of Guise. The English King had just lost his own third wife Jane Seymour, who had died not long after giving birth to a son, and his Council were urging him to marry again. The real reason for his unseemly haste was that he had just heard rumours of James V's plans.

James V was Henry's nephew, but they were scarcely on the best of terms. Personal animosity apart, Henry had broken with Rome and had set himself up as head of the English Church. He was continually urging James to follow suit, but James remained obstinately faithful to the Pope. Worse still, James was an ardent supporter of Scotland's traditional alliance with France, an alliance which was a constant threat to England. Any further strengthening of the friendship between his northern and his southern neighbours was seen by Henry as a source of danger, and so he decided to stop the marriage at all costs. The simplest way to do so would be to marry James's bride himself.

When he heard that Mary would bring with her a dowry of 30,000 francs a year and was both 'lusty and fair', Henry wasted no more time.[4] He told the French ambassador in London to let him know which French brides of suitable rank were available, and he made private investigations into Mary's wealth and lineage.[5]

The ambassador duly conveyed the message to the French King, who was divided between amusement and indignation. The English must choose their wives as they did their horses, he observed: by lining them up and inspecting them. Although he was insulted by the implication that his own daughter should be included in this parade of prospective brides, he replied diplomatically enough. He would count it an honour if Henry chose a French wife, and he was welcome to select any lady in the kingdom – any lady, that is, except the Princess Margaret and except Mary of Guise, who was already promised elsewhere.[6]

The negotiations between Henry and Francis now took on a

distinctly farcical character. Castillon, the French ambassador, was summoned once more to Henry's presence. Knowing very well that monarch's unpredictable nature he was prepared for almost anything, but even he was shaken when Henry launched forth into impassioned declaration. So enamoured was he of Mary, Henry said, that he could consider no other bride, and he went on to elaborate this theme in considerable detail. When he eventually paused for breath, Castillon inquired tartly, 'Would you then marry another man's wife?'

Henry was not deterred. He had discovered, he said, that Mary had not yet given her personal consent to the match with James and was still available. Swallowing his exasperation, Castillon explained that Mary's father had full powers to act on her behalf. The marriage could not have been contemplated had she been unwilling. Henry obstinately refused to believe this. Somewhat nonplussed, the ambassador ventured to inquire why Henry was so set on the Duke of Guise's daughter. With a knowing gleam in his eye, Henry retorted that Mary was big in person, and he had need of a big wife.[7] 'I may be big in person,' observed Mary when they told her what he had said, 'but my neck is small!'[8]

The general attitude at the French Court was one of amused disbelief. When Henry persisted in his protestations of affection, Francis and his advisers began to think that they could turn the situation to their own advantage. What one of them termed 'a pretty comedy' might be played out, with Francis leading Henry on, wringing political concessions from him in return for the promise of a wife who would never be his.[9]

All this might be entertaining enough, and Mary might even be able to joke about it herself, but the question of her future was still causing her the gravest concern and as Christmas approached she received yet another blow. Her baby son Louis died when he was just four months old.[10] Nor was she comforted when she received yet another letter from Francis I ordering her to go through with the marriage.

Francis was now determined to have the contract signed before Henry VIII became any more persistent, but he was so preoccupied with other matters that he scarcely had time to see Cardinal Beaton. The French were about to embark on yet another campaign against the Emperor, military preparations took precedence over all else, and the Court was constantly on the move. The Cardinal grew uneasy and even began to fear that Francis would change his mind and give Mary to the English King instead.

Mary herself was greatly perplexed. She had come to realize that the marriage was inevitable. Like it or not, she would have to accept it, and all she could do now was to try to ensure that the terms of the new marriage contract did not militate against her little son's interests. Because she remained at Châteaudun, in mourning, it was difficult for her to protect his rights but she sent one of her household, Monsieur Puiguillon, to Court to act for her.

When Puiguillon first arrived there he discovered that nothing had actually been put down in writing and that no definite action could be taken until Mary sent her father her first marriage contract. By diligent inquiry, however, he discovered some alarming news. The King had decreed that Mary should take with her a dowry of 150,000 livres tournois, but this sum was not going to be provided by the Guise family. Instead, 120,000 livres would come from the revenues and lands settled on Mary by her first husband, and Francis would supply the 30,000 livres needed to make up the complete sum.

Puiguillon warned Mary that this would never do. The proposals were most unusual, as well as being exceedingly prejudicial to the interests of her son. During her own lifetime Mary was entitled to enjoy the proceeds of her jointure lands, but on her death these lands would revert to the Longueville estates, thus forming part of the little Duke's inheritance. Should the lands instead be taken to provide a dowry for Mary, they would become the property of the Scottish King. Puiguillon explained that he himself had been so astonished when he heard these proposals that he had lost no time in passing them on to the Duke of Guise. Claud was equally vexed. Puiguillon then made sure that all the Court officials realized that such terms would be quite unacceptable to Mary. He would have liked to return to Châteaudun to discuss the

James V and Mary of Guise in the year of their marriage, by an
unknown artist (above)

The Castle of Joinville, Mary's childhood home:
engraved by Skelton (below)

James Hamilton,
Earl of Arran,
Duke of Châtelherault
and Lord Governor
of Scotland,
by Bronckorst

Cardinal David Beaton,
Lord Chancellor
of Scotland,
by an unknown artist

matter with her personally, but he did not dare leave Court lest some agreement be made in his absence.[11]

Puiguillon also wrote to Antoinette about the latest development and she was greatly disturbed. On 28 January she sent her daughter a long letter expressing her concern. The news about the contract was indeed alarming, she said. The King had promised Claud that no further steps would be taken without Mary's consent, but Antoinette feared that Mary was simply being used as a pawn in the political game and that matters would go against her.

The arrangements about the dowry must be altered before the final contract was drawn up, there was no doubt about that. Antoinette recognized, of course, that her daughter was in a delicate position. The King must not be irritated, whatever happened. Mary must deal with him prudently but honestly, pointing out as tactfully as she could just why his proposals were unacceptable.

In conclusion, Antoinette offered some consolation. Friends would do all they could to help: the King's sister, Marguerite of Navarre, had already promised to mediate on Mary's behalf. Harassed as she was, Mary must try not to worry too much. All these tribulations were a sure sign that God must intend great things for her in the future, either in the present world or in the next.[12]

Of course, Mary did continue to worry: how could she do otherwise? The fate of her little son, the distance of Scotland from France, the prospect of living in a foreign country with a virtual stranger – there were problems enough to occupy her every waking hour. All she could do was to concentrate on the immediate, practical arrangements; and concentrate she did, with considerable success. Presumably by a combination of her own direct dealings with Francis and of the efforts of her friends, she persuaded the King to alter the terms of the marriage contract. By the end of March, Puiguillon was able to report that the articles would be in accordance with her wishes, and so indeed they were.[13]

The marriage contract was signed the following Monday at Lyons, in the presence of the entire Court. The dowry remained at 150,000 livres, but the arrangements for paying it were now very different. The King himself would provide no less than 70,000 livres and Claud would contribute the remaining 80,000: in fact, he would be giving the same 80,000 livres as he had settled on Mary at the time of her first marriage. Should James V die, his heirs were bound to give back to Mary one third of the dowry if there were children of the marriage, one half if there were none. She would be able to take back all her own possessions and valuables in such a contingency, and she would not be liable for any of her husband's debts. In return, she would waive all claim to any share in his goods and properties.[14]

The marriage would, of course, bring her lands of her own in Scotland. As her jointure, she would receive the Palace of Falkland and the Castles of Stirling, Dingwall and Threave. Along with these, she would be given the earldoms of Strathearn, Ross, Orkney and Fife and the lordships of Galloway, Ardmannach and the Isles. Were she widowed, Mary would keep these properties as her own. She would also be entitled to remain in Scotland if she so desired, but if she preferred to return to France she could do so, taking with her the specified portion of her dowry together with all her own possessions. In addition, she would continue to draw the revenues from her jointure lands.

The contract was undoubtedly favourable to Mary. It protected her interests very well, without interfering with her son's lands. She had managed to ensure that his revenues would not be diminished in any way and she had seen to it that her own financial future was secure.

With the contract completed, the arrangements could now enter their final phase. James wrote off to the Pope for a dispensation of consanguinity, for he and his bride were within the forbidden degrees. Oddly enough, the link was through Philippa of Gueldres, whose aunt had married an earlier King of Scots. Consequently, Philippa was first cousin of James III and Mary of Guise was third cousin of James V.

This tenuous link with Scotland may have consoled Mary a little in the anguish of parting from her family. She had decided now what she must do with her little son. He would go to Joinville to be brought up by Antoinette. It was the ideal solution, really, for he would be joining a large, affectionate family group. Antoinette's son René was the same age as little Francis and there was also a new baby. He would feel as if he were among brothers and sisters rather than aunts and uncles. The thought of leaving him behind was almost more than Mary could bear, but at least she would know that he was happy and safe.

At this point, Mary received a letter which heartened her greatly. Waiting for his bride, James V had decided to write her a letter explaining to her something of his own situation. He had probably heard of her reluctance to come to him, he may even have feared that she would somehow change her mind yet and go to Henry VIII instead; whatever his motives, he felt that some sort of appeal to her was necessary and he couched that appeal in eloquent terms.

'Madam,' he wrote, 'I am only twenty-seven years old and life already weighs as heavily upon me as my crown does . . . Fatherless since childhood, I have been the prisoner of my ambitious nobles. The powerful house of Douglas kept me in servitude for a long time and I hate their name and everything that reminds me of the sombre days of my captivity. Archibald, Earl of Angus, George, his brother and all their relations now in exile never cease to stir up the King of England against me and mine. There is not a noble in my kingdom who has not been seduced by their promises or suborned with his money. There is no safety for my person, nothing to guarantee the execution of my orders or the enforcement of equitable laws.

'All this alarms me, Madam, and I await your support and counsel. Without money I rely on the help I receive from France and the parsimonious gifts of my opulent clergy. I am trying to embellish my castles, strengthen my fortresses and build up my navy. Unfortunately, my lords believe that a king who wishes truly to reign over them is an insupportable evil. In spite of the friendship of the King of France and the aid of his troops, in spite of the attachment of my people, I

THE HOUSE OF GUELDRES, THE KINGS OF SCOTLAND AND THE KINGS OF FRANCE

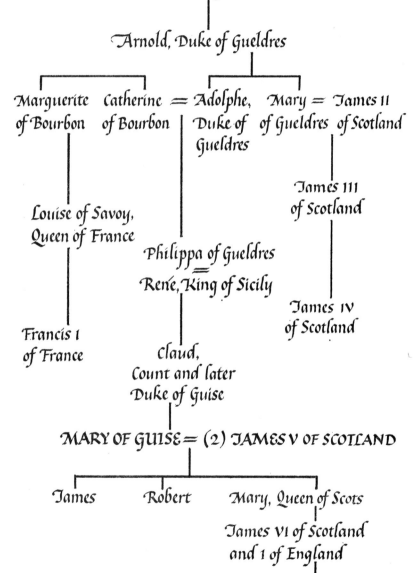

Arnold, Duke of Gueldres

Marguerite of Bourbon

Catherine of Bourbon = Adolphe, Duke of Gueldres

Mary = James II of Gueldres of Scotland

Louise of Savoy, Queen of France

James III of Scotland

Philippa of Gueldres
=
René, King of Sicily

Francis I of France

James IV of Scotland

Claud, Count and later Duke of Guise

MARY OF GUISE = (2) JAMES V OF SCOTLAND

James   Robert   Mary, Queen of Scots

James VI of Scotland and I of England

fear that I shall never gain a decisive victory over my rebellious lords.

'I wish to overcome all obstacles so that I can open up for this nation the way of justice and of peace. I might perhaps attain this end if I had only my noblemen against me, but the King of England does not cease to sow discord between the nobles and myself, and the heresies which he has implanted among my people extend their ravages even into the Church. All along, my power and that of my forbears has rested on the middle class and the clergy, and I am obliged to ask myself if this power can last much longer . . .'[15]

It was more than an appeal, it was a challenge, and nothing could have been better calculated to engage Mary of Guise's sympathies. James could have written promising her high position, wealth, possessions. She would have accepted these impassively as the expected accompaniments of her future rank. Instead, here was not so much a King seeking a consort but a man who needed her support. He was not simply offering her a ceremonial role in life but asking for her advice and assistance. She was to be his partner in a difficult endeavour. Together they would drive back the English, protect the Catholic Church, bring peace and equity to their troubled realm. From the moment that she read his letter, Mary committed herself to her new life. There would be homesickness, there would be regrets, but henceforth she would direct all her energies into helping James achieve his aims. She had a sense of purpose once more.

She was anxious, now, to begin, hurrying forward the plans for the wedding ceremony. James would not be coming himself, but he was sending Lord Maxwell to represent him, along with Lord Erskine and an impressive retinue. For his part, Francis I had promised to send Mary a 'noble guard' to lend dignity to the occasion, and on 22 April she was writing impatiently to a Court official to ask when they would come.[16]

She was married on 9 May 1538 in her Castle of Châteaudun.[17] Robert, Lord Maxwell, acted as proxy for the King of Scots, placing on her finger 'a ring with a diamond to be the Queen's spousing ring'. It had cost James a fraction of what he had paid for Madeleine's ring but it was, after all, its symbolic rather than its financial value which mattered and in the celebrations which followed Lord Maxwell distributed forty crowns among the officials and the minstrels who were in attendance.[18]

They all stayed on at Châteaudun for several weeks, then the entire company set out to escort Mary to Rouen. There the protracted farewells took place. She said goodbye to her little son, to her mother, to her brothers and sisters. More distant relations took their leave too, as did many friends. Ladies who had not been able to attend the wedding sent kind messages, assuring Mary that she would be greatly missed. Her popularity had been real and her departure was sincerely regretted by a very large number of people.

Early in June, she parted from those whom she would leave behind, and went to the coast. To ease the pain of separation from her family, it had been arranged that her father would accompany her to Scotland and so would her sister Louise. She would also take with her a household of French servants who would stay on in Scotland with her. On 10 June they all embarked at Le Havre.[19] Three galleys would carry them to Scotland – the same three galleys which had taken James and Madeleine north the previous year. Sea voyages were dangerous at the best of times, and the hostility of the English made this one doubly so. However, James had taken all necessary precautions and one of his servants, Archie Pennicuik, had been dispatched to sail north in advance to 'inspect the ports of England', and make sure that there was no immediate danger.[20]

At last, everything was ready. The final moments were somewhat marred by a violent quarrel between Cardinal Beaton and Lord Maxwell. The Cardinal was feeling slighted. After all his trouble in arranging this marriage, he had been allowed to play no important part in the actual ceremony. Mary's numerous ecclesiastical relatives had seen to that. Now, when he made to embark with Mary of Guise, he was not 'tholit [allowed] to come in the ship that she was in'. His quick temper was aroused and he and Lord Maxwell exchanged angry words. As Lord Maxwell was also Lord High Admiral of Scotland, the Cardinal was overruled, and it was with a very ill grace that he finally climbed aboard one of the other galleys.[21]

If he was feeling resentful as he watched the coast of France recede into the distance, Mary of Guise's sentiments were much more poignant. The excitement of departure was eclipsed by sorrow as she thought of those she had left behind her, and the cheering words of father and friends did little to relieve her melancholy. There was one consolation. As the voyage progressed, she discovered that sea travel agreed with her. Claud was wretchedly sick, but Mary remained unaffected and so she clung to the notion that the journey between France and Scotland was not so dreadful after all. Having accomplished it successfully once, she could do it again. France was not, after all, lost to her forever.

On Trinity Sunday, 1538, she set foot in Scotland for the first time. The three galleys had sailed up the coast of England, past the shores of southern Scotland and on to the estuary of the River Forth. They were making for St Andrews but for some reason, when they sighted the most easterly point of Fife, they pulled in to the shore. St Andrews lies several miles further on, round the point. Perhaps the winds were unfavourable, or perhaps the French sailors mistook the castle on the headland for the castle at St Andrews. Whatever the reason, Mary landed on the sandy shore at Balcomie.

As she and her companions gazed around, they realized that they would have to wait where they were. They could not arrive unannounced and so they decided to spend the night in nearby Balcomie Castle while a messenger rode hastily to St Andrews. In the meantime, the sailors busied themselves bringing ashore the baggage, taking especial pains with the Queen's bed, while the invaluable Archie Pennicuik saw to the disembarking of her horse. There was time, too, to look around with curiosity at the view from their rather windswept headland. To the north were the waters of the Tay estuary, to the south were the waters of the Forth, to the east lay the North Sea, but to the west lay the pleasant, rolling country of Fife

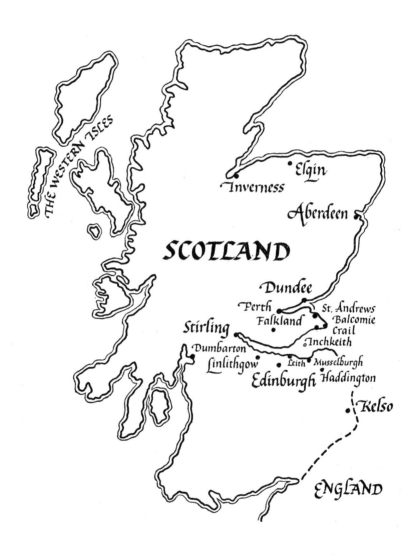

with its gentle hills and its fertile valleys.

St Andrews is only ten miles from Balcomie, so the news of Mary's arrival did not take long to reach there. A breathless messenger announced to James V that his bride had come, and the King gave immediate orders. Early next morning the entire Court was to assemble in their best clothes to ride out and greet their new Queen. So it was that when Mary looked out from the castle next day, she saw a splendid cavalcade approaching: a procession of servants in liveries of scarlet and yellow, noblemen in brilliantly coloured garments and, riding at their head, King James V of Scotland. She met him once again, this time as his wife.

Their words went unrecorded, but no doubt they greeted each other formally, then presented their separate households to each other. The initial civilities over, they mounted their horses, French and Scots now riding side by side. Together, Mary and James made their way over the hilly countryside, past the little villages of Boarhills and Kingsbarns, on until they breasted the final rise and found themselves looking down on St Andrews itself.

The old, walled city of grey stone stood on the edge of the North Sea. Three parallel streets of houses with long, narrow gardens ran from east to west, linked by a series of lanes. Dwarfing the houses and dominating the entire city was the magnificent Cathedral with its soaring spires. Nearby stood a tall square tower, that of the eleventh-century Church of St Regulus, and beside the market was a spacious parish church. Over by the harbour was Cardinal Beaton's residence, the castle. St Andrews was Scotland's ecclesiastical capital, a university city and a frequent resort of the King and his Court.

As befitted the occasion, a ceremonial welcome had been prepared for the new Queen. When Mary arrived at the New Abbey gate, the cavalcade halted and the townspeople pressed round to have their first sight of her. A pageant had been specially arranged for this moment by the King's old friend Sir David Lindsay, the Lord Lyon of Scotland. Before the fascinated gaze of the spectators, a great wooden cloud descended from the arch of the gateway, and out of this cloud emerged 'a fair lady most like an angel'. Clutched in this vision's hand were 'the keys of the whole of Scotland'. These she presented tremulously to Mary, delivering at the same time a pretty speech to the effect that 'all the hearts of Scotland were opened to the receiving of Her Grace'. Various uplifting orations composed by Sir David then followed. Probably they were in Latin, for Mary would not yet have mastered Scots. For years Sir David had been urging James V to abandon his licentious ways and settle down with a virtuous wife. He now took the opportunity of exhorting Mary to serve God, obey her husband and, above all else, remain faithful to him.

Mary received this advice with gracious attention, then, the speeches over, the procession made its way through the Abbey Gate and into the city. Passing along the street known as the Pends, they arrived shortly afterwards at the domestic buildings of the priory. As was customary, the Cathedral had always possessed a guest house for distinguished visitors and there was a Guest Hall dating back to the thirteenth century. Mary, however, was to stay in the recently-built Guest House known in the town as the Novum Hospitium or the New Inns. This handsome mansion, which survived until the beginning of the nineteenth century, had been carefully decorated 'with all necessaries pertaining to a Queen'.

Mary rested there that night. Next morning, she and her ladies rose early to prepare themselves for an important ceremony. At ten o'clock, they left in procession to walk the short distance to the Cathedral. The Cathedral is a ruin now, but even so it retains a measure of its former magnificence. According to legend, the earliest Christian settlement on the site had been in AD 345, but the oldest existing parts of the structure dated from the twelfth century. A new Cathedral had been consecrated in 1318 in the presence of King Robert the Bruce, but a great fire fifty years later had damaged it and an extensive programme of rebuilding had to be undertaken. The resulting church was the largest in the kingdom.[22]

On that June morning, it was crowded. Special scaffolding had been erected to provide seats for the huge congregation, and the entire Court had gathered to witness the confirmation of James V's marriage. As she looked round the Cathedral, Mary could see the smiling, encouraging faces of her French family and friends. She could pick out some Scots who were already well known to her – Cardinal Beaton, Lord Maxwell – and she could recognize others to whom she had recently been introduced; men who were as yet unfamiliar to her but whom she knew to be of importance in her new life.

The most significant, dynastically speaking, was James, Earl of Arran, head of the powerful Hamilton family. Clanship was a concept which applied, technically, only in the Highlands of Scotland, but in the Lowland areas the bonds of kinship were equally strong. The Hamiltons could be expected to support the head of their House, particularly in his feuds with his traditional enemies. Long-established rivalries played a vital part in public affairs, and the head of the House of Hamilton would never be found on the same side as the head of the House of Lennox, his great rival. If Arran supported the English then Lennox would support the French. In this way, traditional prejudices and traditional loyalties greatly complicated events, making it extremely difficult for the King or for anyone else to build up a really strong body of support.

The Earl of Arran himself was a mild enough looking young man with a nervous, ingratiating manner and an inability to look anyone in the eye. His portrait, painted in later life, conveys exactly the air of weakness combined with cunning which his contemporaries found so irritating. The direct descendant of a Stewart princess, he was the heir to the throne of Scotland until such time as James V fathered a legitimate son. This made the Earl of Arran a figure of importance at Court, whatever his personal shortcomings.

His great rival, Lennox, was absent. Also the descendant of a Stewart princess, he disputed Arran's place in the succession, declaring bluntly that his enemy was illegitimate. Fortunately, he was a permanent resident at the Court of France. Likewise conspicuous by their absence were the Earl of Angus and his brother Sir George Douglas, still in exile in England.

Instead, James had near him men like his nephew and great favourite George, Earl of Huntly. The son of an illegitimate daughter of James IV, Huntly had more or less been brought up at Court and, being an almost exact contemporary of the King, was more like his brother than his nephew. For a short time Huntly had been very friendly with the Douglases and he had indeed fled with them to England in 1528. However, it had not been long before he returned to Scotland and was reconciled with James V. He was a member of the Privy Council and when James had gone to France to choose his first wife, Huntly had remained at home to act as one of the regents of the kingdom.

Another longstanding friend was Hugh, 4th Lord Somerville. A supporter of the King ever since James had escaped from the Douglases, Lord Somerville was a relatively poor man who borrowed heavily to finance an extravagant way of life. His clothes were magnificent, his hospitality famous and he frequently played host to the King himself. Then there was Lord Fleming. He had married yet another illegitimate daughter of James IV, so his ties with the royal family were also very close.

Such were the men surrounding the King that June morning in St Andrews Cathedral. The royal marriage was solemnly confirmed and blessed, the organ music thundered out, bells pealed, trumpets sounded and the bride and groom emerged once more into the Cathedral grounds to walk the short distance to the old Guest House. There, James entertained his wife and guests to dinner, then 'there was great mirth, shawms, draught trumpets and war trumpets, with playing and farces after dinner till time of supper'. Even the sophisticated French visitors were impressed, and Claud's secretary wrote home enthusiastically praising 'the magnificent novelties' with which they were entertained.

On the following day, Mary was taken on a tour of St Andrews itself. Accompanied by the provost and burgesses of the town she walked round the university colleges, talking with students and academics alike, before going on to visit the many ecclesiastical foundations, calling on the Blackfriars and the Greyfriars, looking round the parish church and touring the old Culdee church. It was just the sort of procedure she had liked at home when her first husband had been alive, and she seems to have enjoyed herself. Everywhere she went, the townspeople pressed round, anxious to have another glimpse of her, and when she arrived back at her apartments she lost no time in telling her husband how impressed she had been. 'She never saw in France nor no other country so many good faces in so little room [space]', she declared, 'as she saw that day in Scotland. For', she said, 'it was shown to her in France that Scotland was but a barbarous country, destitute and void of all commodity that uses to be in other countries, but now she confesses she saw the contrary, for she saw never so many fair personages of men and women and also young babes and children as she saw that day in these bounds where she had been'.

Lindsay of Pitscottie, the chronicler who reported her words, is better known for his embroidering of events than for his historical accuracy, but when he was dealing with the happenings of his own lifetime his descriptions can be read with more reliance, especially when he was recording events in Fife. A relative of Sir David Lindsay, he lived less than five miles from St Andrews and he probably had first-hand knowledge of Mary's arrival. There is no reason to think that he recorded her words verbatim but they certainly ring true in their general tone. It is possible to interpret her remarks as being yet another example of her famous tact, but there was more to it than that. The French did regard Scotland as a primitive country, an 'infant nation' as they were to put it euphemistically, and they had no doubt painted a grim picture for Mary of life on the northern edge of the world. When she arrived and found herself among civilized men and women she was relieved. She was many miles from home, but the familiar sights of people going about their daily business reassured her and she was able to take a keen interest in all she saw. She was, after all, a young woman visiting a foreign country for the first time and she was eager to begin well. She was therefore anxious to praise what she saw when it pleased her. Her compliments sprang not from a superficial sweetness of manner but from genuine appreciation. She was more than a little relieved that the gloomy tales she had been told had no foundation in reality.

Her comments certainly pleased her husband. 'Forsooth Madam, you shall see better before you leave here, if God pleases,' Lindsay of Pitscottie has him say, 'and before you pass through Scotland you will see many good-like men and women with other commodity that will be to your contentment.'[23]

For the next forty days, however, the Court remained in St Andrews, celebrating the marriage. Amongst the entertainments provided was a series of tournaments in which the Duke of Guise played a prominent part. His secretary proudly noted that Claud defeated all manner of noble opponents, some of whom had come from as far away as London for the pleasure of jousting with him.[24] Then there were archery contests, hunting and hawking, singing and dancing. The Scots were delighted with their new Queen. Madeleine had touched their hearts but her fragility had been all too obvious. Mary, in contrast, was a fine, handsome woman, taller than the King himself, and if she lacked conventional prettiness she had dignity of manner as well as her natural charm.

In August, Claud and the French guests left, and James decided to show her some more of their kingdom. They rode westwards to the ancient burgh of Cupar, in central Fife. There they dined, in the royal castle, before turning south to the Palace of Falkland. The small town of Falkland lies in a sheltered hollow at the foot of the gently-rounded Lomond Hills, and in the sixteenth century it was surrounded by fine oak forests. For centuries past the palace had been used as a hunting lodge by the Stewart kings, a favourite place for relaxation and enjoyment. Mary approached the palace with particular interest, for it was one of the properties settled on her by her marriage contract. There was a sentimental attachment as well, for James II had given Falkland to his bride, Mary of Gueldres, and to this day a walk through the palace woods bears the name of the 'Gilderland Walk'.

The great round tower of the palace dated from the thirteenth century at least. Both James II and James III had extended the accompanying domestic buildings by constructing a new north range. James IV had continued the programme of improvements, adding an eastern and a southern range so that elegant new buildings surrounded the courtyard. James V was equally anxious to embellish the palace, and he had all manner of plans for ornamenting the façade of the wings as well as for beautifying the interior of the building. In preparation for his marriage to Madeleine he had employed painters to decorate his apartments and those of his future wife, directly above his own. The chambers were now a blaze of colour, with intricate patterns on walls and ceilings.

The Chapel Royal in the south block was also the subject of the King's attentions, and in the gardens he planned to erect a fine new tennis court. A vast expanse of lawn stretched northwards to the 'lang butts' where he and his courtiers practised archery, and beyond the butts lay the woods. Whenever the Court came to Falkland, deer were specially brought and released in the parks. On this occasion James and his entourage spent about a week hunting the fallow deer, then they moved westwards, to Stirling.

Very different from the sheltered situation of Falkland was this other castle which Mary had received with her jointure lands. Stirling Castle is built on a steep rock commanding magnificent views over the valley of the River Forth. It was one of Scotland's strongest fortresses but, while retaining its important defensive function, it had been considerably beautified by successive Scottish kings. The handsome, Gothic Great Hall had been the work of James III's architects, and now James V had put in hand ambitious plans for an entirely new palace, to be constructed round the courtyard known as 'the Lion's Den'. There would be an elegant, Renaissance façade, and the exterior would be decorated with stone demons and gargoyles, cherubs and carved heads.

Inside, the palace was to be equally impressive. The King's Presence Chamber would have a fine Renaissance ceiling consisting of carved wooden roundels, each with its own central design – a jester, a King's head, a child. Twenty-eight of these roundels have survived and, along with the magnificent fire-

places decorated with birds, beasts and foliage, they give some
indication of the elegance of Stirling Castle. From the outside
it was very different from the airy, turreted buildings of
Joinville, but inside the disparity was not so great.

There remained the third royal residence, the Palace of
Linlithgow. With the approach of winter, James decided that
it was time to move on once more, and they rode eastwards.
When Mary first saw Linlithgow Palace, she was enchanted.
It was, she declared, as fine as any castle in France. A handsome
building looking out over a small, pretty lake, it probably did
remind her of the châteaux of her own country. James V
had been born at Linlithgow and he had ambitious plans for
it, too, but on this occasion he did not linger. After only a
few days, they left for Edinburgh.[25]

The entry into the capital was the climax of the royal progress, and on 16 November, Mary of Guise rode into the town
for the first time. The date had been carefully chosen for it was
St Margaret's day, the feast of a previous Queen of Scots.
Few details of the occasion are known, but one account noted
that Mary 'made her entrance in Edinburgh with great
triumph, and as with order of the whole nobles. Her Grace
came in first at the West Port and rode down the High Street
to the Abbey of Holyroodhouse, with great sport played to
Her Grace all through the town'.[26] There were pageants, there
was dancing, there was feasting. The townspeople had turned
out in full force to see her, and an army of servants had been
busy for weeks beforehand preparing the Palace of Holyroodhouse for her arrival. Windows had been repaired, drains had
been cleaned, the stables had been renovated. Butts for
archery had been put up in the gardens, with turf brought
specially from Liberton, on the edge of the town. Tapestries
had been hung up, silver plate polished, fine linen washed.
Everything was now in readiness, and when Mary rode down
the Royal Mile and arrived at Holyrood, it was to see her own
newly-carved coat of arms decorating the front of the palace
alongside the newly-painted and gilded great arms of Scotland.

3

The Queen of Scots

'Madam,' Antoinette wrote to her eldest daughter on 3 August 1538, 'I must tell you what joy your letters have brought your father and me . . . I assure you we took great pleasure in learning of the health of the King and yourself and of the honest welcome and the honour which greeted your arrival. We and you have good cause to thank God that you are so well settled.'[1]

The predominant feeling of both Mary and her family was one of relief. The marriage, which had not been of her own seeking, looked as if it would turn out well. Conscious of her daughter's new dignity, Antoinette now addressed her letters to 'The Queen of Scotland' and signed herself 'Your humble and good mother' where before she had simply begun 'My daughter, my dear' and ended 'Your good mother'. Nothing else in their relationship had changed, however, and personal concern for Mary was uppermost in the Duchess's mind. She continued in the same vein when she wrote again, a few weeks later, commenting that she had been delighted to hear of 'the good treatment which you have received in the place to which Our Lord has sent you'.[2]

They were all missing each other keenly in the aftermath of their parting, and the Duchess hastened to send cheerful reassurances, dwelling on the thought that Mary might come back to see them some day. 'If only I were younger I would be tempted to risk it myself and come to see you,' she said, 'but I can't think of it at my age. As soon as there is peace, however, your father says that he will make the trip.'[3]

As well as holding out hopes of a family reunion, Antoinette was careful to give news of Francis, Mary's little son. In her

JAMES V AND THE ENGLISH

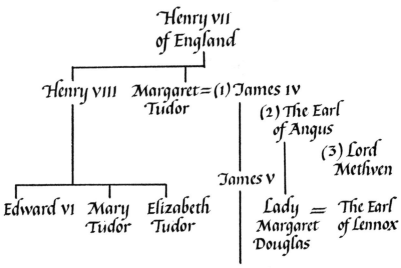

Henry VII
of England

Henry VIII   Margaret = (1) James IV
            Tudor   (2) The Earl
                          of Angus
                                  (3) Lord
                                      Methven
                    James V
Edward VI Mary Elizabeth   Lady = The Earl
          Tudor Tudor   Margaret   of Lennox
                            Douglas

letter of 3 August she had lost no time in 'coming back to
what I believe you most want to hear. Our grandson is as
well as possible and I have never seen him in such good health.
His grandfather is taking care of him and such a friendship
has grown up between them that there are tears whenever they
are separated . . . For three days he did not stop talking about
Madam the Queen and he remembered all sorts of things
about Châteaudun.'[4] A month later, she reported that 'our
little grandson is as well as he has always been', and, although
he had suffered a touch of scurvy, he was recovering and was
eating well. News of brothers and sisters, gossip about aunts
and uncles, snippets of information about friends, Court
gossip – Antoinette relayed them all in her frequent, affectionate letters although she in her turn did not hear as often from
Scotland as she would have liked. 'I know very well that you
take after your father,' she was scolding Mary that autumn,
'and are lazy about writing, unless Scotland has changed you.
I have only had your first letters and I am longing to know
how you have been since then.'[5]

Absorbed as she was in her new life, it was hardly surprising that Mary did not find time to write often. To dull the pain of parting from her son and from everything she knew, she had deliberately seized upon her new role as Queen of Scots. She would do everything James wanted and more. She would learn all she could about his country, she would show her husband that she was an intelligent, capable, experienced woman, worthy of the life he offered her. She was anxious to please, and she turned to her task with the apparently limitless energy which characterized the Guise family.

Of course it was difficult, more difficult than she had ever imagined. For one thing, the homesickness was much worse than she had feared. She found herself longing for the next messenger from France, listening eagerly to any little detail anyone could bring her about what was happening at Joinville. It took all her determination to force a more cheerful outlook and to occupy herself with adapting to life in Scotland.

That, in itself, was not as she had expected. True, the country and the climate were far better than she had envisaged. The royal palaces might be old-fashioned still, but the building work was going ahead and they were comfortable enough inside. There were Continental tapestries on the walls, fine linen cloths on the tables, and a pleasant variety of food laid out on the gold and silver vessels. James V might have inherited an empty exchequer, but he had transformed that situation entirely. His careful management had enabled him to accumulate a considerable amount of money, and this had recently been increased by the dowries of his two brides and by a Great Tax granted to him by the Pope, ostensibly for the foundation of a College of Justice. One contemporary was to estimate the royal fortune at 300,000 livres, and in consequence, James had no hesitation in spending lavishly.

He wished to live as a monarch should live and so he dressed, for instance, in splendid garments. He and Mary kept their first Christmas together in Edinburgh, and throughout the festivities he appeared in a series of magnificent outfits. One day he would wear his new purple satin doublet with the gold buttons. Next morning he would be in crimson silk, another time in white velvet trimmed with gold. His new crimson velvet cassock was lined with red taffeta and sewn with gold and silver, and he had gowns of cloth of gold and crimson velvet.[6]

He saw to it, too, that his household was well run and he kept a large complement of servants. There were over a hundred of them, in the charge of his steward, Sir David Christison. Two master households saw to the actual domestic running of the Court and in 1538 these were both men from Fife, James Learmonth of Dairsie and Patrick Wemyss of Pittencrieff. They organized the various departments within the household. The catering arrangements, for instance, were divided between the master cook, who prepared food for the King and his immediate circle, and the Court cook, who provided for the rest of the household. Similarly there were royal bakers and Court bakers, pastry cooks, poultrymen, turnspits and keepers of the spice house. All purchases and expenditure had to be recorded, of course, so there was a small army of clerks attached to each department.

Another important office was that of master of the wardrobe. Thomas Arthur occupied this position, looking after the royal garments and the royal jewels. He had in his charge not only existing clothes but bolt upon bolt of cloth waiting to be made up – flowered velvets, rich satins, cloth of gold. The royal tailor, Malcolm Gourlay, would come each month with directions from the King and receive from the wardrobe lengths of material for each new royal outfit. Shirts and nightlinen were made for James by Kate Bellenden, his seamstress.

Out of doors, the servants were equally numerous. Robert Gibb occupied the important position of squire of the King's Stables, which was the equivalent of the later master of the horse. At least fourteen grooms and eight pages worked for him, along with four yeomen of the stables. Arthur Sinclair and eight more grooms were specially employed to look after the King's Danish war chargers while John Sprotty and his son were the royal smiths.

These were what might be termed the ordinary, working servants. There was also a large number of men employed in more or less honorary positions. Well-born men sought positions as ushers in the King's chamber. One stood by the door of his inner chamber, two guarded the outer chamber and a fourth watched the hall door. There were four yeomen of the chamber, and several cupbearers, one of whom was the King's great favourite, Oliver Sinclair of Pitcairns. No fewer than nine pages were kept to run errands and generally make themselves useful, then of course there were servants connected with the royal recreations. Four men kept the King's dogs and four children looked after his hounds. The curiously named 'Badman' found hares for the royal sport, and five falconers accompanied the royal hunts. Finally, and of special interest to Mary of Guise, there were the musicians. Under the direction of Anton the taborer, five Italian minstrels, four violers, four trumpeters and two other taborers entertained the Court with music in the evenings.

As she sat with her husband at the Christmas banquets, Mary must have been taken with the colour of the scene around her. Most of the royal servants wore liveries of scarlet and yellow, echoing the royal standard with its red lion rampant on a yellow ground. Pantrymen, kitchenboys and men bearing dishes hurried past in parti-coloured doublets of red and yellow, with matching red and yellow hose. The pages wore black, but they had red bonnets, and the musicians were in red and yellow too, though Jacques Collumbell the violer wore an entirely red livery and Anton refused point blank to dress as the other minstrels did. After a fine show of temperament he had persuaded the royal officials to pay him a special allowance of £9 17/– a year for his livery, 'because that he would not wear red and yellow as his servants'.[7]

Now, as she watched her own black-clad servants mingling with the vivid red and yellow, Mary may have felt that the contrast in colours somehow underlined her own position and her own difficulties. She had come to Scotland with James's letter of appeal firmly in the forefront of her mind. He needed her help, so an important new task awaited her. But when she arrived, of course, she was confronted with all the things she had forgotten. James had lived most of his life as a bachelor.

His way of life was long established. He had his habits, his daily occupations, his friends and his advisers. Poor Madeleine had not lived long enough to make a place for herself at the Scottish Court. Mary was not coming to take up an existing position as the Scottish King's wife. His bride she certainly was, but she was also a foreigner coming to live at his Court with a large entourage of her own people. Somehow or other they would all have to learn to exist together and it was not going to be as easy as she had supposed.

An important factor was that she spoke French, and many of her household were French. She had her own master household who had come to Scotland with her, her secretary, her almoner and her physicians. She had a female French fool called Senat, and she had a little French dwarf named Jane. Her ladies were Frenchwomen like Mary Pierres, whose father had served her in France, and Joanna Grisenoir, who was later to be known in Scotland as Joanna Delareynville. They all spoke French together and the King spoke French to them. They even had their French tailor who could make sure that they dressed in the latest Paris fashions.

If she had so wished, Mary could have lived out her days in a little French enclave, speaking nothing but French, reading French, seeing scarcely anyone outside her immediate circle. But this was far from being what she wanted. She did not wish to be an isolated figure on the periphery of her husband's Court. She wanted to be his real wife and companion and to play an active, public part as his Queen. She was accordingly anxious to integrate herself and her entourage into James's existing way of life as quickly as possible.

It was not easy. He was surrounded by friends and courtiers. He went on much as he had done before. He did not take her into his confidence. It seemed to her sometimes that he had little time for her during the day. For the past ten years now he had been ruling his realm personally, and this meant that he was very much taken up with problems of state. There was the English threat to worry about, the French alliance, the problems of finance, the troubles of keeping the peace among quarrelsome subjects. The Scottish nobility did not treat him with the distant deference Mary had known at the Court of France. From the beginning the Stewart Kings had suffered from the fact that they had begun as just another noble family. A Stewart had married the daughter of King Robert the Bruce, and so the crown of Scotland had come to them, but their fellow nobles did not forget that at one time they had all been of equal status. The royal minorities had not helped, and with surprise Mary saw her husband's leading subjects thrust their advice bluntly upon him and treat him with rather less than the respect which she herself would have demanded. There was little opportunity to talk with him when Fleming, Huntly, Arran and the rest were pressing importunately round him, when Cardinal Beaton was always at his elbow to advise him and when there were favourites like Oliver Sinclair to take up his attention.

However, time would cure that, Mary consoled herself, and she set out on a deliberate policy of making herself necessary to the King and seeing that her household was acceptable to his. With prudent management, she would replace the others as his principal adviser and the petty jealousies and quarrelling among the servants would fade away as the 'foreigners' settled down.

Mary therefore began to foster friendship and understanding by every possible method. She began by introducing Scots into her household. Scottish ladies could lay claim by right to be in attendance on her, and if she were to understand and befriend the Scots, the ladies would help her in the doing of it. Lady Drummond and Lady Craigie accordingly came to help Mary Pierres and the rest, all dressing in gowns of purple and white, and in the spring they were joined by the Earl of Lennox's sisters.[8]

There were other Scottish servants too. The four grooms in her chamber were all Scots, Andrew Drummond, Walter Scrimgeour, Gibbie Moncrieff and John Moncrieff. Although her pantryman was a Monsieur Beglatt, the man who looked after her spices was Sandy Durham and it was William Gib who took care of her geldings. The Scots and French might squabble and grumble about each other at first but, working together daily, they would surely come to a better understanding.

One of the basic difficulties, of course, was that of language. It was all very well that James and many of his courtiers could speak French, but it still meant that there were long hours when Mary sat and listened to the unfamiliar Scottish language eddying around her. At home she had been at the centre always of a laughing group of ladies and courtiers who had appreciated her ready wit. Now she had to sit silent, listening to the jocularity and to the arguments, but taking no part. Obviously, she would have to learn Scots as quickly as possible.

She did so with considerable success, and eventually she was able to switch easily from one language to the other, even if her mastery of the foreign syntax was not complete. John Knox, amid his many bitter criticisms of her, has left us a description of how she spoke. Noting the events of 1558 and Mary's dealings with the Protestants, he records that 'There was heard nothing of the Queen's part but, "My joys, my hearts, what ails you? Me means no evil to you, nor to your preachers. . . . Me knew nothing of this proclamation . . ." ' He intended his readers to share his scorn for Mary, but instead he gave an unintentionally touching description and it is possible to catch in his satire an echo of a pretty voice speaking Scots with an engaging accent.

Eager to pursue her policy of assimilation into Scottish life, Mary encouraged her ladies to make friends with the Scottish courtiers. It was not long, indeed, before she arranged a marriage for Mary Pierres. One of James's most faithful supporters was Lord Seton. He had recently been left a widower with a large family, and when he began to show an interest in Mary, the Queen approved and arranged their betrothal. Joanna Grisenoir also became the wife of a Scot.[9]

Mary herself spared no effort in winning the friendship of her husband's family and in doing so she scored a notable success with her mother-in-law. Margaret Tudor was an awkward person to deal with at the best of times. She had quarrelled with her brother, she had fallen out with her son and she was now trying to divorce her third husband, Lord Methven, so that she could remarry her second husband, the Earl of Angus. Needless to say, James V refused to countenance this and so Margaret was continually complaining about him, alleging that he kept her scandalously short of money. It is no small tribute to Mary of Guise that she won over her difficult mother-in-law, who was soon praising her for her honourable behaviour.[10]

Her diplomacy was even more in evidence in her dealings with her husband's children. Several of his illegitimate sons were away at school in St Andrews, but there remained his little daughter Lady Jane Stewart. Missing her own son as she did, Mary found solace in the small girl's company and took her into her household, caring for her almost as though she were her daughter.[11] Her pleasing ways soon earned her the friendship of many of James's relatives, and that first New Year they all exchanged gifts of gold rings, gold bracelets and gold chains.[12]

When the festivities were over, the Court resumed its peripatetic existence. January was spent in Linlithgow. After that they moved to Falkland, travelling west again to spend Easter at Stirling. By mid-April they were back in Falkland once more, and they divided their time that summer between there and St Andrews.

The more Mary saw of the Scottish way of life, the more eager did she become to show James what improvements could be introduced. In many ways, the Scottish Court for all its comfort and liveliness seemed to her to be medieval in outlook. The noblemen dressed with the splendour of the Middle Ages, hunted and listened to music but there were no fine paintings, no cabinets of jewels, no lengthy discussions on philosophy or political theory. Many things could be improved, and contact with France could bring to the Scots all the benefits of Renaissance civilization.

Scotland, of course, had always had close contacts with the Continent and many Scots had travelled abroad and had seen the ways of others. The trouble was that constant warfare had occupied their energies and depleted their resources. Now, if

THE FAMILY OF JAMES V

James IV = Margaret Tudor = (2) Archibald, Earl of Angus
                      (3) Lord Methven

James V = (2) Mary of Guise
(1) Princess Madeleine

and the following
illegitimate children
of James V

James   Robert   Mary
(1540–1)   (b. and d. 1541)   (1542–87)

John,
Prior of Coldingham,
son of Elizabeth
Carmichael
(c. 1531–)

Robert,
Prior of Whithorn,
son of
Lady Elizabeth Stewart

Adam,
Prior of Charterhouse, Perth,
son of
Lady Elizabeth Stewart

Margaret   James,
Commendator of Melrose
and Kelso, son of
Elizabeth Shaw
(1529–77)

Jane,
daughter of
Elizabeth Bethune

The Lord James,
Prior of St Andrews
and later Earl of Moray,
son of Margaret Erskine
(–1570)

James, son of
Christina Barclay

Robert,
Commendator of
Holyrood, later
Earl of Orkney,
son of Euphemia
Elphinstone

peace could be maintained, a more sophisticated way of life could begin. Because of these thoughts and because of her natural anxiety to have news from home, Mary fostered communication with France. Members of her own household were constantly coming and going, taking messages, attending to their own affairs at home, bearing gifts. That first Christmas, the French King's emissary, Monsieur Lassenze, came over to Edinburgh and stayed on until early March. One of the French pursuivants was with him, and the Duke of Guise's master household had come too.[13]

Then again, Mary sent emissaries to make purchases for her abroad. Her master household was dispatched regularly to buy wine and dried fruit for her in France, and most of the cloth for her garments came from there.[14] She even sent over John Mossman, the royal jeweller, to purchase fifty pounds' worth of gold work for her.[15]

Not surprisingly, the French influence did make itself felt in Scotland. James gave orders for 'a saddle of the French fashion' to be covered in leather for him and he had a new black velvet coat made up 'of a new fashion come out of France'.[16] Mary's servants went about in clothes made of 'French black' or 'Paris black' and had hose of 'French grey'.[17] The Earl of Lennox's sisters had kirtles lined with 'French red' and each received a 'French hat'.[18] Naturally enough, Scottish ladies took with enthusiasm to the latest French fashions and it was not merely the courtiers who imitated the Queen. The townspeople of Edinburgh began to follow suit, thereby bringing down on themselves the wrath of Sir David Lindsay. Trains, he declared, were all very well for a monarch, but merchants' wives looked ridiculous with their dress hems trailing behind them in the mud and dust. 'The Queen they should not counterfeit,' he admonished them severely.[19]

On a less frivolous note, Mary enlisted her mother's help for two important projects. Anxious to have a personal hand in the improvements being made at her residences of Falkland and Stirling, she determined to send for some French masons. After considerable delay, Antoinette managed to locate six who were willing to come to Scotland, though they did not arrive until the summer of 1539.[20] Nor did Mary neglect the gardens outside her palace. She sought the help of an old friend, Mademoiselle de Tern, asking her specially to send over cuttings of fruit trees when the season was right. Scotland had an abundance of apples, pears and plums but there was not the variety that she had known at home. She realized, of course, that some of the fruit grown in the warm gardens at Joinville would never flourish in the colder Scottish air, but certain species could be cultivated. Mademoiselle de Tern was eager to be of service, and she sent off a parcel of cuttings of three kinds of plums of the best eating sort and two varieties of delicious pears. These, she told Mary, would allow her the happiness of seeing them grown in her country, where her people would never have known such pleasure before.[21]

There were, too, the forests at Falkland to be considered. Her father's master household therefore received instructions to send over several young, wild boars. He was at the French Court when her letter arrived, but he set off obediently for Elboeuf, hoping to capture some. Unfortunately, he had no sooner arrived than the King recalled him, so his mission remained unfulfilled and he had to send Mary an apologetic reply.[22]

Rather more serious in intent was Mary's other principal project. Quantities of valuable minerals had always been found in Scotland and when she heard that there was even gold to be had, she was immediately interested. Here, surely, was a solution to future economic difficulties. She decided that experienced miners from Lorraine would know best how to exploit the minerals of Crawfordmuir, high up in the hills of western Scotland, so once more she sought the assistance of her mother.

In the autumn of 1538 Antoinette made investigations and found that the miners would prefer to wait until spring. The thought of the voyage north was enough to deter them unless it could be undertaken in better weather. Mary was impatient, for she liked things to be done at once, but there was nothing for it but to wait. By March of the following year

Antoinette was assuring her that the miners would set out at Easter and that Duke Antony's wife might be able to supply two more. By June, she was promising that the miners would be in Scotland soon after midsummer, but it was not until well into July that they finally arrived at St Andrews. After seeing Mary and the King they went to the west accompanied by 'a Scots boy that speaks French . . . to serve them until they get the language'.

In the end, they could have picked up only a smattering of Scots, for their stay was short. They worked at the mine in August and September, but on 9 October 1539 they took their leave of James V and set sail once more for France. In spite of the brevity of their visit, the King seems to have been pleased with them for he paid them eighty pounds.[23]

By that summer, when Mary had been in Scotland for a year, she began to feel that her efforts were being rewarded. Scots and French did seem to be settling down together more amicably, and in innumerable little ways she was making her influence felt. There was one outstanding source of anxiety, however, which had begun to occupy her mind increasingly. She was still not pregnant. From the earliest days of her marriage she had been confidently expecting to find herself with child again, and she was looking forward to that time with deep longing. More than anything else, she wanted a son. Her desire was twofold. At a personal level, she was desperate to have a baby to replace Francis, whom she had left behind, and Louis, whom she had lost so soon after his birth. Her mother was good at sending her descriptions of Francis. She even sent drawings, and a portrait, but it was not enough. Mary's sense of loss could only be assuaged by the birth of another child.

Even more important, her husband required an heir. She knew perfectly well that he had married her in the expectation of her bearing sons. Her suitable stature and her previous fecundity had been a common topic of conversation at the courts of Europe during her second marriage negotiations. Moreover, as if the matter needed any emphasis, it had escaped no one that Mary had not yet been crowned Queen of

Scots. Her own grandfather had repudiated the wife who had failed to bear him children and everyone knew how Henry VIII, her husband's uncle, had treated his first two wives when they did not give him an heir. For the honour of her family and for her own security, Mary needed to bear a son as soon as possible. Once she was the mother of his children, James would withhold his trust from her no longer and her position as his consort would be firmly established.

Her mother and her uncles shared her anxiety, promising each time they wrote to pray for 'the fine son you so much desire'.[24] The first year of marriage had passed and the second summer had gone by. In August 1539, she and James went on a pilgrimage to the Isle of May in the Firth of Forth. St Adrian's shrine there was a well-known source of help for barren women. In September she accompanied her husband on a hunting expedition to the west of Scotland, but it was probably when she was back at Falkland that her happy suspicions were confirmed. Her child would be born the following spring.[25]

Mary now entered one of the most hopeful and contented periods of her life. Her pregnancy had the effect she had desired, and her husband was now loving and attentive. The new warmth in their relationship was reflected in Mary's correspondence with her mother. When she wrote Antoinette a letter that autumn, James added a few lines in his own hand. The Duchess was charmed, and responded by teasing her daughter, threatening to tell James all her faults. James replied by sending his mother-in-law the gift of a diamond, along with his portrait. 'I find his picture so handsome,' Antoinette jokingly told Mary, 'that you would be jealous if you knew how much I loved him!'[26]

All this was very different in tone from the polite deference with which Antoinette had previously treated James, and her happiness was completed when Mary wrote to tell her that her coronation was now being planned. At long last, she was to be crowned Queen of Scots. James was not even waiting to see if his child was a boy: the ceremony would take place that winter, several months before the baby's birth.

The Christmas season was spent at Linlithgow, where the festivities had a distinct air of happy anticipation. By the end of January, the Court was in a fever of preparation for the coronation. Letters were being sent out to the nobles and their ladies, summoning them to attend the ceremony. The magnificent chapel vessels and furnishings were being carefully transported from the Chapel Royal at Stirling to the Abbey at Holyrood. Cardinal Beaton was fussing about his own wardrobe, ordering a new pair of red damask sandals for the great day. Down in Leith, John Gogar the carter was instructing his men to drag eighteen loads of munitions up to Edinburgh Castle and quantities of fir spars were being taken up to Holyrood to the Abbey to be made into the usual scaffolding for the congregation. The palace chambers were being hung with tapestry, and in February Edinburgh began to fill with people from all parts of the country, from the peers and their wives to the chaplains from Stirling who would take part in the service.[27]

At last everything was ready, and Mary was crowned Queen of Scots on 22 February 1540, by Cardinal Beaton. She was six months pregnant, but she was splendidly dressed in royal robes of purple velvet lined with white corded taffeta. Over her robes she wore a fine gold belt set with a single sapphire. Her silver sceptre had been specially made for her by James Mossman, and gilded with four rose nobles. He, too, had made her crown. He had been paid £45 'for making of the Queen's crown and furnishing of stones thereto, which weighed thirty-five ounces of gold of the mine'.

By her side was the King, an equally magnificent figure in his royal robes of purple velvet lined with ermine. His crown was slightly larger than Mary's, weighing forty-one and a quarter ounces, and it was set with twenty-four precious stones including three great garnets and a great emerald. On his finger was a ring set with a turquoise.

Cardinal Beaton sang Mass: the crown was placed on Mary's head, and her position as Scotland's Queen was finally affirmed.[28] The day had been something of an ordeal as well as a triumph, and once the celebrations were over she was glad to be able to relax and await the birth of her child. Even so, her life had to be lived in public, and an interesting glimpse of her that February is afforded by Sir Ralph Sadler, envoy of Henry VIII.

Sir Ralph had been sent north ostensibly with a gift of geldings from uncle to nephew but actually to try to arrange a meeting between the two and to urge James to dissolve the Scottish monasteries. Supreme Head of the English Church since 1531, Henry had severed his links with the Pope and had seized large quantities of Church property for himself. His parliament of 1536 passed an act dissolving 370 lesser religious houses, whose lands he promptly sold or rented out. Pleased with the results, he proceeded enthusiastically with this policy and by 1540 most of the monasteries had been suppressed. Knowing that his nephew was equally anxious to accumulate wealth, he hoped to persuade James to abandon his support of the papacy by pointing out to him the financial benefits of turning against Rome.

Sir Ralph Sadler was eager to have an audience of James V, but his first sight of the Scottish Court was scarcely encouraging. When he was taken there at nine o'clock in the morning, the day after his arrival in Edinburgh, he found the King at Mass, surrounded by bishops, monks, priests, nobles and gentlemen. The Queen was absent because she was not feeling too well, but Sir Ralph's guide assured him that if he lingered in the chapel at 'any season' he would see her come to Mass.

Next morning at the same time he went back to the chapel and there, sure enough, was 'the Queen, the King's wife, hearing a sermon in French, accompanied with a number of ladies and gentlewomen'. After the service was over, Sir David Lindsay presented Sir Ralph, who told Mary that Henry VIII sent her his greetings. She replied decorously that she was most grateful and promised that if she could, she would do everything possible in the interests of amity between her husband and Henry. Sir Ralph then saw James himself, and finished his duties for the day by talking with Margaret Tudor. 'She told me much . . . of her own affairs,' he reported, 'how she was well treated and much made of, of the new Queen.'[29]

Not long after the coronation, the Court moved to Stirling. In these final days, Mary was spending leisurely hours with her ladies, working at her favourite embroidery. At the beginning of April, twelve double hanks of sewing gold were sent to her from the wardrobe, with sixteen ounces of white sewing silk. Her female fool, Senat, was still with her, keeping her amused, and there were all manner of happy plans to be talked over with her ladies.

The King had decreed that his child should be born in St Andrews, so in early May the Court moved there, Mary presumably travelling in a litter. Her chambers at St Andrews were now prepared carefully for her confinement. Two beds were set aside for her use. One was hung with curtains of white damask fringed with white silk, and the other had curtains of yellow damask fringed with gold. Both had matching covers, with sheets of white taffeta. Mary herself ordered a loose-fitting gown of flowered purple damask and Andrew Mansioun, a French carver, was at work on an ornate cradle for the expected baby.[30]

As ever, James was himself occupied with affairs of state, and he had decided that the best way to deal with current disorders in the Western Isles was to make a personal visit. What is puzzling is that the voyage north seems to have been planned to coincide with Mary's confinement. Even if James, with his nervous disposition, dreaded the actual event, it would have been only natural for him to wish to be on hand when the baby came. Instead, he seems to have gone to the west, to prepare for his expedition. Perhaps the simplest explanation is the correct one: Mary may have miscalculated the date of the baby's birth. She did not always recognize her pregnancies for what they were in the early weeks, and she may have thought that the child was not due until June or even July. Again, the birth may have been slightly premature.

Whatever the explanation, 'the King scarce had taken anchor at Dumbarton, when . . . came messengers that his wife was lighter of a lad, a fair and wellfavoured lad unto him, both fair and lusty'.[31] The baby was born on 22 May 1540, and his parents were delighted. James rewarded Andrew Michelson, the messenger who brought him the news, with the promise of a new suit of clothes, and the royal accounts duly record the making of a Paris black gown, a serge coat, a black velvet doublet and hose with a bonnet for him, noting that 'This livery was given to him for bringing of tidings to the King's Grace of the nativity of My Lord Prince'.[32]

James then disembarked rapidly and rode at once to St Andrews to see his wife and son. Triumphant messengers were dispatched throughout Scotland to announce the news and to invite the nobles and their wives to the baptism. Special messengers were also dispatched to England and to France.

When he was a week old, Mary's son was baptized in St Andrews, by torchlight. He was named James and he was given the titles of Duke of Rothesay and Prince of Scotland. His godfathers were the Archbishop of St Andrews and James, Earl of Arran, who was now displaced from his position as heir to the throne. His godmother was Margaret Tudor. Throughout Scotland bonfires were lit that night. James at last had his legitimate male heir.[33]

No one rejoiced more at the birth than Mary did herself. Her dearest wish had been satisfied and during her lying-in she saw as much of the baby as she possibly could for she knew that she would not be able to bring him up as Antoinette had brought up her sons or as she herself had planned to raise little Francis. This baby was Prince of Scotland. From the very beginning he would have his own household, and his upbringing would not be in her hands. James had ordained that he should live in St Andrews, so there he would remain, while Mary moved around with the Court. For the time being he was hers, though, and while James set off on his postponed northern voyage, Mary stayed on at St Andrews.

While she recovered her strength gradually she must often have gone to admire the little Prince as he lay in his richly-carved cradle with its crimson and red velvet covers. Once she was able to go out, she travelled short distances in her fine new litter. It had been specially made for her and it was of black velvet, the harness decorated with gilded brass thistles and fleurs-de-lys. Wrapped warmly in her black taffeta gown lined with rabbit skins, she enjoyed the bracing sea air and she soon regained her former vigour. By the time James returned from the north, she was ready to move on with him once more and the beginning of August found her in Falkland, preparing for the autumn's activities by ordering a new riding cloak of scarlet cloth trimmed with crimson velvet.[34]

Wherever she went, her new son was never far from her mind. Prince James was now in the care of a group of specially chosen ladies. He had his wet-nurse of course, but he also had a complete household which even included his own chaplains. He lacked for nothing. His little coats of white satin and his shirts of white linen were made up by the King's own tailor, and James took a delight in lavishing gifts upon him – a silver spoon, a gold whistle, a bear's tooth set in gold, presumably for him to suck when he was teething.[35]

Even in the midst of his pleasure at his son's birth, however, James remained a prey to melancholy and neurotic suspicions. He was often ill, and Mary anxiously sent to France for drugs for him. That autumn, he caused her considerable unease and startled his entire Court when he suddenly turned against an old friend. For many years past, one of his close companions had been Sir James Hamilton of Finnart. An illegitimate son of a previous Lord Hamilton, Sir James was master of works and as such was intimately involved in the important building programmes going on at Falkland and Stirling. High in the royal favour, Sir James received both financial rewards and the King's trust.

In the early autumn of 1540, however, James suddenly had his old friend arrested. With mysterious haste he was accused of plotting against the King, was sentenced to death and was executed. There had been no previous hint of trouble. Some thought that James had become a prey to imaginary fears, others said that Hamilton must have had some scheme to kill the Prince and the King both, so that the crown would come to his own family; most people declared that the charge of treason was merely an excuse for James to seize his wealthy subject's possessions.

Whatever the truth of the matter, the King certainly went on to take the dead man's property and amongst the belongings which came into his hands were the furnishings from Hamilton's chapel. These James proceeded to give to his own infant son. He delivered to John Mossman 'Sir James Hamilton's chapel gear', that is to say, his silver cross, his candlesticks, a holy water stoup, the bell and the box for the Host, with instructions that Prince James's arms be engraved upon them.[36]

Whether Mary of Guise felt any qualm of superstitious distaste at her husband's action remains unknown, but the death of Sir James Hamilton certainly preyed on the King's mind. During one of his periodic bouts of depression, he began to suffer from terrible nightmares. He awoke from one of these in a panic, describing to his alarmed servant how in his dream the dead man had come to him with a drawn sword in his hand and had struck off both his arms, then had vanished, promising to return soon after to cut off his head.

If Mary was troubled by her husband's state of mind, she was soon even more worried by news which came to her from St Andrews. The Prince was not too well. Hitherto he had been a fine, thriving baby but now his wet-nurse's milk had failed and there was nothing for it but to replace her. The woman was reluctantly dismissed and a substitute named Janet McGie was found instead but, as normally happened in such cases, the baby's digestion was upset by the change. Mary was thrown into a fever of anxiety by the news. What if he became really ill? Perhaps the women looking after him had exaggerated or perhaps, worse still, they had minimized his sickness so as not to alarm the King and herself. She had experience of babies and she had always been interested in nursing and in medical matters. If only she could have been with the child, she could have judged for herself. As it was, all she could do was to pour out her anxiety in her next letter home.

Antoinette wrote back reassuringly. It had not in the least

surprised her, she said, that the baby had taken badly with the different nurse. That was only to be expected, and most babies who had a change of this sort were unwell for a few days but soon picked up again. No doubt this would be the case with little Prince James. However, Mary must be sure to write again soon with the latest news for, she declared, great was her affection 'for this little creature whom I have never seen'.[37]

In her same letter, Antoinette made inquiries about a rather happier subject. Was it true, as rumours suggested, that Mary was pregnant again? It was indeed. Only two months after the birth of Prince James, she had conceived once more, and her child was expected the following spring. Before she knew that she was pregnant, Mary accompanied her husband on a visit to Glamis and Dundee, but when she realized her condition she retired to her favourite residence of Falkland. There she spent most of her pregnancy, within easy reach of the little Prince in St Andrews.

As her mother had predicted, the baby recovered quickly from his upset and was thriving once more. Mary was able to enjoy peace of mind on that score. She did not see much of the King that winter, though she did join him at Stirling for the Christmas celebrations, but she was happy enough away from him. They had grown into an agreeable relationship together. Mary was still only twenty-five, but she had a maturity and a strength of character which her husband lacked, and he had come to depend on her. He had, since his marriage, apparently given up his liaisons with other women, and he was now turning to his wife for reassurance and consolation when he was troubled or harassed. He listened to Mary's advice and he often did as she suggested. No longer anxious about her own position at Court, she was able to enjoy life in her own household during this peaceful interlude. The time would come when she would take up her active role as his consort once more, but for the moment she was content to rest at Falkland while James and his Court made their accustomed circuit of the royal residences.

It had been decided this time that the coming child should be born at Stirling, and so in March Mary made the journey westwards by litter. There she found James in a state of nervous apprehension, still troubled in his mind by thoughts of Sir James Hamilton of Finnart and by morbid fears for the future. She did what she could to cheer him, then on 24 April she went into labour. The great cannon at Stirling were dragged up to the highest point of the castle wall in readiness to fire off a salvo when the new child arrived, and a few hours later they thundered out over the town. Mary had given birth to a second son.

Here then was a fine way of ridding James of his melancholy thoughts. The succession was secure. Scotland had two royal princes, and Mary had proved once again that she could be the mother of sons. Immediate preparations were made for the christening, which took place three days later in the castle chapel. The baby was given the name of Robert, after the earlier Stewart kings, and he bore the titles of Duke of Albany, Earl of Fife and Earl of Menteith.[38]

For a week there were celebrations and festivities, but on the seventh day the rejoicings were cut short. A distraught messenger came riding into the castle, demanding to see the King at once. He was shown into the royal presence, and there he delivered his alarming news. He had come from St Andrews, to say that Prince James was critically ill: they feared the worst.

The King was appalled. There had been no hint of trouble. True, there had been that upset the previous autumn, but ever since the baby had been thriving. Only two days earlier the royal tailor had been ordered to make a new taffeta coat for the Prince, who was growing fast. Shocked and alarmed, James immediately took horse for St Andrews. He rode urgently through the Lowlands of Scotland, through Stirlingshire and Fife, past Cupar and on at last to St Andrews but he was too late. He arrived to find the little Prince already dead.

Dazed with grief, he left the chamber where his son lay and came out to find yet another white-faced messenger awaiting him. The King had scarcely left Stirling when the new baby, Robert, had fallen ill and now seemed at the point of death. Scarcely able to assimilate this dreadful news, James hurried back to Stirling. Prince Robert was still alive when he got there, but he passed away shortly afterwards, within hours of his brother's death.[39]

The entire nation was stunned by this unexpected tragedy. That one Prince should die was sad enough, but that both should die on the same day was too appalling to contemplate. There was a terrible feeling of doom about it and all who had heard of James's nightmare saw the parallel: in his dream he had lost both arms: in life he had lost both sons.

Mary and James were inconsolable. The little Prince Robert's body was placed in a lead coffin and taken to Edinburgh. Prince James's body was brought there too, and they were buried together in the Abbey of Holyroodhouse. 'The death of both the King of Scots's sons . . . doth much perplex the said King and divers other nobles and councillors there . . .' an English emissary in Scotland reported to Henry VIII, while Margaret Tudor wrote to tell her brother that the King and Queen were both in great distress. To add to their anguish, there were the usual disquieting rumours. 'The occasion of their deaths,' said Henry's correspondent, 'is suspected to be by poison, as I am informed, and the Queen [is] very sickly and full of heaviness.'[40]

Rumours of poison were always common when a high-born person died suddenly, and so untoward were the circumstances on this occasion that it was all too easy to attribute them to some unnatural agency. Mary herself seems to have shared in these fears. She wrote wretchedly to her mother, apparently alluding to the possibility of poison and referring to the physical appearance of the dead babies. Antoinette realized that in her weakened condition Mary was vulnerable to all manner of terrible doubts, so she wrote back as consolingly as she could, telling her daughter gently to put such thoughts from her mind. She herself believed that Prince James had died from overfeeding, and emphasized that she had always distrusted the change of nurse. It had probably been an excess of concern which had killed the little Prince, nothing more sinister, and as to Prince Robert, many infants' lives were tragically brief. Mary must seek comfort in God and in the company of her husband: she had told her mother that James was taking the loss so well that she had decided she must follow his example. Antoinette had no doubt that she would bear her grief with all the courage she could muster. After all, she and her husband were young yet. There was plenty of time.[41]

4

The Death of the King

⁓ᵛᶜᵃᵛ⁓

With the loss of the Princes, so much else was lost. Nothing could have had a worse effect on James V than the death of both his sons. Superficially, he had seemed to bear his grief well, but in fact his confidence in the future was shattered and he was plunged into the deepest depression. If before he had been overly suspicious of those around him, his distrust now bordered on paranoia. From childhood he had never been able to rely upon his nobles. Now he was convinced that they were all plotting his overthrow and death. They might stand smilingly before him, but they were having secret correspondence with England and some of them might even have murdered his sons. Nothing would ever be right again.

For their part, his lords viewed his behaviour with alarm. He was liable to turn on any of them at a moment's notice. Had he not caused Lady Glamis to be burned as a witch? Had he not ordered the execution of Sir James Hamilton of Finnart? None of them felt safe from his unpredictable wrath, and there were those among them who were now driven to seek the friendship of England in a desperate search for a measure of security.

In such an atmosphere of suspicion, fear and envy were contagious and it was perhaps not surprising that the death of the babies marked the beginning of a steady decline in Mary's relationship with her husband. United at first in their grief, they now began to drift apart. Even before Prince Robert's birth there had been a hint that all was not well between them, that James's pathological suspicions were turning against even his wife. On 14 May 1541, Sir Thomas Wharton had written to Henry VIII, repeating the latest

89

news given to him by one of his spies in Scotland. The man was of the opinion that James V would not make war on England in the near future, for 'the King's nature, his disposition and his qualities are not given to war, but daily labouring in his mind covetously for profit, with most suspicion of his own nobles and subjects, and jealousy over the Queen'.[1]

John Knox, in one of his many unpleasant innuendoes, was later to hint that James suspected his wife of being too friendly with Cardinal Beaton. This was a highly unlikely suggestion. Mary did not particularly care for the Cardinal, for all he was so enthusiastic for the French alliance. Apart from anything else, he was old enough to be her father and he had for many years enjoyed a permanent relationship with the woman who was the mother of his numerous children. Considering Mary's advanced state of pregnancy in the winter of 1541, it seems extraordinary that anyone could have suspected her of an illicit liaison.

In any event, Mary was simply not the type of woman to be interested in extramarital affairs. She had always been much admired for her dignity and her virtue. Highly intelligent, she was more readily diverted by intellectual pleasures than by physical passion. She had been trained from childhood to take her place in society as a virtuous wife, to direct her energies into the upbringing of her children and the running of her household. She was perfectly content in the company of her ladies, and a maternal solicitude for all the members of her staff was one of her most marked characteristics.

Of course, she had spent several years at a Court where lighthearted dalliance was a convention, and it is possible that James invested some of her merry, joking ways of talking to his nobles with a significance which they did not possess. Then again, there were always those who were ready to make trouble. Seeing Mary's increasing influence over her husband, some courtiers found themselves or fancied themselves neglected, and grew jealous. The Queen was a foreigner. She had brought a train of foreigners with her. They were gaining a hold over James, a hold which must be broken. There were accordingly always men ready to magnify any little difficulty, to misrepresent the Queen to the King, the King to the Queen.

Had Mary been in her normal health she could have dealt with the situation. As it was, she was suffering from the same feelings of despair which engulfed her husband, and she was in a lowered condition physically. All the doubts and fears which had plagued her in the early months of her marriage now returned with redoubled intensity. She had failed to give James the healthy, living sons he needed and she had failed to rescue him from despondency. She felt out of sympathy with the Scottish courtiers, unwanted and insecure. Her husband was preoccupied with the threat from England, with his determination to amass a fortune. He was spending more and more time away from her, and he seemed to have returned to all his old ways, hurling himself into an exhausting round of hunting and riding which left him little leisure for his wife and gave the troublemakers the opportunity of sympathizing odiously with her over his neglect. They also said that he had taken up once more with other women.

A few of James's letters to his wife survive from this period, giving a clear indication of the growing misunderstanding between them. Some time during the early spring, James wrote to her in peevish tones. 'I have received the letter which it has pleased you to write to me,' he told her, 'and which I find very strange, being as ill as I have been for these three days past. I entreat you to deem me a man of my word and promise, in which I shall never fail. The rest of my reply you shall have by my own hand immediately . . . Your servant and friend, James Rex.'[2]

A letter of the following autumn gives an even more explicit mention of difficulties created deliberately by others. Towards the end of the year, Margaret Tudor died. James had entertained scant affection for his mother while she lived, but he saw her death as yet another omen of disaster. She had died near Perth, so he went there to clear up her affairs and see to the funeral. While he was doing this, he received a reproachful message from Mary. Her letter has not survived, but his reply gives an indication of its content.

'I have received the letter which it has pleased you to write to me, for which I thank you humbly', he began. 'But those who have told you that I do not want to leave here have falsely lied, because I have no thought but of being with you on Sunday. As for my mother's things, I will not forget, begging you not to be so thundering until you know the truth. Praying you to be of good cheer until my return, which will be on Sunday, and praying Our Lord to give you a good and long life, your humble husband, James Rex.'[3]

In her unhappiness, Mary was ready to believe the rumours she heard, and she apparently reacted by being somewhat imperious in her dealings with her husband. It was his turn to write again to her in conciliatory tones a few days later, telling her that 'Following your command, I am sending by this bearer the gown and the laces which I promised you, along with my most humble commendations to your good grace, praying you to take the occasion to treat me well and to keep the promise you have made me as a good wife must do to him who merits and always will merit it, for the rest of my life, with the aid of God. Entreating Our Lord to give you a good and long life, Your most humble husband, James Rex.'[4]

The talk of a promise is cryptic; presumably he had asked her not to believe the rumours she had heard about him, but to be assured of his fidelity. The gravity of the trouble between them is indicated by the fact that news of their differences spread to France, where Mary's own family were distressed to hear from various sources that all was not well between them. Her mother wrote to her at once, anxiously referring to a rumour that Mary was suffering great annoyances. This had been a source of considerable concern to herself and to Claud, the Duchess said, and if the trouble continued the Duke would come to Scotland himself to see what was wrong.

Mary was dismayed when she received her mother's message. It was hurtful enough that James should stay away from her, it was humiliating to have the entire Court buzzing with speculation about their relationship, but it was unendurable to have her own family hear of these things. From her earliest days Mary had been proud, and now that she was a Queen she was all the more conscious of the dignity of her position. She sent one of her ladies to Joinville at once, to tell her mother that there was no truth in the rumours she had heard, but in private her bitterness increased.[5]

According to one chronicler, James V had no sooner become the father of two sons than he decided that he 'needed not to care for nothing but his own pleasure . . . and sensual lusts in using of his own body'. In view of the brief time during which James actually had two living sons, the chronology of this is unacceptable, and it is more probable that James turned to physical pleasures from despair rather than from self-satisfaction. There is no direct evidence that he kept a mistress until the end of 1542, but his pursuit of other women seems the most likely explanation for Mary's distress.

The attitude towards mistresses was in the sixteenth century somewhat ambivalent. It was well known that monarchs fathered children who were then publicly recognized and brought up at Court. Mary had known from the start about James's illegitimate sons and she had accepted his natural daughter into her own household without question. Nevertheless, she had a right to demand a certain degree of discretion from her husband. Before his marriage his various affairs could be regarded as proof of his virility: after his marriage, he should keep them a secret.

The outlook of the virtuous wives of the time is perhaps best illustrated by the amusing story of Mary's own parents. While he remained at the French Court, Claud conducted his amours with the utmost decorum, but in middle age he retired from public life and settled at Joinville with his wife. Not long afterwards, his attention was taken by a pretty young girl who lived in the town of Joinville and he began to pay regular visits to her house. Now, unfortunately, the castle looked directly down on to the town, and it was not long before Antoinette realized what he was doing. Such a public insult to her honour could not be tolerated. She did not confront Claud with her knowledge, however. There would be no undignified scene. Instead, a plan occurred to her which appealed to her sense of humour. She called several servants to her. They were ordered to collect a number of the finest tapestries in the castle, some handsome pieces of furniture, several velvet cushions and a selection of silver dishes. These they were to carry down to the house of the Duke's mistress. When the startled girl opened her door, they explained that the furnishings were for her house, since the Duchess wished the Duke to enjoy all his accustomed home comforts.

Brushing aside the girl's protests, the servants put the expensive furnishings in position, then left. That afternoon Claud arrived for his usual visit. He went in, saw his own belongings, and fell back. The excited girl babbled forth an explanation, repeating Antoinette's words to him. Claud turned on his heel, marched out and went back to the castle. Never again did he visit his friend in Joinville. He said not a word to his wife and she never once mentioned the subject to him, but he immediately began to lay out a beautiful new garden for her as a token of his love and respect. He had broken the unwritten code of conduct, and he knew it. By acknowledging his fault, he retained intact his affectionate relationship with his wife.[6]

Mary of Guise's outlook was much the same. So long as James visited his mistresses in secret, she could keep up the polite fiction that they did not exist. Unfortunately, James did not possess his father-in-law's tact and his courtiers were all too ready to pounce on any hint of scandal, with the result that Mary was humiliated and affronted by his behaviour.

At first, they did try to keep up appearances. In the summer of 1541, in deep mourning, they had made a progress through Perth and Aberdeen. In the latter city, they visited the university there, entertained by pageants performed by the burgesses and students: 'No day passed but when either they had not a comedy or some controversy [debate] or orations in Greek or Latin tongue'.[7]

They returned to Edinburgh by way of Dundee and Falkland. Christmas came and went, and with the spring Mary put off her sombre black and ordered a new gown of crimson damask with a yellow velvet kirtle. May found her in St Andrews, joining in the celebrations for the marriage of the Countess of Errol, but the outward rejoicing did not match her

94

inward mood.[8] She was not in good health. She suffered from frequent colds, and she was feeling generally debilitated. Once more she was longing for a child, and her need for a son had a new poignancy. If only there could be another baby prince, she could start again. The King would be pleased, he would make much of her once more and his neglect would be a thing of the past. The thought that there might not be another prince was something she dared not contemplate.

In her restlessness, her thoughts began to turn to the part she played in public affairs. So far, it seemed to her that her role had been a formal, ceremonial one. She appeared at Court as the gracious Queen, she toured the country with her husband as his consort, yet she felt dissatisfied. She had always taken a keen interest in public affairs. Along with the news of family and friends sent to her from France there were regular bulletins on the latest political events, the military campaigns, the manoeuvrings of King and Emperor. Mary was in her late twenties now, and with increasing maturity came a need for wider interests. Her active mind was all too liable to dwell on morbid subjects if she had nothing to distract her and she had not enough outlets for her formidable energies. She needed more, much more, to occupy her thoughts. In spite of her very real longing for another child, she was insensibly turning away from the narrow, domestic sphere. She had always been a highly intelligent woman. At first, she had thought that she could find fulfilment with her young French husband, bringing up his family and running his estates. When that future was denied her, she had entertained hopes of performing an active and useful public role as James's consort. When this in its turn seemed impractical, she had devoted herself wholeheartedly to the role of mother to his children, but even then her interest in a wide range of public affairs had merely been lying dormant. Now, with the loss of the Princes, with the waning of James's affection, she put behind her the passive, domestic way of life. To focus all one's hopes on husband or children was to invite pain, grief and disillusion.

She now therefore took into her own hands the financial

administration of her household, and she persuaded James to allow her to help with his. She had always found satisfaction in exercising her talents for organization, and if James were to leave her bed for the company of other women, it would be some consolation if he relied on her in other ways. Gradually, she began to feel happier about her increased involvement and so taken up did she become with her new activities that she did not think of the obvious explanation for her continuing ill health.[9] Apart from the frequent colds, she was experiencing other disquieting symptoms, and she wrote to her mother for advice. Antoinette pondered over her letter, considered the details of the indisposition, and reached a happy conclusion. Mary must be pregnant, she decided, and she was right. A few days later, a message from Scotland confirmed her hopes. The baby would be born the following winter.

Divided between relief and anxiety, Mary was determined to do everything she could to have a safe pregnancy. There is a hint that everything did not go smoothly at first, for in July the sum of twenty pounds was paid to Anthony Bassett, a surgeon, 'for his labours done by him to the Queen's Grace at this time only'. Whatever the trouble, it could not have been too serious, for Mary was able to visit Peebles, in the south of Scotland, later in the month. The purpose of her visit is not disclosed in the accounts, but she was probably making a pilgrimage to the church there, for her husband had presented a fragment of the True Cross to that ecclesiastical foundation.[10]

It was possibly at this time, too, that Mary drew up in her own handwriting a touching memorandum of various matters to be undertaken in the event of her death. This took the form of a list of pilgrimages which she hoped to make in person. Some were to shrines in Scotland – to St Adrian's, on the Isle of May, the help for barren women, and to Peebles. Some were to places in France, such as Our Lady of Chartres and St Nicholas of Lorraine, while another was to St James in Spain, the offering of wax made there to be the weight of a child of four months old. If she did not manage to undertake these journeys herself, Mary asked her mother to see that they were carried out.[11]

No doubt James and Mary both rejoiced at the thought of the coming child, but any feeling of carefree anticipation had long since been dispelled. Everything else that year was overshadowed by political events and in particular by the threat of war. Henry VIII's discontent with his nephew had been growing daily. Not only was James persisting in his adherence to the Roman Catholic Church, but he was remaining equally faithful to his alliance with France. Henry decided that he could no longer tolerate the threat from his northern neighbour, and in the spring of 1542 he instructed the Archbishop of Canterbury to search through the ancient records for any document which would prove his claim to the overlordship of Scotland. Claiming this overlordship, he would then invade the northern kingdom. So obsessed had he become with this ambition that he even considered the cheaper and quicker expedient of having his agents kidnap the King of Scots.

The Archbishop's search failed to yield what he sought, and in August Henry decided that the time had come to take military action. He sent a small force north, accompanied by the Earl of Angus and his brother Sir George Douglas. They were defeated by the Scots at Kelso, and forced to retreat south once more. Everyone knew, however, that the crisis had not passed but had merely been deferred. The real invasion would come later. When she heard about the encounter at Kelso, Mary 'took journey from Edinburgh to Musselburgh on foot [a distance of some seven miles] religiously, feeling herself heavy with bairn: whom the King convoyed to that holy place of Our Lady of Loretto'. There she prayed not only for her own good health but for the safety of her husband and his kingdom.[12]

Shortly afterwards James himself rode to the Borders, apparently intent on a retaliatory expedition into England. Whatever his plans were, he was unable to carry them out. Once again, the divided loyalties of his lords caused him the utmost difficulty. Those who received English pensions combined with those who feared defeat at English hands and they refused to march into England with him. So numerous were the defectors that he had to abandon the expedition entirely.

This latest evidence of his lords' treachery brought James to the verge of nervous collapse. He felt himself incapable of taking any decision, and more or less resigned the government of the realm to his old friend Cardinal Beaton and to his more recent favourite, Oliver Sinclair. He then rode to Linlithgow to spend some days with his wife.[13] With her strength of character, she could give him the support and consolation no mistress could provide. Even in this extremity, she was able to put new heart into him. Cardinal Beaton was urging him to try again, declaring that it was vital that they should forestall the inevitable English invasion by themselves taking the initiative. When James went to Linlithgow he wanted nothing to do with any new expedition, yet by 19 November, he was back in Edinburgh planning a new advance. Two days later he marched south with his army. It had been agreed that the Cardinal should remain at Haddington with part of their forces to protect the eastern route against any invasion. For his part, James would take the rest of the forces to the south-west, crossing the Solway Firth into England.

When he arrived at the estuary of the Solway, he had to wait for a suitable tide before he could take his men across, so he encamped at Lochmaben, sending Oliver Sinclair with the royal forces to a position a little further east. On 24 November, Sinclair and his troops sighted an English army marching towards them. They met near the River Esk, on a stretch of marshy ground known as Solway Moss, and the encounter was disastrous. According to one account, the nobles were furious at being commanded by a lowborn upstart such as Sinclair, and in their rage they threw down their weapons and surrendered to the English. Other versions suggest that Lord Maxwell and his companions saw the enemy, panicked, and galloped hastily to the rear of their own army, determined to save themselves at all costs and in the process causing alarm and confusion in the Scottish ranks. Others said that the Borderers turned on their own leaders and handed them over to the English. Whatever the exact details, few Scots were killed that day but over a thousand were taken prisoner including Lord Maxwell, the Earls of Cassilis and Glencairn, Lord Fleming and Lord Gray. Their capture was to have a far-reaching significance in the years to come.[14]

The English were triumphant. For James V it was the end. He had not been present on the battlefield himself, and as soon as he heard of the English victory he abandoned all plans for his expedition. He could not fight back. His confidence, his energy, his very will to survive were gone. He left Lochmaben and he rode north. According to the English spies, he made for Tantallon Castle 'where he has a mistress, being in the keeping of Oliver Sinclair's wife, and by report he sets not much store by the Queen'. Even so, he rode on through Edinburgh to Linlithgow, where Mary was spending the last weeks of her pregnancy.[15]

Their meeting must have been a distressing one. James was distraught, 'his mind near gone through dolour and care'.[16] He had confused thoughts of vengeance. It was not the English he wanted to punish, though, but his own faithless lords. He sent out messengers to seek all who had fled from the battlefield, frantically determined that he would question them and make them suffer for their desertion. He inveighed against Cardinal Beaton, blaming him as 'chief procurer and setter forward' of the disastrous expedition.[17]

Mary could only try to cheer him with hopes that France would send help and that their son would soon be born, but he was beyond comfort. He left her, and rode to Falkland. There, on 6 December, he took to his bed, fevered and delirious. Less than forty-eight hours later, Mary went into labour. Contemporary reports suggest that her confinement was premature and if this was so it must have increased her anxiety as she lay in her room in the north-west corner of the palace, overlooking Linlithgow Loch. Early or not, the birth was uncomplicated and, with her fifth child, her labour was probably short. On 7 December the baby was born, alive and well, but it was not the hoped-for prince. Instead, Mary had given birth to her first daughter.[18]

The news was taken to James V at Falkland. It is said that

when he was told, he commented wryly, 'It cam wi' a lass and it will gang wi' a lass', meaning that the House of Stewart had gained the crown of Scotland through a woman, Marjorie Bruce, and that in these troubled times no woman could rule Scotland. If he did indeed make that celebrated remark, it was one of his last coherent utterances, for he soon lapsed into delirium again. Sir George Douglas remarked that 'all the time of his illness he did rage and cry out and spoke but few wise [i.e. sensible] words'. He was still obsessed by the desertion of so many of his lords at Solway Moss. 'Fie, fled Oliver? Is Oliver ta'en?' he repeated over and over again, his mind dwelling on his favourite, Oliver Sinclair.

It was obvious to those who were with him that he was dying, and in the midst of their anxiety for him it was only natural that even those who were genuinely concerned for him should also be extremely worried about the government of the kingdom. What was to happen when James died, leaving only this infant daughter? Cardinal Beaton was particularly anxious to ensure that the Regency would pass into the hands of someone who would continue his own policies of alliance with France and opposition to England. He would have liked the Regency for himself, but he recognized full well that his own cousin had a better claim. Although the birth of the Princess had displaced the Earl of Arran from his position as heir to the throne, he remained the nearest adult male in the succession and he would obviously expect to assume the Regency. Knowing Arran as he did, Beaton feared that this might prove fatal to his policies, and so he set about trying to ensure that the government of the realm would not pass solely to the Earl.

As James lay dying, Beaton was at his bedside, plying him with questions about the future of Scotland. Who should become Regent? Would the King name Cardinal Beaton? If so, who should be the principal advisers? Over and over again he asked his questions, but James lay raving in delirium and could give no coherent reply, 'albeit the Cardinal reported otherwise'. According to some accounts, Beaton's efforts to secure supreme power for himself did not stop there. He was said by some to have guided the dying man's hand to sign a blank sheet of paper which he then filled up, naming himself, Moray, Huntly and Argyll as a Council of Regency. Others alleged that he had actually forged the King's Will.

On the night of 14 December, Cardinal Beaton was keeping watch at his bedside along with a few other friends, including the faithful Sir David Lindsay of the Mount. Just before midnight, James turned over in bed, looked at them, and seemed to recognize them for the first time in many days. He gave a little smile, laughed weakly and kissed his hand to them, then he died.[19]

At the age of twenty-seven, Mary of Guise found herself widowed for a second time. There is no record of how she received the news of her husband's death. His condition when he paid her his last visit, and the reports brought to her from Falkland, must have made her suspect that there could be no future for him. Unsatisfactory as he had been, however, she probably recalled the happier days they had spent together when she first came to Scotland, and regretted him. Certainly the news of his death must have brought fear and foreboding as well as grief. There she was, in a foreign country amongst jealous nobles, with her six-day-old daughter, the monarch of the kingdom.

Mary had to make a swift decision about her future. According to the terms of her marriage contract, she was now free to return to France if she so wished. The prospect was a tempting one. She had known little real happiness in Scotland: now she could return to Châteaudun, to her son, to the close proximity of her parents and her friends. Yet she knew that it was impossible. She could not contemplate leaving her newborn child behind, and the lords were most unlikely to allow her to remove the Scottish Queen from Scottish soil. Even if she did manage to strike some sort of bargain with Arran, allowing him the Regency with the promise that she would bring her daughter back later, there were other considerations.

It is sometimes said that Mary decided in an entirely selfless way to stay on in Scotland in order to protect her daughter's interests, but there was more to it than that. Mary of Guise had been crowned Queen of Scots, and she regarded herself as exactly that. So indeed did her contemporaries. For many months they termed her 'Queen of Scots' in their letters, for instance, referring to her child as 'the Princess of Scotland'. Mary believed firmly that God had sent her to Scotland for a purpose, and that she must continue to work towards that purpose. From the early days when James had written and spoken of his problems, she had resolved to do all she could to bring to this nation law and justice, financial stability and a peaceful way of life. For a time she had seen herself in a supporting role, providing security and a family life for her husband. Later, she had felt the need to play a more active part in this task, and now that James had gone she felt that it had fallen to her to bring all these things about by herself. She would strive to give Scotland peace and good government, she would strengthen the French alliance. By the time her daughter came of age, the young Queen would rule over a well-organized, efficient country firmly in the French interest.

Yet how was it to be done? Mary knew that, traditionally, a widowed Scottish Queen acted as Regent for her child. Joan Beaufort and her own kinswoman Mary of Gueldres had both done so. It seemed obvious to her that the position of Regent was naturally her own. Unfortunately, her husband's death had come at the very time when she was forced to play a largely passive role. Lying in childbed at Linlithgow she was at a distinct disadvantage, and could only wait with impatience and anxiety for news of what was happening.

Cardinal Beaton and the Earl of Arran were now engaged in a determined struggle for the Regency. When the Privy Council met to decide what was to be done, Beaton produced the document naming himself as Governor, with Moray, Huntly and Argyll associated in the Regency with him. On the production of this document, a violent quarrel erupted between the two main contenders. Alarmed and furious at the prospect of seeing power pass him by, Arran 'called the Cardinal "false churl" and would have drawn his sword at him, saving that other[s] of the Council went betwixt them'. The Cardinal retaliated by giving a moving description of how James had died in his arms, entrusting the government to him.[20]

Arran's agitation was understandable. Had it not been for the existence of the week-old baby in Linlithgow, he himself would have been sitting on the throne of Scotland. Only the life of a frail infant stood between him and the crown, and he still had hopes, for after all, many children did die in the first few weeks of life. If the Princess succumbed, all his dreams would be realized. Personal ambition at that moment came first with him, international politics a long way behind. On the virtues of an English or a French alliance he was open to conviction. What mattered to him was that his own rights should not be infringed. As second person of the realm, he must be its Regent.

If Lindsay of Pitscottie is to be believed, despite her grief and her physical weakness, Mary of Guise gave Cardinal Beaton her active support 'because she knew him to favour France . . . and so did many of the lords by her means'.[21] No doubt she shared the Cardinal's opinion that Arran was 'too facile and inconstant to be Governor of the Realm': her later comments on the Earl bear this out. More than that, though, she feared for her daughter's safety should the baby Queen be entrusted to the heir to the throne. Were Arran in a position of power, how could he resist the temptation of eliminating the one person who stood between him and the throne?

Mary's implacable enemy, John Knox, was to declare that 'she mended with as great expedition of that daughter as ever she did before of any son she bore. The time of her purification was sooner than the Levitical law appoints'.[22] As always, his comments on her were vindictive, but there may have been more than a grain of truth in this particular statement. The baby had been small at birth, it was her fifth child, and she probably did make a rapid recovery physically, spurred on by her desperate need to influence events. The leading men of the country would be calling on her to offer their condolences and to ask after the little Queen. Mary no doubt used the opportunity to try to persuade them to give their support to Cardinal Beaton. She did not particularly trust the Cardinal, she wanted the Regency for herself, but for the moment it was necessary to do all she could for him in an attempt to displace Arran.

Meanwhile, there was to be a brief respite from the threat of war. Lord Lisle had been busily preparing to follow up the English victory at Solway Moss when he had received news of the death of the King of Scots. He was taken by surprise, but he quickly composed a message to Henry VIII telling him that he 'thought it should not be to your Majesty's honour that we, your soldiers, should make war or invade upon a dead body or upon a widow or on a young suckling his daughter, and specially upon the time of the funerals of the said King which time all his realm must lament the same'. He accordingly held his hand.[23]

His royal master, however, was far from idle. The death of his nephew and the succession of the baby Queen opened up a whole new prospect for Henry in Scotland. He had a young son, Edward. He would take the Scottish Queen as a wife for Edward, and once she was in his hands, Scotland would be his. Of course, the Scots would not readily agree to such a marriage, but he would persuade them. After all, he had at Court the ideal instruments for his new policy – the Solway Moss prisoners.

On Christmas Day 1542 he summoned to his presence the Earls of Cassilis and Glencairn, Lord Maxwell, Lord Fleming, Lord Gray and the others. He received them graciously, presenting each with a gold chain according to his rank. He then told them of his intentions. He would release them, he said, and they would be free to return to Scotland, on condition that they promised to work for the marriage. They must do all they could to deliver the baby Queen into Henry's hands, and they should also hand over to him Henry's arch-enemy Cardinal Beaton, along with the principal fortresses of the country.

They agreed. Some of them favoured union with England, others thought that, once in Scotland, they could do as they wished, even if they were to deliver up hostages for their good behaviour. Ten of them signed an additional, secret article, promising that, should the baby Queen die, Henry would rule Scotland. They were given horses and money, and they set out for home.[24]

Apart from the Solway prisoners, there were two other important Scotsmen who were still in England: the Earl of Angus and his brother Sir George Douglas. The Earl of Arran was anxious to have them at home with him. They would act as powerful allies against Cardinal Beaton and the pro-French lords. The Earl of Angus and Sir George themselves were not so eager. Certainly, now that James V was dead, the main obstacle to their return had been removed, but they had made many enemies in Scotland. The result was that when Henry ordered them to go north too, they lingered. Henry sent further commands, more peremptory in tone. The brothers conferred anxiously, and at last decided that Sir George should go on ahead to see what sort of reception awaited them. Even when this decision had been taken, Sir George made no move apart from writing lengthy letters to his English friends complaining about the difficulty of his mission.[25]

The New Year began in an atmosphere of great uneasiness. The Scottish lords assembled in Edinburgh to hold the convention at which they would choose their Regent or Lord Governor. Suspicion and distrust filled the air. 'Every man suspecteth other amongst them' a spy told Lord Lisle, and added that the gentlemen attending the meeting in Edinburgh rode in defensible array, each man with double the number of attendants he was accustomed to have. Discontented soldiers filled the town, complaining about unpaid wages and, in the temporary lull in hostilities, rumours were rife about the return of the Solway Moss prisoners.[26]

On 3 January 1543 the Earl of Arran was proclaimed Lord Governor of Scotland. It seemed that, vacillating and unsatisfactory as many of his contemporaries judged him to be, he had gained enough support to defeat the Cardinal. Even so, his victory was not complete, for a week later it was announced that Beaton was to be the Chancellor of Scotland. The Cardinal remained in a position of power, and was probably more or less content to bide his time, convinced that he could outmanoeuvre Arran whenever he wished.

With the announcement of the new appointments, an unnatural calm descended on the country, as all thoughts turned to the funeral of the King. Throughout December, James's body had lain in the Palace of Falkland. Both his household and Mary's were in deepest mourning. On 21 December Mary's comptroller collected from the Royal Wardrobe yard upon yard of French black, Paris black and black velvet to make garments for the Queen and her servants. Preparations for the funeral were well advanced by that time, and on the same day thirty ells of black velvet and ten ells of white velvet were taken from the Wardrobe to make the cloth of state for the funeral. The tailors also made a black covering for the bier, and the embroiderers were at work on a gold and crimson satin coat of arms. Andrew Watson, the herald painter, provided not only a taffeta banner 'with an effigy, crown and sceptre' but supplied 16,048 coats of arms, both great and small, for use in the funeral procession. The Dolorous Chapel at Holyrood was painted black and Andrew Mansioun the carver went to work on the tomb. The tomb has long since been destroyed, but the Lord Treasurer's Accounts reveal that it was surmounted by a carved lion set above a crown, and that Mansioun was paid fifty shillings 'for the [en]graving of the superscription of the tomb in Roman letters containing in length eighteen feet'.[27]

Messengers were sent throughout the country, summoning the lords and barons 'to come and give presence at the King's Grace's interment', and the Earl of Arran crossed over to Fife with a solemn procession of lords, ecclesiastics and servants. They escorted James V's body from Falkland to Edinburgh, the final ceremonies being conducted with sombre magnificence. 'Whatever could be devised in solemn pomp or honourable decorum or doleful dolour and dole [mourning] . . . here all was done,' wrote Bishop Lesley, describing the scene almost forty years later, 'fulfilled with all due ceremonies and all diligence, torches lighted, places spread with tapestry, with notable cloth and well painted, lamentable trumpets, whistles of dole, Cardinals in sadness as their [bowed] heads show, the Earls of Argyll, Arran, Rothes and Marischal and others in great number of the nobility sombre in dole weed, were all in the meantime so dressed that albeit you may marvel much at their pomp in order, in colour nevertheless easily you might see sorrow, for all were in dole weed, when in Edinburgh in the Abbey of Holyroodhouse, in the same sepulchre where Madeleine his sweet wife was buried was he laid.'

Mary of Guise remained at Linlithgow, where her baby daughter had been christened Mary in the Church of St Michael.

5

The Lord Governor

As the widow of the King of Scots, Mary of Guise found the daily circumstances of her life altered to a significant degree. Certainly she retained her own household, and she possessed in addition her residences of Stirling and Falkland under the terms of her marriage contract, but otherwise much had changed. James V's household had been taken over by the Lord Governor. It was Arran who now occupied Edinburgh Castle and the Palace of Holyroodhouse. It was he who controlled the royal revenues. It was he who dictated the foreign policy of the country, who saw to the actual business of government, who exercised the considerable powers of patronage. He was now the centre of all influence and there was a danger that Mary of Guise would become more and more isolated from affairs of state. This she could not allow to happen. Apart from anything else, her daughter's future if not her very life depended on the course taken by Arran with regard to the threat from England.

Mary soon came to hear of Henry VIII's plan to marry her daughter to his son. So determined was Henry to carry through this scheme that he was blind to all possible difficulties. His emissary in the north of England, Lord Lisle, was not so oblivious to the problems involved and he felt impelled to point out to the King that the Scots would never agree to a union with England for, he said, Scotland 'evermore hath been a realm of itself'. In the event of any union, Scotland would be 'clearly undone, for albeit the realm of Scotland is but a poor thing to England, yet having the state of a King in itself, all the revenues thereof should be spent within the realm, whereas if both the realms were under one, all should go to the King of England out of the country of Scotland not to be spent there, whereby Scotland now being poor already should be utterly beggared and undone'.[1]

Henry ignored all warnings, economic or otherwise. It was a simple enough matter. Certainly the appointment of Arran as Lord Governor had been something approaching a setback, for he had wanted the position of Regent for himself. No matter; Arran was a fool and could be manipulated. The Solway lords and the Douglas brothers were the instruments of English policy and through them Henry would soon have the baby Queen in his hands, along with the strongholds of Scotland and his old enemy Cardinal Beaton. By encouraging the spread of the Reformed doctrines north of the border he would wean the people away from their old allegiance to Rome and to France, transforming them instead into Protestants who would look to England for advice and support. The only person liable to put up any serious opposition to his plans was Mary of Guise and so he sent her a series of letters containing thinly-veiled threats about how her child would be in actual danger if Mary did not look favourably upon the marriage.

Needless to say, Mary viewed Henry's schemes with apprehension and distaste. She had come to Scotland in the first place to strengthen the alliance between James V and France. She saw help from France as Scotland's only hope of salvation in the existing situation, and the last thing she intended to do was to hand over her child to a man like Henry VIII. Other considerations apart, she would never serve the interests of France's longstanding enemy. Yet what was she to do? In her present position she was virtually powerless. There had been no time to build up a party of supporters who would oppose the English marriage. There was no knowing what Arran might do, and if she wrote back too coldly to Henry VIII she might precipitate an invasion.

There was, of course, the possibility of giving the little Queen in marriage to someone else and, ludicrous as it may seem, Mary, the Scottish lords, and the Kings of France and England spent long hours in the early days of 1543 worrying about finding a suitable husband for a child a few weeks old.

From Mary of Guise's point of view, she wanted for her daughter a prince of a nation which would be a powerful ally for Scotland in the struggle to retain independence from England. The trouble was that no such prince existed. If only the French King had fathered a suitable son the way ahead would have been clear. Unfortunately, there was no French prince available. The heir to the French throne had been married for years to Catherine de Medici, and the union was barren. There seemed no prospect that Catherine would ever bear a child. True, the King of France did have another son, but as Lord Lisle had sensibly pointed out to Henry VIII, he was already a grown man and 'would not tarry for a suckling child'.[2]

There remained the possibility of marrying the baby Queen to a Scotsman, but this was as impractical as it was undesirable. No powerful ally for Scotland would be forthcoming. Instead, the monarch would be dragged into all the petty feuds which had for so long bedevilled Scotland. She would be disparaged, in that she would have married a man far below her own position, and she would be delivered into the hands of unscrupulous schemers interested only in their own advancement. A marriage with a Scot was out of the question.

Mary of Guise's only possible line of action was to procrastinate, to dissemble if necessary, but at all costs to play for time until she could strengthen her own hand. What she needed most was a powerful ally within Scotland, someone to act as a counterpoise to Arran. When Henry VIII had heard that the Scots had chosen Arran to be their Governor, he had remarked that 'the face of this erection may be more in appearance than it is in deed', adding hopefully, 'the Earl of Arran being but a sober man in goods and wits shall not be able to support that room [position]'.[3] Mary of Guise, however, did not make the mistake of writing Arran off as negligible: she knew him too well. He had been at her marriage. He had been godfather to one of her sons. He had been in constant attendance at Court, heir to the throne, before the birth and after the death of the Princes. With her accustomed perspicacity, she saw him exactly for what he was. Personal ambition was almost invariably the key to all he did. Second person of the realm, father of a young son . . . might he not be tempted to have the baby Queen killed, so that the throne would be his? Could he not be persuaded to hand the child over to Henry VIII in return for a promise of the crown of Scotland? Might he not take the child and marry her to his own son, thinking that if he could not be King himself he would at least be the father of Kings?

Arran might pretend to be simple, but beneath the simplicity lay craftiness, guile, determination to protect his own interests at all costs. He would play a double game, a triple game, agreeing with everyone so that he might be in the best possible position to manoeuvre for his own advantage. It was therefore impossible to bribe him successfully or to manipulate him satisfactorily. He would take the money, he would make the promises, but no reliance could be placed upon him.

There was all the more reason, therefore, to continue to support Cardinal Beaton. He too could not be trusted, of course. He had not kept secret the fact that he thought a baby girl a most unsuitable monarch for the country in its present necessity. He had said openly that he would like to make the young Earl of Lennox King of Scots by virtue of his royal descent. He wanted to be in a position of supreme power, as Kingmaker if not as Regent. Even so, at least he was firm in his support of the French alliance and he would never deliver the baby Queen to the English.

Events were moving swiftly, and Mary had to quieten her lingering doubts about him. She summoned him to her presence and asked his advice about the English marriage. She found that he agreed with her own feelings. When approached by Henry VIII, she should dissemble. She should let it be thought that she favoured Prince Edward as a husband for her daughter. Beaton, too, feared that any refusal on her part would precipitate the English invasion and, for the time being, they concluded that it was safe enough for her to agree to the match. The Scottish parliament would not consent to hand over the baby to Henry VIII at once and a projected marriage could easily be repudiated at a future date. Mary therefore told the English that nothing would please her better than that her child should become the wife of Prince Edward.

The dangers of the situation were at this point underlined by the reappearance in Edinburgh in mid-January of the sinister figure of Sir George Douglas. Finding it impossible to delay his return any longer, Sir George had at last crossed the Border. A wily, scheming adventurer, he was for the moment the wholehearted supporter of Henry VIII – or at least, so he would have had Henry believe. His instructions from England were that he should do everything in his power to bind Arran to the English interest and to remove Beaton from the scene. According to his own account, he set about accomplishing these two objectives with all speed. Returning from his exile with only eight companions, he boasted that he found a thousand horsemen waiting to welcome him home. He rode at once to Edinburgh, and asked where he could find the Lord Governor. Somewhat to his disappointment, he was told that Arran had been to Linlithgow to see Mary of Guise, after which he had returned to his own palace at Hamilton. Sir George was forced to cool his heels for several days at his cousin's Castle of Dalkeith, a few miles from Edinburgh.

As soon as Arran came back to town, however, he sent for Sir George and, to the latter's gratification, 'used him very familiarly', keeping him up talking until well after midnight, then giving him a chamber just two doors along from his own. Less enthusiastic in his welcome of the returned exile was Cardinal Beaton. When Sir George presented himself before the Privy Council on the following day, the Cardinal told him in no uncertain terms that 'he was come for no good to the realm of Scotland, and he and his brother [Angus] had been so long nourished in England that they would never be profitable for their own country, and that it was not meet that they should be suddenly admitted unto their peace and lands'. He accordingly insisted that Sir George and the Earl of Angus should both have to swear that they had come back for the good of the realm of Scotland before they were allowed to stay permanently.

A heated debate thereupon broke out in Council, to be interrupted at last by the Earl of Arran. Rising to his feet, he announced piously that now was the moment to set aside all malice and receive 'his kinsmen' back into the realm. The babble of argument immediately broke out once again and Sir George was eventually asked to withdraw. After a seemingly interminable wait outside the door, he was admitted once more. The Cardinal drew him to one side and questioned him closely about his religious beliefs, asking him 'whether he was a good Christian man or not, or whether he was given to the new learning after the fashion of England or not?'

Sir George replied with masterful evasion that he was christened, adding that if he was not a good Christian he prayed to God to make him one, and wished that in the realm of Scotland there were no worse Christians than there were in the realm of England. Realizing that he had met his match in verbal skirmishing, the Cardinal 'gave a great sigh' and told Sir George that he was now welcome, promised to be his friend, and offered him twenty thousand crowns. They parted on the best of terms, Sir George to return smugly to his lodgings, the Cardinal to berate Arran for his support of Sir George and to warn him to 'take good heed of himself, for they would do him a shrewd turn if it lay in their powers'. Arran afterwards reported this conversation to Sir George, whereupon they agreed together that as soon as Angus returned to lend them his support, Arran 'would lay hands upon the said Cardinal and pluck him from his pomp', sending him to England as a prisoner.[4]

Whether he would put these threats into practice remained to be seen. Listening night after night to the Lord Governor's outpourings, Sir George soon began to wonder if Arran would ever prove a suitable instrument for anyone's plans. He was ready enough with his assurances that he would arrest Beaton but as a practical conspirator he left much to be desired. There was, for instance, the unfortunate episode of the letter.

Lord Lisle was in regular correspondence with Arran, and one day he wrote secretly about their plans for Beaton. As luck would have it, his messenger arrived to find Arran and the Cardinal together, deep in conversation. There was nothing for it but to hand the letter over under the Cardinal's watchful eye. Arran took it with a furtive look, then thrust it deep into the pocket of his gown, chattering nervously in an attempt to divert his companion's attention. For a few moments all seemed well. The conversation continued, then Arran, in order to make some point or other, decided to produce a paper he had brought with him. Forgetting all about the incriminating English letter, he dug into his pocket and drew out a document which he handed to Beaton. It was the secret letter.

Prepared to cast a brief glance over its contents, the Cardinal looked, looked again, then began to peruse it closely. As he read his expression darkened. 'This letter speaks of a special message touching myself!' he exclaimed, turning on his companion. Realization flooded over the unfortunate Earl. For a moment he could only stand appalled, then he snatched the offending paper from his cousin's hand and rushed off to tell Sir George 'how he had overshot himself'.

Sir George, listening with growing exasperation to his visitor's tale of woe, was convinced that Arran was a fool. Sometimes he suspected the Earl of deceiving him: of pretending a hostility to Beaton which he did not really feel. After all, he and the Cardinal were cousins. On Beaton's instructions, the Governor might simply be pretending amity with England. On this occasion, however, he could only marvel at the man's stupidity, and he probably felt inclined to agree with the comment of another observer, who had declared laconically that the Governor was 'half an idiot and quite unfit for the crown'.[5]

Sir George advised Arran to do his best to allay the Cardinal's suspicions. He should go back and invite Beaton to answer the letter himself: that should quieten his fears. Finally ushering out his tiresome confederate, Sir George shook his head over his behaviour and looked forward to the return of his own brother, the Earl of Angus, who was expected on the following day.[6]

News of Sir George's own return had long since reached

Mary of Guise in Linlithgow, followed swiftly by all manner of rumours about his intentions. Mary's uneasiness grew, and she decided that as soon as she was able, she must go to Edinburgh to investigate the situation for herself. Her chariot was accordingly made ready, her ladies packed up her mourning gowns, and towards the end of January she took up residence in the apartments set aside for her at Holyrood.

Once installed there, she decided that she had come not a moment too soon. The Earl of Angus had arrived a few days earlier and already he had gained an alarming ascendancy over the Governor. What was more, the whole Court was buzzing with the rumour that the Duke of Guise was about to sail to Scotland with an army to take the government of his grandaughter's kingdom into his own hands. These stories had actually been put about by Angus and Sir George, who estimated that the thought of any such intervention would drive Arran permanently into the English camp.

In fact, Mary and Cardinal Beaton were waiting for rather different news from France. In casting around for ways of counteracting Arran's influence in Scotland, they had remembered about the Earl of Lennox. The traditional enemy of the Hamiltons, Lennox was still in permanent residence at the French Court. If only he were back in Scotland, he could lead a powerful opposition to the Governor. The problem was that he had no desire to leave France. There would have to be some strong inducement. Talking it over together, Mary and the Cardinal agreed to write to Lennox, promising that if he came back, not only would he be made Governor of Scotland in place of Arran, but he would become the husband of Mary of Guise. Needless to say, Mary had no intention of fulfilling that particular promise, but she hoped that it would have the desired effect. Any day now she should hear how their offer had been received.

At this point, events took a dramatic turn. Arran was holding a series of meetings of the Privy Council to discuss affairs of state. These meetings were held in his chamber at Holyroodhouse, and although Mary of Guise had no part to play and did not attend, the Cardinal and all the other lords were present. On one such occasion, as the Governor and the others sat round the long table in his room, arguing and debating in the usual way, the door suddenly burst open. A detachment of armed guards marched in. They went straight to where Cardinal Beaton sat, dragged him from his place and, ignoring his cries of protest, hustled him from the room. They took him down to the courtyard, bundled him on to a horse, still protesting furiously, and rode with him to the Douglas's castle at Dalkeith.

Back in the palace, the Council chamber was in uproar. Everything had happened so swiftly that those who were unprepared hardly knew what was going on. There was a great deal of banging, shouting and clattering of feet on the stairs. The outcry was clearly audible in Mary of Guise's chamber above, and 'she was therewith in very great fear and gave a great shriek'. Hearing her scream, the Earl of Angus and the Earl of Arran exchanged significant looks. Arran made no move, so it was Angus who ran quickly up to her room to quieten her. There was no cause for alarm, he said. The disturbance had been caused by nothing more than the arrest of a false, lying fellow who was going to have to answer for his behaviour. This seemed to reassure Mary. She was relieved, she said, 'for she had thought the lords had been together by the ears'.[7]

Evading her questions about the identity of the man arrested, Angus withdrew and made his way downstairs again. On the landing, he paused to speak to one of his servants, whom he found gazing out of a window overlooking the palace forecourt. The man pointed out a small figure hurrying towards the gates, and together they watched 'a priest that carried the Cardinal's cross trudge out of the gate as fast as he could, carrying it under his arm'. Why, the servant asked, did not Angus order the man's arrest? 'Peace, carl,' the Earl replied carelessly, 'he shall pay better than his cross ere he have done,' and he turned away.

He had cause to be confident. He and Sir George had done all they were supposed to do. The Cardinal had been taken, and Arran seemed firmer than ever before in his support of the English. As one of their friends told Henry VIII, 'the Earl of Angus and his brother rule the roost about the Governor'.[8]

When Mary learned the real identity of the 'false, lying fellow', she was greatly alarmed. No one seemed to know what had happened to the Cardinal. He might even now be on his way, a prisoner, to Henry VIII. Her thoughts immediately flew to her daughter, and she returned at once to Linlithgow where she could protect her child and take stock of her own position.

The weeks which followed seemed something of an anticlimax. Word of the Cardinal's actual whereabouts soon leaked out. It seemed that he was not to be given to Henry VIII after all. After the drama of his arrest, there was a period of calm, although the tension remained. On the surface, life in Mary's household went on unaltered. The Palace of Linlithgow stood by its loch, little changed since that day when she had first seen it and praised its charms. She still occupied the apartments where her daughter had been born, and she still went to pray in the little oratory overlooking the loch. The palace was her familiar, comfortable home. With the coming of Lent, of course, there were the usual dietary restrictions, but the plentiful supply of fish from the loch could be supplemented by barrels of herring and salmon imported specially. Claret and other wines were brought across from France to the port of Blackness, a few miles away, along with other luxuries like barrels of figs and raisins, baskets of apples and onions. Sugar, spices and flour were brought out in white leather bags from Edinburgh, and there was plenty of butter, milk and eggs from the royal estates.[9]

In that winter season the days were short, but it was not the long hours of darkness which provoked Mary of Guise's feelings of foreboding. She was, for the time being, comfortable enough in her own palace. The Cardinal seemed reasonably safe at Dalkeith. Arran seemed to be inactive — yet still Mary felt a sense of danger, for she saw that a recent innovation in her household had ominous implications.

With the death of her husband, her servants had been

augmented by a number of men from James's household who did not care to stay on and serve Arran. Some of the royal servants, like Malcolm Gourlay the tailor, were perfectly content to work for the Governor, but there were those like Robert Gibb, the squire of the King's Stable, and Thomas Marshall, the master cook who preferred to transfer themselves to Mary's establishment.[10] That was perfectly acceptable, but her household had also suffered a distinctly sinister augmentation. She was no sooner back in Linlithgow than Arran announced that he intended to appoint a much greater company to wait upon her and the little Queen.[11] He cloaked his true intentions by explaining that their status demanded a more dignified retinue, but his real motive was all too obvious to Mary. By infiltrating her household with his own men, he would sever her communications with her friends and family and he would be able to keep her under constant surveillance. She would become virtually a prisoner in her own household.

Mary could not allow that to happen. First there had been Beaton's arrest, and now there was this threat to her own liberty. She felt as though a net were closing in about her and her child. At all costs, she must retain her freedom of action, so that she could maintain her communications with France and work for the release of the Cardinal. She was already building up an efficient intelligence system by careful use of bribes, and the news she was receiving from it did little to reassure her. A temporary truce with England had been signed, but the danger from England remained, not to mention the danger from those Scots working in the English interest.

Mary determined that she and her daughter must move from Linlithgow. It simply was not safe. It had been built as a domestic residence, not as a defensible fortress. It could not withstand a siege and it did not offer sufficient protection against more insidious dangers. It had come to her ears that Lord Bothwell, for instance, was writing to the English Privy Council offering to seize the baby Queen and take her to London, and she knew that the laird of Buccleuch had been making similar threats. The English spies themselves were busily reporting that the little Queen was 'in great peril either to be conveyed [to England] or destroyed amongst them'.[12]

It was small wonder that Mary felt a rising sense of panic. At Linlithgow she and the baby were far too vulnerable. Some reckless adventurer might easily force his way into the Palace or gain entry with the connivance of Arran's men. What might happen then did not bear thinking about. It was imperative that she should move the little Queen to a place of safety.

Turning the matter over in her mind, Mary concluded that her own Castle of Stirling would provide the ideal solution. Set on its rock high above the River Forth, it was wellnigh impregnable and it was near enough the west coast to have communication with shipping to France. Before the end of February, Mary therefore sent her servant Alan LeBoeuf to Stirling with coffers and other household belongings. She gave orders that all her clothes were to be packed in trunks. These were strapped to the backs of horses, and they too were taken to Stirling. A further sixteen horses then set out with all the utensils from the Court kitchen. By the beginning of March, the ladies' beds had been folded up and taken west, along with another horse loaded with more baskets and boxes.[13] Everything was ready for Mary and her household to go too when the blow fell. The Earl of Arran announced that they must not leave Linlithgow. Apparently he had been willing enough to give his consent, but at the last minute he had mentioned the move to Sir George Douglas and Sir George immediately pointed out the undesirability of any such change. Henry VIII would not like it, he said, and his persuasions convinced Arran.[14]

Mary heard the news with frustration and dismay. If the Governor refused to let her take her daughter from Linlithgow, there was nothing she could do. She became even more sure that Arran meant to keep her prisoner in her own palace. All she could do now was to hope that the coming parliament to be held in Edinburgh would bring about some improvement in her circumstances. She knew well that the ecclesiastics attending were far from content with recent events. It was rumoured that 'the priests that come to the parliament bring all their men in coats of plate and long spears', and their dislike of Arran was well known.[15]

They had various reasons for being displeased. For one thing, Arran was now giving open support to the Protestant cause. He had written to his friends in the south for Testaments in English, and had so encouraged an interest in the Reformed doctrines that, according to one Scottish source, the Old and New Testaments, the primer and the psalter 'be marvellously desired now of the people in Scotland and . . . if there were a cartload sent thither they would be bought, every one'.[16]

Naturally enough, they were even angrier at the arrest of the primate, Cardinal Beaton, and as supporters of his policies they feared the Governor's intentions with regard to the little Queen. They therefore came to the Edinburgh parliament with three demands: that Beaton be released, that the clergy be continued in their present condition and not expected to follow the English example, and that the little Queen be put into the keeping of four Scottish noblemen until she was old enough to agree to marry.[17] Unfortunately for the clergy, the influence of Angus and his brother remained paramount and on 17 March parliament was prorogued without any of the requests being granted.

By now, Henry VIII was anxious to find out just exactly what was happening in Scotland. Conflicting rumours suggested that Mary, Queen of Scots was a sickly child – and that she was strong and healthy. Her real condition was of the utmost interest to him. Then again, there was the question of the Solway prisoners. Since their return to Scotland they had achieved singularly little. They must be forced to do more. There was also the business of the Earl of Lennox. His spies reported that Lennox was seriously considering returning to Scotland. What was Arran doing to prevent his return? Finally, there was the attitude of Mary of Guise herself. Was she as much in favour of the English alliance as she would have him believe?

Eager to hear the details from a reliable source, Henry decided to send an ambassador to Edinburgh, and he chose as his emissary Sir Ralph Sadler. Sir Ralph was, of course, no stranger to the Scottish Court, and he knew the principal protagonists of old. He would go to Edinburgh to weigh up the situation for himself, and, more important, he would settle the details of the marriage of Mary, Queen of Scots to Prince Edward.[18]

Sir Ralph duly arrived in Edinburgh on 18 March and met the Earl of Arran strolling in the gardens of Holyroodhouse. The Governor expressed pleasure at seeing him, but although he swore that Henry VIII 'had his heart above all princes', he was as evasive as ever. Sir Ralph then sought out Sir George Douglas, who spoke at great length of how all the success of Henry's plans for Scotland was due entirely to Sir George himself. The capture of Beaton, the attachment of Arran to the English cause, the favourable attitude towards the English marriage proposal – all these were the result of Sir George's diligence.

When Sir George finally paused for breath, Sir Ralph managed to slip in a pertinent inquiry. Why, he asked, was Arran still in power when Henry VIII had long desired his removal? Sir George was not to be outfaced. He gave a lengthy and complicated explanation, to the effect that, were Arran deposed, it would be impossible to bring Scotland into obedience to England, for 'there is not so little a boy but he will hurl stones against it. The wives will come out with their distaffs and the commons universally will rather die in it, yea and many noblemen and all the clergy fully against it'. Depose Arran, he warned, and there would be such an outcry that Beaton would be released, the French army summoned to Scotland for help, and the Governor driven into the arms of France.[19]

Sir Ralph was dissatisfied. In the days that followed, he had interviews with all the other leading nobles: Angus, Glencairn, Somerville, Bothwell and the rest. Meanwhile, Mary of Guise was pondering how she could turn his visit to advantage. The English marriage must never become a reality. Perhaps by some careful intrigue she could sow dissension amongst the lords who favoured England and so form an opposition party which would refuse to agree to the marriage. She decided to summon Sir Ralph to her presence.

When he arrived at Linlithgow, she received him graciously. Exercising all her considerable charm, she told him that she was delighted at the prospect of a marriage between her daughter and Prince Edward. She was, she declared, perfectly willing for the baby to go at once to Henry VIII for, she confessed with a sigh, that alone would ensure the little Queen's safety. The English marriage plan she praised as the work of God, who had given her only sons before but had now sent her a daughter who would accomplish the union of the two kingdoms.

These remarks were well received by Sir Ralph, who was all too willing to believe them. Seeing that he was receptive, Mary even assured him that she would be advised by Henry in all things. Having thus lulled her listener's suspicions, she then embarked on the delicate business of discrediting Arran in the eyes of the English. 'Whatsoever pretence or fair weather he made', she declared, the last thing the Governor really wanted was this marriage. He had told her so in so many words, she said, urging her to agree to the contract but to keep the baby with her until the child came of age. By that time Henry VIII would probably be dead and the contract could be broken.

Looking covertly at her companion, Mary could see that he was shaken, and so she pressed on. This was the reason, she murmured, why she had asked to see Sadler personally. She could trust no one, be they Scottish or French, for none of her own servants was about her. Her troubles all stemmed from the fact that Arran wanted the baby Queen for his own son. If only Cardinal Beaton were free, he would see to it that the English marriage was accomplished.

That brought Sir Ralph up with a jerk. Cardinal Beaton help Henry VIII? It was unthinkable. Skilled though she was in diplomacy, Mary had come close to overplaying her hand. Surely, Sadler exclaimed, the Cardinal would do more harm than good, since his sympathies were well known to all and his hatred of the English was notorious.

Mary hastily tried to retrieve the situation. The Cardinal was a wise man, she said judiciously, 'and could better consider the benefit of the realm than all the rest'. She then returned quickly to the safer theme of the Governor and his deficiencies. As soon as Sadler had left, she said, Arran would come hurrying to see her so that he could find out what had been said between them. 'And,' continued Mary, 'when he comes I shall, as my custom is, make as though I were not well willing to this marriage and then . . . as he is but a simple man, he will tell me his whole intent in that part.' If she did not play this game, Mary said, 'He would keep himself the more covert and close and tell me nothing.'

Not surprisingly, Sadler was now becoming thoroughly confused. Mary was employing a subtle mixture of truth and invention to try to turn Sadler against Arran. Her interview with Sir Ralph that day was a long one, and in the course of their conversation she denied categorically that there was any truth in the rumours of a proposed marriage between herself and Lennox. She was certainly speaking sincerely when she declared that 'now, since she had been a King's wife, her heart was too high to look any lower'. She also denied that there were any plans for her father to come to Scotland. Claud was far too busy with military preparations for a campaign against the Emperor. Finally, after a lengthy discussion of the European situation, Mary returned again to the subject of her daughter, emphasizing that the custody of a child monarch was never given to his heir. Arran must on no account be put in charge of the baby Queen. The Governor had alleged that the child was unlikely to live but, said Mary, 'You shall see whether he says true or not'. With these words, she led Sadler through various chambers until they came to the nursery. Mary, Queen of Scots, lay there in her cradle. Her mother ordered the nurse to unwrap the child's swaddling bands so that he could see her properly, and he was forced to admit that 'it is as goodly a child as I have seen of her age'. Mary drew attention proudly to the baby's size, commenting that it looked as though her daughter would be as tall as she herself was and, Sadler remarked afterwards, Mary of Guise was 'of the largest stature of women'.[20]

The interview between Mary and Sir Ralph, described in his

own report to Henry VIII, is particularly illuminating for it shows vividly how Mary conducted her business: how she used all her intelligence and her diplomacy to manipulate those around her. Despite her comparative youth, she was obviously no novice at the game of intrigue and it is easy to see why her enemies were always to fear her subtlety. Having sown the seeds of doubt in Sir Ralph's mind, she continued her campaign to persuade Arran to let her go to Stirling. She had failed in a direct approach to him but she hoped that an intermediary might achieve success and so she asked the Earl of Moray, her late husband's half-brother, to speak to the Governor about it. Once again Arran seemed on the verge of agreeing, but once again Sir George Douglas intervened and no permission was forthcoming.[21]

This was a sad disappointment, but at least Mary's other plans were making some progress. Slowly and carefully she was working for the release of the Cardinal. Her principal instrument in this plan was James V's young cousin, the Earl of Huntly. Huntly had always been a favourite at Court, and now he and Mary somehow managed to persuade Arran that the Cardinal should be placed in the custody of none other than Lord Seton. Lord Seton was Mary's faithful supporter, all the more so because he had married one of her French ladies. It was not surprising that, as soon as the move took place, everyone began to speak of the imminent release of the Cardinal.[22]

Henry VIII was furious when he heard the news, and sent immediate instructions to Sir Ralph Sadler that he must find out what Arran thought he was doing. When questioned, the Governor was all innocence. 'Release the Cardinal!' he cried in horror, protesting that nothing was further from his mind. He would be the last person to set Beaton free. After all, had not Beaton told James V that Arran was the greatest heretic in the world? Set him at large, declared Arran dramatically, and 'I should surely go to the fire!'[23]

Wary by now, Sir Ralph listened to this fine speech with some scepticism. A little later, he sought out Sir George Douglas to ask him for his reading of the situation. If Arran had been vehement, Sir George flew into a positive passion at the thought of Beaton being set free, and his remarks about Arran were scarcely complimentary. The Governor, he declared, was 'the most wavering and unstable person in the world, and the soonest would be altered and changed with every man's flattery or fair speech'. As for Huntly, it was all his fault. He was 'the falsest and vilest young man in the world' and he had gained such a hold over Arran that the latter would do anything he asked.[24]

Was Sir George sincere or was he acting a part? Sadler did not know. He went back to Arran again and, to test his reaction, suggested that Beaton be sent to England. When he heard this, Arran burst out laughing. Obviously not devoid of a sense of humour, he told Sadler merrily 'The Cardinal had liefer go into Hell'. Sir Ralph was almost convinced of his sincerity. 'Unless he be the greatest dissembler that ever was,' he told the English Privy Council, 'he mindeth to hold surely the Cardinal in prison.'[25]

Reassured as to Arran's intentions, Sir Ralph turned back once more to the question of Mary of Guise and her attitude to the English marriage. When he told Arran that he was to go to Linlithgow again, it was Arran's turn to warn Sir Ralph. He would, said Arran, find Mary 'in end, whatsoever she pretends, a right Frenchwoman'. He complained bitterly about Mary's remarks that he wanted to marry his own son to her daughter. She had done this simply to get him into trouble with Henry VIII and to widen the rift between the Scots and the English so that the Scots would maintain their alliance with France. 'This,' he said, 'is her only device which,' he added, 'as she is both subtle and wily, so she hath a vengeable engine [vengeful mind] and wit to work her purpose. And still she labours,' he continued, 'by all means she can to have the Cardinal at liberty.'[26]

For all his apparent 'simplicity', Arran had summed up Mary of Guise rather well. Sadler, however, remained of the opinion that her proceedings were frank and open, and the next day he rode to Linlithgow once more to see her. His second audience was very much a repetition of his first. Mary warned him against Arran, and urged that Henry VIII demand immediate custody of the little Queen. Once more she praised the Cardinal, declaring with obvious mendacity that if Beaton were at liberty 'she thought he would go into England to offer his service to the King's majesty'.

She and Sadler then engaged in a long and complicated discussion, each trying to find out just exactly what the other knew. When Sir Ralph questioned Mary about the allegiance of the various lords, she skilfully avoided committing herself. Arran was 'assuredly a simple and the most inconstant man in the world, for whatsoever he determined today he changed tomorrow'. Angus was 'of no policy or engine' and was wholly directed by his brother Sir George who, for his part, was 'as wily and crafty a man as any was in all Scotland'.

Sadler felt that he had gained no information at all from her and he came away with a growing sense of frustration. He could no longer believe Mary or Arran; he had listened to each miscall the other so much that he did not know if either of them spoke the truth. He could obviously trust neither of them.[27]

A few days later, Mary's fortunes took an abrupt turn for the better when messengers brought the news that the Earl of Lennox had arrived at Dumbarton with two ships and a small company of men. Encouraged to believe that the government of Scotland would soon be in his hands, he was also anxious to rescue Mary of Guise from her captivity. As long as she and Beaton were in the hands of Arran there was the danger that they and the little Queen would be sent to England. Lennox therefore rode at once to see Mary in Linlithgow, then set about gathering his supporters. At the same time, Cardinal Beaton regained his freedom. Lord Seton had been persuaded to let him go to his own castle at St Andrews and by some fortunate mischance had failed to install any of Seton's own servants there to keep him in custody. The Cardinal, in his own castle and among his own people, was a prisoner no longer.

Contemporaries were inclined to attribute the Cardinal's release to the efforts of Mary of Guise. Others blamed Huntly, but Huntly was acting in Mary of Guise's interest at that time, as of course was Lord Seton. Arran, it appeared, had simply stood back and allowed events to take their course. Henry VIII had warned him of what was about to happen, but when Sadler taxed the Governor with negligence he swore that he had known nothing about the move to St Andrews. He cried 'I am a Christian man and if I should swear to you as I do and lie, I were worse than a Jew!' He even laid his hand on the hilt of his sword, 'offering to stick himself to the heart if he knew of it till he [Beaton] was at liberty'.[28]

Be that as it might, he himself was now under the influence of a new force at work in the affairs of Scotland. His half-brother, John Hamilton, the Abbot of Paisley, had returned from France and was strongly in favour of the French alliance.[29] From the moment of his return, Arran's already wavering support for England grew even weaker and Henry VIII was forced to hold out promises of Princess Elizabeth as a wife for Arran's son in order to prevent him from changing sides.

In fact, the arrival of Lennox had as much to do with keeping Arran in the English camp as did the machinations of Henry VIII. As soon as Lennox returned, everyone was agog to see how the rivals would receive each other. At the end of April, Lennox came to Edinburgh and exchanged civilities with the Governor but their apparent amity did not last long. Only two days later the anticipated trouble began when Arran demanded that Lennox sign and seal the act of parliament ratifying Arran's position as second person of the realm. In view of what he regarded as his superior claim to that title, Lennox refused and it seemed to observers that there would be 'a great strife and controversy' between them.[30] Lennox left Edinburgh abruptly and Arran retired to his own lands, vowing vengeance. The Governor then sent a herald to Lennox ordering him to deliver up Dumbarton Castle and repeating his demand that Lennox recognize him as second person of the realm. Acting on the advice of Cardinal Beaton, Lennox pretended to be agreeable but before Arran could come and see him he withdrew to the Highlands with a band of followers.[31]

The direct result of all this wrangling was that, so long as Lennox was acting in the French interest, Arran would support the English. As everyone had always suspected, the two Earls would inevitably be on different sides in any struggle. In spite of the efforts of Lennox himself and of Beaton, who gathered the clergy together in a convocation at St Andrews, the English supporters remained in the ascendant that spring and when the question of the marriage of the little Queen came before parliament, those who opposed it seemed power-less to offer direct resistance to Henry VIII. There were heated debates about what should be done. An English spy reported that even Arran was opposed to the marriage but that he had told his Council that they had not the power to resist Henry and should therefore give him fair words and promises as a means of gaining time. There were many Scots who existed by playing off England against Scotland, but in the end there were few who would willingly see their country lose its independence.

The consequence was that on 1 July the Treaties of Green-wich were finally concluded. One treaty agreed on peace between England and Scotland during the lives of Henry VIII and Mary, Queen of Scots, while the other settled the marriage of the little Queen and Prince Edward. As soon as she reached the age of eleven the young Queen was to be taken to England and married. The kingdom of Scotland was to remain in-dependent with Arran as Lord Governor and should Prince Edward die childless, Mary would be free to return to Scot-land.[32] The treaties would be ratified two months later. The announcement of their terms was received with great hostility. Popular feeling against the English was by now considerable, particularly in Edinburgh, as Sir Ralph Sadler found to his cost. One day while he walked behind his lodgings with some friends a shot was fired at them, missing one of his men by no more than four inches, and he suffered further indignities from the mob who broke into his garden and despoiled his archery targets.[33] Everyone spoke against Arran and the English alliance. In the west, Lennox was gathering together an army. In the east, Cardinal Beaton was assembling forces.

A small French fleet was sighted off the east coast and there were immediately rumours that the ships had come to remove Mary of Guise and her daughter to France.

The Earl of Arran was for once galvanized into instant activity by the news of the French fleet. He went to Linlithgow and began to fortify the palace with his own men and with artillery.[34] Highly alarmed, Mary of Guise sent urgent messages to Cardinal Beaton, who had gone to Stirling to join forces with Lennox, Huntly, Argyll and the other supporters of France. When they heard of developments at Linlithgow, the Cardinal and Lennox marched east with some six or seven thousand men, hoping to surprise the Governor. Arran's preparations at Linlithgow had been too successful, however, and they were not able to seize the palace as they had planned to do.

The town of Linlithgow lies just outside the palace, and there Lennox and his men took up their position. They had no artillery, and without artillery they could not capture the palace. Arran had withdrawn again to Edinburgh with his army. It was estimated that he had about eight thousand men with him, but he was unwilling to take the field and he complained to Sadler about his lack of money. In an atmosphere of mounting tension, emissaries came and went between the two opposing camps, while Mary of Guise waited impatiently in her palace, more of a prisoner than ever. Eventually, representatives from both sides met at the little village of Kirkliston, approximately half-way between Edinburgh and Linlithgow. The Cardinal's men there put forward four demands. They asked that Mary, Queen of Scots be given into the custody of four Scottish lords. They asked that in future Arran rule by advice of a Council 'without following the advice of such private persons as he now does'. They said that, if he refused to take the advice of that Council, he should be forced to resign, and they demanded that Angus and Sir George absent themselves from Court for a season.

After much heated discussion, the first two demands were granted but the other two were refused. However, the representatives agreed to meet again and said that if they could not come to an amicable conclusion, they would fight it out on the following day. The second meeting duly took place and the warlike show put on by both parties dissolved abruptly. 'There was shaking of hands one with another, friendly embracing and familiar communications and very good agreement amongst them and long and familiar talk betwixt the Earl of Angus and the Cardinal', Sadler reported to Henry VIII.[35]

With an enormous sense of relief, Mary of Guise heard that the Earl of Glencairn was riding to Linlithgow to dismiss all of Arran's people from about the little Queen. Instead, she was to be put in the care of Lords Graham, Erskine, Lindsay and Livingston, two of whom had been chosen by Arran and two by Beaton. At last she and her daughter were free from the Lord Governor and they could now leave Linlithgow. Twenty-four carriage horses set off for Stirling bearing Mary of Guise's great bed and the beds of all her ladies. A man was paid four shillings to carry the baby Queen's cradle to the west, and another was paid two shillings to take the pictures from Mary of Guise's chamber to her new residence. Nineteen carriage horses transported the great larder, all the kitchen utensils, the wine cellar and bakehouse equipment and the coffers from the bread pantry. At last everything was ready and on 26 July Mary of Guise rode from the Palace of Linlithgow with her small daughter. Escorted by the Earl of Lennox and two thousand five hundred mounted men with a thousand heavily armed footsoldiers, they made the journey to Stirling Castle.[36]

Once installed in the castle, Mary was in a position of greatly increased power. When Livingston and Lindsay, the two lords named by Arran to have custody of the little Queen, arrived at Stirling it was not long before they realized that they would have no influence at all. They resolved to go back to Edinburgh at once but by the simple expedient of seizing their baggage, Mary prevented them from going. Lord Erskine was the keeper of the castle and had all the keys. The castle belonged to Mary of Guise by her marriage contract, and so this fact alone gave her considerable influence. Henry VIII might send orders that Mary of Guise should be separated from her daughter, but as Arran himself admitted 'it is not possible to be accomplished, specially because the Castle of Stirling is her own house'.[37]

Of course, Mary's troubles were far from being over. At first she was afraid that Arran might bring his army and beseige Stirling Castle in an attempt to take her daughter back. She sent anxious messages to Huntly telling him that she had heard to her displeasure that this might happen; Huntly reassured her, promising his support and that of Lennox and the others should the Governor make any such move, and it became obvious soon enough that Arran had no military ambitions of that description. He remained Governor, of course, but the Treaties of Greenwich were not yet ratified and Mary herself was emerging as a figure of considerable importance. For the first time there was talk of her 'party', of those lords and gentlemen who owed their first allegiance to her rather than to Beaton or to Arran.

With growing confidence in her own prospects, Mary continued to play her game of procrastination by summoning Sir Ralph Sadler to her presence once more. She then assured him 'that she was now the same woman that I left her at my last being with her, both for her good mind and zeal to accomplish all things which might be to your highness's [i.e. Henry VIII's] good contention', especially the accomplishment of the English marriage. She declared that she was now more hopeful than ever that the marriage would take place, for the Scottish noblemen had delivered her out of Arran's hands. She assured Sadler that 'she desired the perfection' of the marriage 'with all her heart' and when he criticized the action of Lennox and the others in rebelling against their lawful Governor, she replied most earnestly that it had been necessary, for 'she and her daughter were held as it were in a prison, whereof she had many times complained and could find no remedy'.[38]

Arran himself was by now subject to increasing pressure from both sides. His half-brother the Abbot of Paisley, a close friend of Beaton, was constantly urging him to desert the English cause. Henry VIII, on the other hand, was repeating his offer of the English princess as a wife for Arran's son, and he now went so far as to suggest that he might make Arran King of all Scotland to the north of the Forth. Since Arran's own considerable territories all lay in the far richer area to the south of the Forth, the offer was not as tempting as Henry supposed, but even so, Arran was still inclined to believe that the English alliance would bring him more advantage than any alignment with the French would do. A prey to all manner of doubts, he nevertheless went ahead with the ratification of the treaties and on 25 August in the Abbey of Holyroodhouse he attended a High Mass 'solemnly sung with shawms and sackbuts' and swore that he would observe the terms agreed.[39]

Cardinal Beaton did not attend the ceremony, although he had let it be known that the treaties had his support, and the next day Arran rode to St Andrews to see him. The Cardinal refused to meet him and so on 27 August the Governor returned to Edinburgh.

The atmosphere in the capital was by now more fraught with tension than ever. Several Scottish ships had been seized by the English, and public feeling was running high. Observing the Governor narrowly, Sadler decided that Arran already regretted having ratified the treaties and 'seems as though he would fain slip from a great part of the same'. Like the French, the Scots did not hesitate to make all manner of promises but then did nothing.

Almost a week passed in this atmosphere of suspicion and unrest until, on the afternoon of 3 September, Arran slipped out of Edinburgh accompanied by only three or four men. He left word that he was going to Blackness Castle to visit his wife who was lying dangerously ill in childbirth there. As soon as the news of his going leaked out, the whole town was astonished, and everyone was full of speculation. Where had he really gone and what were his intentions?

It was the following day before the truth was known. Arran had ridden to Blackness, certainly, but from there he had gone on to Lord Livingston's house near Falkirk, where he had been reunited with Cardinal Beaton. After 'very friendly embracings' and 'a good long communication' they rode together to Stirling.[40]

Mary of Guise and Cardinal Beaton were triumphant. On 8 September Arran went to the Franciscan Friary in the burgh of Stirling and there did penance for his support of the Protestants. In recent months he had been encouraging the distribution of the Scriptures in English and his protection of friars also suggested that his allegiance to the Catholic Church was no longer all that might be desired. The Cardinal granted him absolution, then he heard Mass, the Earls of Argyll and Bothwell holding the towel above his head while he received the sacraments.

That same afternoon he remitted all his proceedings to the advice of the Cardinal and his supporters, promising to do nothing without their consent and counsel. On the following day, the baby Queen was crowned in the Chapel Royal 'with great solemnity, triumph, plays, farces and banqueting, and great dancing before the Queen with great lords and French ladies'. At the actual coronation ceremony the Earl of Arran carried the crown, Lennox bore the sceptre and Argyll held the sword of state. The Earl of Angus and the English party stayed away.[41]

6

The Struggle for Power

In September, communications between Mary and France having been restored, the Duchess of Guise wrote to her daughter praising God 'who, lending you His aid, has set you at liberty and out of such a great and long captivity'. Antoinette confessed that she herself had almost despaired of seeing Mary's affairs prosper once more, while Claud had often discussed the possibility of bringing their daughter back to France. Now, however, the danger had passed. Mary must put her trust in the wise and good Cardinal Beaton, and she should soon receive word from the King of France who was most anxious to help.[1]

Mary did indeed find herself in a position most marvellously improved. The Earl of Arran was in effect powerless. He was to be directed in all things by a Council of Regency, and the principal member of that Council was Mary of Guise.[2] At last she had regained a position of real influence. Of course, there were problems ahead. A mere glance round the Council chamber at the very different members present would be enough to remind her of the difficulties of her task. Cardinal Beaton and the other ecclesiastics would give firm enough support to the pro-French policies, and Huntly and Moray, both related by blood to James V, were surely reliable. But the pro-English Earl of Angus sat near the pro-French Earl of Lennox, and who knew how Bothwell or Glencairn would act in an emergency?

For the time being, though, Mary was content to celebrate her new-found freedom. According to one chronicler, her Court 'was then like Venus and Cupido in the time of fresh May, for there was such dancing, singing, playing and merriness into the Court at that time that no man would have tired therein'.³ All this romantic activity centred around the Earl of Lennox and the Earl of Bothwell, suitors both for the hand of Mary of Guise. Lennox, of course, had come to Scotland in the expectation of marrying her. He was disappointed to find that the matter was not as settled as he had imagined. As the weeks went by Mary was encouraging, but she was not encouraging enough. She even seemed to look with favour on his rival, Bothwell. In spite of the fact that he was a married man with a family, Bothwell had been unable to resist the prospect of such a matrimonial prize and he was prepared to divorce his wife so that he could marry the Queen Dowager.

'Earl Bothwell,' the chronicler noted, 'was a young, lusty gentleman, fair and pleasant in the sight of women, therefore he intended to have the Queen in marriage as well as did the Earl of Lennox, and therefore daily these two lords pursued the Court and the Queen with bravery, with dancing, singing and playing on instruments and arrayed every day in sundry garments and prided every one of them who should be most gallant in their clothing and behave themselves in the Queen's presence, sometimes in shooting, sometimes in singing and jousting and running of great horse at the lists with all other kindly games that might satisfy the Queen or do her pleasure.'

Annoyingly enough for Bothwell, Lennox had two distinct advantages. He had been brought up in France by his uncle and so he knew that language and all the pretty French ways of behaving. He was also considered a good deal more handsome. Lennox was 'a strong man of personage well shaped . . . fair and pleasant faced, with a good and manly countenance . . . and upright in his passage. Therefore at that time he was most pleasant for a lady'. Bothwell, by comparison, was 'fair and whitely and something hanging-shouldered and went something forward with a gentle and humane countenance, but yet he was not thought to do a gentlewoman so great pleasure as the other'.⁴ Contemporary evidence suggests that he was indeed consumptive.

For all his manly charm, Lennox soon realized that he was

making no progress. Mary gave him fair words but no indication that she would ever fulfil her promises. Bothwell was even hinting that she had sworn to marry him. By mid-September Lennox had grown impatient, and one day he left Stirling Castle abruptly and without permission. Mary was none too pleased. She wrote him a letter rebuking him for his sudden departure, which, she said, she found very strange. He replied in huffy tones, declaring that he found it even stranger that she should find fault with him. He had, after all, explained that his sister's illness and other private business required his presence in Glasgow. However, he ended on a conciliatory note, hoping to see her that Wednesday evening and assuring her of his loyalty.[5]

Mary was too astute to be convinced by these protestations. Lennox was becoming an embarrassment. It was growing increasingly difficult to keep him in hopes of marrying her without committing herself in any way. She knew perfectly well, too, that the strange presence of both Arran and Lennox on the same side would not be of long duration. However, she was determined to do all she could to keep the lords united. Towards the end of the month the Court moved to Edinburgh, then she went across to St Andrews where she stayed on at the castle with the Cardinal and the Earl of Bothwell for quite some time before returning to Stirling.[6]

No doubt her intelligence network kept her informed of the fact that Lennox was now deeply involved in secret dealings with Henry VIII. The Earl was writing to assure the English that he was most anxious to be of their party, and he was declaring with enthusiasm that, above all else, he wished to marry Lady Margaret Douglas. Not only was she so ravishingly beautiful that he had fallen in love with her, but she was the daughter of Angus and the niece of Henry VIII himself. Knowing of his disappointed hopes with regard to Mary of Guise, the English party had offered him a very desirable alternative.

While he waited for some definite message from the south, Lennox therefore played the double game of trying to please both sides. Nevertheless, at the beginning of October, he was forced out into the open. On the evening of the first Thursday of the month, six ships sailed into the anchorage at Greenock, in the west of Scotland. Faithful to his promise to the Guises, the King of France had sent help. On board was Marco Grimani, Patriarch of Aquileia, along with the French ambassador Jacques de la Brosse, who was an old friend of the Guise family, and another French statesman named Jacques Menage. They brought with them a significant quantity of silver and artillery for Mary of Guise.[7]

Shortly after calling at Greenock, the ships sailed on to Dumbarton, and there the money was landed. Now Dumbarton Castle was in the Earl of Lennox's possession, and he was in residence. Delighted at this opportunity of compensating himself for all his disappointment at the hands of Mary of Guise and the Cardinal, he seized the money and refused to give it up.[8]

Naturally enough, Mary and Beaton were furious when they heard the news. Lennox was supposed to be acting in the French King's interest but instead here he was behaving in the most obstructive way imaginable. However, the arrival of Jacques de la Brosse meant that Mary had a powerful new ally in Scotland, someone who actively represented the French King and who, looking at the situation with a fresh and objective eye, could offer advice on how best to deal with the present difficulties.

Mary therefore summoned La Brosse and his friends to Stirling to see her at once. In order to get there, they had to pass through Glasgow, where Lennox was now staying. The Earl ordered the Frenchmen to be brought to him, and he questioned them closely as to their mission. He also took the opportunity of justifying his own erratic behaviour. The real trouble was, he explained, that the promises made to him had not been kept. Arran was still Governor and since he had taken over the direction of affairs he had been favourably disposed towards the heretics. Moreover, he had recklessly squandered the entire personal estate of the late King, valued at more than £300,000. Was it any wonder, he demanded, that he was tempted by Henry VIII's offer to use force to make him

Governor of Scotland and to marry him to a wealthy bride, Henry's own niece?[9]

La Brosse was not impressed. He reproached Lennox, reminding him of how much the French King relied upon him, and he took the occasion to warn the Earl of how little Henry VIII's promises might be trusted. He then left hastily for Stirling, for an audience with Mary of Guise.

Mary's pleasure in welcoming her fellow countrymen was somewhat marred by the problem of Lennox. His behaviour was at the forefront of her mind, and she was soon explaining to La Brosse that the divisions caused by Lennox were most harmful. La Brosse could indeed see for himself that private quarrels and feuds were rampant. 'Because of the aforesaid divisions,' he noted, 'the realm of Scotland was and still is at the present time under arms. For all the friends of one faction mistrust all those of the other faction, so much so that not merely is the nobility in arms, but churchmen, friars and the country people only travel through the countryside in large companies, all armed with pikes, swords and bucklers.'[10]

Civil unrest was exacerbated by a combination of anti-English feeling on one hand and anti-ecclesiastical feeling stirred up by the English on the other. Thanks to the encouragement of Henry VIII, La Brosse discovered that 'when we arrived in Scotland some five or six thousand men had assembled, who had undertaken within four days to destroy all the monasteries and convents in the town of Edinburgh, and the inhabitants of that town were in arms to resist them. But as soon as they heard of our coming they wholly abandoned this attempt and the churches and religious estate remain as they were when we first arrived'. Talking the situation over with La Brosse, Mary of Guise was inclined to blame Arran for all these troubles, declaring that 'through the fault of the said Governor heresies had abounded and do abound in this realm'. She also echoed Lennox's complaint about Arran's financial dealings, telling La Brosse that the Governor was administering the revenues of the realm in an evil and reckless way.[11]

After much discussion, La Brosse advised Mary that

138

Lennox must be drawn back into their party once and for all. He would be the chief instrument in removing Arran from power and so he must be firmly attached to the French party. It is interesting to discover that this advice was supported by an anonymous Scotsman, probably Lord Methven, who sent a memorandum to Mary about that time urging her to win Lennox over and advising her how best to comport herself. Even if Lennox would not agree to what she wanted, and even if contrary things were done, Mary should 'bear you as pleasantly as you may goodly, and by continual labours, as I hope your wisdom can better do nor a hundred men can devise, you shall bring things to good address . . . that now appear not to come. And treat all the lords being with you, and treat the Governor, and take no displeasure but think to overset this and after to have all you desire'.[12]

Whatever the identity of the anonymous friend, his advice is enlightening. He was obviously addressing someone who was liable to lose patience, to let her annoyance show. He felt the need to warn her that by so doing she would put herself at a disadvantage, and he took it that she had enough intelligence to realize the force of what he said. In a way, his recommendations recall the Duchess of Guise's admonitions to her daughter to accept the will of God and to submit to whatever was visited upon her. Both advisers, although speaking of very different subjects, were thinking along the same lines. Her friend spoke of political manoeuvring, her mother of spiritual life, but both were advising someone who was apt to chafe against restrictions, to lose her temper with the devious ways of others. Be patient, be subtle and bide your time was what the friend advised, and for the most part Mary followed his advice.

She certainly tried once more to retain the allegiance of Lennox. She summoned him to Stirling and made him the best possible offer. If he would hand over the money from France and promise to uphold the French alliance, he should have the hand in marriage of the baby Queen.[13]

This startling *volte-face* was designed to keep Lennox interested for a number of years. It was safe enough to offer the baby Queen in marriage: she would not be old enough for the promise to be fulfilled for quite some time to come. Disappointed though he had been over Mary of Guise, Lennox would surely be unable to resist this glittering prize.

Lennox did agree to the proposal. He had no intention of waiting ten or fifteen years in the hope of marrying Mary, Queen of Scots. He had privately resolved to throw in his lot with the English. So much did the pro-English lords distrust him, however, that he was forced to rely for the time being on Mary of Guise's support. The promise of marriage was merely an expedient to bind him to the French interest, and he recognized it as such. For a few months more he found it desirable to remain with the pro-French party.[14]

Lennox's tiresome behaviour was by this time paling into insignificance by comparison with the threat from England. With the increase of patriotic feeling in Scotland, with the growing power of Mary of Guise and her allies, and with the active support of France in the person of La Brosse, it was becoming obvious that Mary and the Cardinal would soon be able to accomplish their design and have the Treaties of Greenwich repealed. The more Henry VIII became aware of the worsening climate of Scottish opinion, the more vehement did he grow in his desire to conquer his northern neighbour, and the more imperious did he become in his demands that his agents should seize the baby Queen and effect the capture of Beaton.

Aware that he would soon act, Mary decided that she must take the initiative. On the late afternoon of 1 November 1543, Lord Maxwell, a supporter of the English, had gone to visit his pro-English friend Lord Somerville at a house in Edinburgh. As they sat talking, a commotion was heard outside. Emerging into the street to investigate, they found John Hamilton, the Commendator of Paisley, waiting for them accompanied by sixty horsemen 'all with red bonnets on their heads and steel bonnets under their arms, beneath their cloaks'. The Abbot escorted the two lords up to the gates of Edinburgh Castle where eighty more men were waiting. When Lord Somerville saw them he cried: 'Treason! We are betrayed!

Let us help ourselves,' but his words were in vain. He and his companion were arrested in the name of the Queen and the Governor. As Sir Ralph Sadler remarked, 'Now it is thought the game will begin,' and he left Scotland soon afterwards.[15]

Lord Somerville was imprisoned in Blackness Castle, Lord Maxwell in Edinburgh Castle. Six days later the Earl of Arran captured the Douglas Castle of Dalkeith. Sir George Douglas was in the castle, but, elusive as ever, he managed to escape.[16] On 25 November the Cardinal and the Governor went to Dundee and arrested Lord Gray, the Earl of Rothes and Henry Balneaves who were also suspected of having dealings with the English.[17] The climax to all this activity came at the beginning of December when parliament met in Edinburgh. For several weeks past La Brosse and Menage had been searching through the parliamentary registers for some pretext under which the Treaties of Greenwich could be broken: some error in the formalities when the marriage treaty was made, for instance. By December they had their excuse. Parliament declared that because Henry VIII had broken the peace by seizing Scottish ships the marriage contract was invalidated. The Treaties of Greenwich were therefore solemnly declared to be null. On 15 December parliament renewed Scotland's ancient treaties of alliance with France.[18] The Earl of Arran then sent to Henry VIII to ask for a new truce, and Mary of Guise set out on foot to walk in pilgrimage the seven miles to Musselburgh, 'to Our Lady [of] Loretto, praying for peace among her lords with the realm of England, and remained there by the space of twenty days in her prayers'.[19]

Mary's motives in all this have frequently been misunderstood. It is often assumed that she was from the start the willing tool of the French King, a pawn in his political game, concerned only in doing whatever he commanded. This is to put too simple an interpretation on events. Above all else, Mary was a woman with a mind of her own, and when La Brosse came to Scotland he was not seeking out someone totally committed to his master's policies. Indeed, he recorded with a faintly relieved air that he found her 'as well disposed and as desirous of doing service to the King [of France] as he could wish'.[20] Certainly Mary would act in the French interest, but her complete support was not a foregone conclusion and it was given for her own motives. She wished to become the ruler of a fully independent realm freed from the threat of English interference. Having learned from bitter experience that she could trust no one in Scotland, she would only feel safe when she held power once more in her own hands. When that day came, the French alliance would be safe, Scotland would be secure and her daughter's future would be untroubled.

With the repeal of the Treaties of Greenwich and the renewal of the French alliance she was well on the way to success. Even so, the reconciling of the lords was a wellnigh impossible task. Angus and his followers had evinced great annoyance at the repeal of the treaties, and the coming of the new year saw him and his friends marching to Leith in battle array to confront Cardinal Beaton and the Earl of Arran. The Governor was in Edinburgh, which was well defended, and for five days Angus and his men were drawn up ready for battle half a mile from the town.

It was a repetition of the encounter at Kirkliston. Messengers passed to and fro between the two sides. This time it was Angus who did not have the necessary artillery to assault Edinburgh, and Arran would not emerge from safety to take the field. In the end, so many of Angus's followers deserted his cause that he was forced to surrender, agreeing that henceforth he would help to defend Scotland against the English.[21] Pledges were given by Angus's party, and the provost of Edinburgh was able to report to Mary of Guise with satisfaction that 'All is well and surely done to your pleasure . . . My Lord Governor and the lords here will be at Your Grace incontinent and make the final resolution and order with Your Grace's advice and counsel and lose nothing but at your pleasure'.[22]

Hopeful though these words might be, the reality was rather different. The rest of the winter was spent uneasily, with much plotting and counter-plotting. Mary was busy bribing friends by distributing the money brought over by La

Brosse. Henry VIII was bribing the same people with his rather more considerable wealth, and all the time he was preparing for war. Fixing a date in March for his invasion of Scotland, he already planned to increase his garrison on the Borders, then keep the Scots occupied with Border raids.[23]

Angus, in spite of his promises to support Mary against the English, was still writing to assure Henry VIII of his fidelity.[24] Arran was taken up with a startling new plan of his own. He had resolved to divorce his wife, a move which would leave him free to marry the lady of his choice – Mary of Guise.[25] Lennox, for his part, was writing to Mary to complain about Arran, who had accused him of causing the 'daily insurrections and disobedience contrary [to] the authority' of the realm. He was also in close touch with the English Court, sending his secretary back and forth with messages to Lady Margaret Douglas, protesting his undying affection.[26]

Lennox's own friends on the French side were by this time heartily tired of his behaviour. Mr John Campbell, one of his associates then acting as Mary of Guise's messenger to the French King, went so far as to write to Lennox from Dieppe, reproaching him for his attitude. He warned that Lennox was liable to lose all favour 'through your own misguiding and that you have had yourself marvellous evil to the Queen's Grace in many cases since my departing which, my lord, will not fail to come to your great displeasure'. It was said openly in France, he reported, that Lennox was 'all the cause of the whole break and division that is in Scotland which, were not you, all would be well, and that the Queen's Grace has not so great an enemy or unfriend as you are, and that you have wasted and spent and daily spends and wastes the King of France's money, holding a guard of thieves and broken men about you and will not answer the Queen's Grace nor ambassadors of none of the said money'. In conclusion, he declared that he had only ever served Lennox at Mary of Guise's command, 'And if all things be of verity that I hear, I would I had been prisoner to the Turks that hour I took such charges for you or any Scottish man'.[27]

By the end of March, Mary had had enough of Lennox.

Taking artillery from Edinburgh Castle, Cardinal Beaton and the Earl of Arran marched west to besiege Glasgow Castle where they believed him to be. After a siege lasting ten days, the garrison was bribed to surrender. This they did, whereupon Arran hanged all twenty-eight of them as soon as they emerged. Lennox was not there. Mary and her supporters had therefore to satisfy themselves with arresting the Earl of Angus and his adherents, apparently not without his own consent.[28]

In the meantime, the Earl of Lennox was sending frantic messages to the English Court, anxiously demanding the hand of Lady Margaret Douglas. At last he set out in person for the south, but the ship in which he was travelling was driven back to Dumbarton by contrary winds and he was forced to spend further weeks in Scotland.[29] By this time, Mary had given up all hopes of binding him to the French interest. She and Cardinal Beaton had long since lived to regret the day they ever invited him to return to Scotland. Almost from the start he had been a liability instead of an asset, and although there was no knowing what mischief he might now make, they no longer saw any point in trying to win him back by promises or by any other means. They had thought they could exploit the traditional rivalry between Lennox and Arran, but their attempts had rebounded to their own disadvantage and their failure said much about any effort to manipulate the Scottish nobles as if they were their Continental counterparts.

March came and went, and there was still no sign of the threatened English invasion. Even so, Mary knew that the crisis was imminent. Her own spies kept her well informed about the troop movements in the south and she was aware that it was simply a matter of time before Henry's armies came to avenge the repeal of the Treaties of Greenwich. When the invasion did come, it nevertheless took the Scots by surprise. April had passed without incident but at the beginning of May 1544 English ships arrived in the River Forth and the Earl of Hertford and his men disembarked near Leith. The invasion had begun.

La mere de la Royne descoce
de la me son de guile

Drawing of Mary of Guise, attributed to Clouet

Holyrood Abbey, Edinburgh, scene of Mary's coronation and burial place of her second husband and sons

Falkland Palace, Fife, one of Mary's own residences

The English army marched towards Edinburgh, taking their light ordnance with them. Urgent messengers rode to Stirling to warn the Queen of their coming. With him, Hertford carried his instructions from Henry VIII, passed on to him by the English Privy Council. These instructions were as ruthless as they were specific. Hertford was ordered to 'put all to fire and sword, burn Edinburgh town, so razed and defaced when you have sacked and gotten what you can of it as there may remain forever a perpetual memory of the vengeance of God lightened upon [them] for their falsehood and disobedience'. They were to beat down and overthrow Edinburgh Castle, sack Holyroodhouse and as many towns and villages in the surrounding area 'as you may conveniently do'. They were to sack Leith, burn it and subvert it, 'putting man, woman and child to fire and sword, without exception, where any resistance shall be made against you'. They were then instructed to cross to Fife and do the same there, not forgetting so to 'spoil and turn upside down the Cardinal's town of St Andrews as the upper stone may be the nether, and not one stick stand by another, sparing no creature alive within the same, specially such as either in friendship or blood be allied to the Cardinal'.[30]

When Hertford and his forces had marched about a mile towards Edinburgh, they were confronted by an army of some six thousand Scots drawn up in battle array, Cardinal Beaton and the Earl of Arran at their head. These the English put to flight, driving the fleeing soldiers to Edinburgh. A little before nightfall the English captured Leith and there they encamped. Cardinal Beaton, the Earl of Arran and the other leaders of the Scottish army fled to Linlithgow.[31]

Alarmed by the proportions of the invading army and the precipitate flight of Beaton and the rest, the provost of Edinburgh sent anxious messages to Hertford, begging him to negotiate a truce. He refused. He then attacked the town. Initially, the English were thrown back in confusion by the vigour of the Scottish defence. Hand guns were being fired at them in quick succession from every available window and loophole. Taken aback, the English shot at random, doing more harm to their own companions than to the enemy. Then they brought up their artillery, and after three or four shots of an English culverin, the town gates flew open and the English surged in. Only the castle held out against them still. Hertford judged it to be impregnable and decided against attacking it. Instead, he gave orders to set fire to various parts of the town and 'made a jolly fire and smoke'.

On the following day, the Scots tried once more to attack, but once more they were driven back and Hertford was able to report with satisfaction to Henry VIII that his commission was now well executed, 'for the town and also the abbey of Holyroodhouse is in manner wholly burned down and desolate'. He had been able to stand with his men on a neighbouring hillside and watch the town burn, while the wind brought to their ears the wailing of the women and the other poor folk of Edinburgh.[32]

Arran, Beaton and the lords were now in St Andrews, planning to assemble the Scottish forces for the attack and discussing the possibility of sending the baby Queen to a place of safety in the Highlands. Taking advantage of their inactivity, Hertford sent his men across the Forth to devastate Fife. He also gave orders to a party of soldiers to ride to within six miles of Stirling Castle, destroying houses and farms as they were 'in such sort as there shall not only . . . remain a perpetual memory of our being here but also . . . the enemies shall neither be able to recover this damage while we live, nor yet to assemble any power this year in these parts of the realm, whatsoever aid be sent unto them out of France or Denmark'.[33]

Hertford then set fire to the town of Leith, destroying the harbour pier and setting light to the ships in the harbour From there, he and his men made their way eastwards along the coast, burning according to their own account 'the town of Musselburgh, Preston, Seton with the Lord Seton's principal house . . . the towns of Haddington and Dunbar, which we dare assure your majesty be well burned with as many other piles, gentlemen's and others' houses and villages which we might conveniently reach, within the limits or compass of our way homewards'. Their mission was fully accomplished and Hertford noted with satisfaction that 'the like devastation hath not been made in Scotland these many years'.[34]

During the invasion, Mary of Guise had remained in Stirling Castle, listening to each new report of the English outrages with a growing anger. Personal distress was added to public indignation when news reached her of the burning of the Abbey of Holyrood. Her dead husband and her baby sons lay there: the attack on the abbey was a hideous desecration.

When the English had gone, she was left with a feeling of bitter rage against the man who had let it all happen – the Earl of Arran. As Lord Governor, he was responsible for the protection of the realm and he had been a miserable failure. This, then, was the moment for her to act. There were many who shared her feelings of disillusion with the present government. Even those who had previously supported him now felt that Arran was completely unfitted for his role. The only salvation against a further English invasion must surely lie in the French alliance and, realizing that, the lords would now turn to Mary of Guise as the person best able to get help from France. The time had come for her to have Arran deposed so that she could assume the Regency herself.

On 16 May, as Hertford was preparing to march south, Mary's supporter Alexander Gordon, the Postulate of Caithness, was already in Perth, issuing proclamations on her orders, probably for the convention which she was about to summon. He then moved on to Dundee, to win over to her side the Governor's former friends Lord Gray and Lord Glamis.[35] Already, she had evidence that she had read the situation correctly. Sir George Douglas was writing to her before the month was out to assure her that 'I am and ever shall be ready to do Your Grace service according to your honour and the common weal of this realm, at the utmost of my power'.[36] Throughout a long political career, Sir George had almost always possessed the happy knack of being on the winning side. It was significant indeed that Mary was about to number him among her most active supporters. The Earl of

Angus likewise decided that the wisest course was to support her, and at the end of May he joined her in Stirling.

Much quarrelling among the nobles then ensued, each blaming the other for the recent disaster. Arran, alarmed and displeased at rumours of the moves against him, retired to his home in Hamilton. Cardinal Beaton withdrew to St Andrews, and on 28 May the Earl of Lennox left Scotland. This time the winds were in his favour when he sailed from Dumbarton, and he was able to land at Chester. He made his way at once to the English Court. There he was honourably received by Henry VIII and married to Lady Margaret Douglas.

The Earl of Arran had summoned a general Council to meet at Linlithgow on 28 May. Instead, it was held at Stirling a day late. Mary and the Governor were both present, along with almost the entire nobility. On 3 June the lords solemnly accused Arran of destroying the realm and breaking the truce with England. He was ordered to resign his office forthwith into the hands of Mary of Guise and themselves.

Clinging desperately to his position, Arran declared that he must take advice but promised to answer the charges against him on the following day. Instead, he stole secretly out of Stirling with only two companions and rode for Blackness. When the Council convened next morning, they discovered his absence with indignation and declared that he was discharged from the governorship. Proclamations to that effect were made in all the principal towns throughout the country, and Arran himself was summoned to appear in Edinburgh on 28 July to hear himself degraded from his governorship in the presence of parliament.[37]

A week later, the lords met again to discuss the problem of the government of the realm. They agreed that Mary of Guise should now become Regent of Scotland, and they appointed a Privy Council of twelve to advise her.[38] It seemed that Mary's day of triumph had arrived. For eighteen months she had been working steadily towards this moment. From a position of absolute weakness at the time of her husband's death, she had gradually built up a party of supporters, using every method at her command, bribing, cajoling, charming and threatening all whom it seemed might help her cause. Quarrelsome nobles, foreign invasion, lack of money, downright treachery had all seemed to conspire against her, but at last she was strong enough to seize power for herself.

Having convinced her supporters that she would get for them the much-needed help from France, Mary had to set about making her promises a reality. She had to convince the King of France that she was in control of the situation, and to let him see that Scotland was once more in a position to be his active ally. Unless he were persuaded that those governing Scotland would now wholeheartedly pursue the policies of James V with regard to France, he would never send aid. Mary therefore had to be very careful in what she said to him. Far from being his obedient agent, she was in the position of seeking his support.

She therefore sought the advice of that most experienced of diplomats, Sir George Douglas. Sir George went to Stirling to see her, and later confided to a friend that he had urged her to be very circumspect. She was to describe to the King of France 'how the Governor uses him [i.e. behaves] and how she has joined together all the noblemen of the realm for the serving of the Queen's Grace her daughter and defence of this realm against the old enemies and how Her Grace is put in authority herself . . . and that the support they might have should be hastened on to Her Grace, and that mention be made unto the King of France that Her Grace has all the whole noblemen of the realm united together which was never before since the death of the King's Grace, whom God assoil, and will be ready both she and they for to do the King of France both pleasure and service as firmly as ever the King of Scotland was'. Above all else, Francis had to see that it was now Mary who ruled the country. The danger was that he would be persuaded to continue to treat Arran as Governor. By referring to her daughter's authority Mary hoped to convince Francis of her own, and she and Sir George were also careful to warn the French King that 'if any private person such as the Governor or the Cardinal would write to the King of France in contrary of Her Grace, he [the King] being advertised before how wisely she has ordered her matters, he will not esteem their information . . .'[39]

The letter to France agreed, Sir George then turned to his old advocacy of peace with England. As his correspondence shows, he was still playing his double game even now that he was one of Mary's principal advisers. He reported every move to Henry VIII with protestations of fidelity, describing the deposition of Arran, for instance, as a great step forward in Henry's policies while all the time swearing to Mary's supporters that he would always serve her and 'be a good Scotsman'.[40] It is pointless to seek any consistent political conviction behind Sir George's machinations. He was no more permanently committed to Henry VIII than he was to Mary of Guise, but by professing friendship for both he would ensure that he himself would not be the loser whatever happened.

Mary of Guise certainly agreed with him on the need for peace with England. The Scots simply did not have the resources to stand up to another English attack, and so on 21 June she wrote to Henry VIII complaining of his ill-usage of the Scots but asking to send ambassadors to him with a view to seeking peace.[41]

Unfortunately for her plans, her own position as Regent was far from secure. The Earl of Arran might have left Stirling in confusion and haste, but he was not going to sit calmly waiting to be deposed by parliament on 28 July. When his own interests were at stake he could be energetic enough. After slipping away to Blackness, he rode from Edinburgh and began his own defensive preparations. He had gunpowder brought from Dunbar to Leith and laid up in Edinburgh Castle. The day after it arrived, six barrels of barley were delivered on his orders to Edward Stewart 'who then with certain men of war' were in Holyroodhouse 'for keeping of the said palace because it was understood by My Lord Governor that the Queen and lords being with her should have come to Edinburgh to have held a parliament there'.[42]

By fortifying the royal strongholds against Mary, he meant to prevent her from having the opportunity of deposing him. On 20 June he felt strong enough to issue proclamations throughout the country discharging Mary of Guise of her assumed authority. He even dispatched a messenger to Stirling itself with his proclamation. He followed this up on 13 July with letters forbidding the acceptance as legal tender of bawbees coined by Mary of Guise, and declaring that the lords must not come to Edinburgh to 'the pretended parliament'. If any parliament were held, he had arranged that sixty-two hagbutters should attend him as his bodyguard and he had gone so far as to put a further eighteen in the steeple of the Church of St Giles, overlooking Edinburgh High Street.[43]

News of his activities made Mary even more anxious to hear from France. Towards the end of the month, she wrote urgent letters to the King of France, asking for aid. These she entrusted to the Sieur de Bauldreul, who was also given similar letters from members of the Scottish nobility. Bauldreul embarked without interference, but as his ship sailed down the English coast, it was intercepted off Scarborough by some Sussex fishermen from Rye. Realizing what was going to happen, Bauldreul hastily wrapped his precious bundle in a linen cloth, weighted it down with a piece of coal, and threw it overboard. Not to be so easily outwitted, the Rye fishermen managed to retrieve the package before it sank and sent its contents to the English Council of the North, whose members eagerly perused this further evidence of Scottish perfidy. Mary's anxious messages would never reach France. Some of her supporters began to say that help would not be forthcoming from that quarter.[44]

The struggle for power continued. The parliament proclaimed for the purpose of deposing Arran did not take place. Instead, Mary postponed its meeting until 12 November. She knew that she still did not have sufficient support to deal with the Governor. The Scots might complain volubly about his shortcomings, yet they retained their allegiance to him. Again and again Mary was to find that the traditional loyalties of the Scots would upset her calculations. Dislike Arran as they might, many of the nobility still preferred his rule to that of a woman and a foreigner.

The difficulties of dealing with the nobility and the lawless state of the country were demonstrated once again by Sir George Douglas's dealings that autumn. Out hawking one day, he came upon Arran's friend, Lord Borthwick, whom he promptly seized and imprisoned in Dalkeith Castle. Lord Borthwick, however, had a wife who was a lady of considerable ingenuity. She lured Lord Bothwell to her castle one night, had her men take him, and kept him captive until she managed to exchange him for her husband. Somehow or other, Sir George triumphed, though, for he persuaded both Borthwick and Bothwell to support Mary of Guise.[45]

Their adherence was but little help in the face of Arran's activities. Not only were his people harassing her servants, but he issued proclamations ordering his parliament to meet on 6 November, six days before hers, and he summoned Angus, Bothwell and Sir George Douglas to appear on a charge of treason.[46] In view of this threat hanging over him, Mary deemed it prudent to bribe Sir George, not for the first time. Her gesture had the desired effect, and on 28 September he was writing effusively to thank her for her 'gentle letter written with your own hand, which promises to me one thousand crowns in pension for my service, which have not deserved so great reward, but I shall be ready to serve Your Grace at all times to the best of my power and shall neither spare for fear of life nor goods to do that thing according to my honour and the pleasure of Your Grace and common weal of this realm'. For good measure, he added that 'if there be but two men in Scotland that will bide at your opinion, I shall be one, and this is not for Your Grace's gear [i.e. goods] but for my promise and honour'.[47]

These noble sentiments did not prevent Sir George from continuing to assure the English of his loyalty, but Mary enjoyed his practical counsel.[48] As the date for her parliament approached, she was alarmed by Arran's growing confidence and, unreliable though he might be, she was glad enough to seek Sir George's advice. Sir George agreed that 'the Governor waxes proud', and commented that 'the country falls to him more for fear nor for love'. It would be best if Mary could convene her own supporters before Arran's parliament actually met, for otherwise 'the most part of Scotland will come to him and then have you lost your purpose'. Mary should also make sure that the summonses to her own parliament were properly sealed. Previous 'slack handling' of such business had not helped matters. The earlier letters had not been sent out correctly sealed. This time she should be firm in her summoning of the lords and she should let it be known that any who failed to answer the summons would be accounted enemies to herself and to her daughter.[49]

Mary took his advice and sent out summonses which were entirely legal in form. She continued her desperate efforts to win support. She even made approaches to Cardinal Beaton in the hope of winning him back to her cause, but she met with no success. The Cardinal and Arran were acting together, these days.[50]

In the end, the struggle between Mary and Arran was temporarily resolved not by bribery and threats but by the inescapable necessities of the political situation. Arran held his parliament in Edinburgh. Mary held hers in Stirling, a week later. Mary was not strong enough to depose Arran. He knew that in view of the threat from England help from France was desperately needed. Some form of reconciliation was the only answer. It fell to Cardinal Beaton to act as mediator, travelling between Edinburgh and Stirling and delivering to Mary a set of proposals drawn up by the Edinburgh parliament. After much negotiation, the terms were finally agreed. Arran would remain Lord Governor of the realm but in all he did he would be guided by a special Council. Principal member of that Council was to be Mary of Guise. It was, in effect, a return to the situation of the previous summer. Mary had lost her bid for supreme power but she knew that, for the time being, all thoughts had to turn to the defence of Scotland against another English invasion. She had not given up the struggle for the Regency, though. She would patiently bide her time and when the opportunity came once more she would be ready.

7
The Rough Wooing

War and the rumour of war were to dominate the Scottish scene for the next five years. It was obvious to everyone that the English would not accept the repudiation of the Treaties of Greenwich, and the uneasy reconciliation of 1544 came not a moment too soon. Mary might be eager to reorganize Scotland's internal government and to assert her own authority, but all such considerations would have to take second place until the country was safe from invasion.

In that desperate winter of 1544–5, Mary devoted all her energies to helping to raise money for defence and trying to keep the lords together. The old year ended badly enough with Cardinal Beaton and the Earl of Arran involved in yet another of their quarrels. The cause was obscure, but an English spy reported with relish that Arran 'clapped his hand on his sword and drew it half out and the Cardinal did go from him in that reason'.[1] Nerves were on edge, tempers uncertain and Mary could only wait in Stirling Castle, chafing against her own enforced inactivity. Queen she might be, but she had no seat in parliament nor could she ride at the head of the Scottish army as a masculine member of the House of Guise would undoubtedly have done. In February, though, she travelled to Edinburgh with her lords and joined in the deliberations of the Privy Council. One of the English spies saw her at Mass in the town, kneeling in apparent amity beside Arran, Beaton, Bothwell, Argyll and the others.[2]

Perhaps her enthusiastic urgings inspired Arran with a new vitality. Before the month was out he was riding to the Borders with a Scottish force to attack the English holding Jedburgh and Kelso and to punish the 'assured Scots', those who openly supported England. Hearing of his coming Sir Ralph Eure, Warden of the Middle Marches, assembled his men and advanced towards Jedburgh. At first the Scots were driven back, but they reassembled and on 17 February 1545 they fell upon the English at Ancrum Moor and won a resounding victory.

Not only were the English defeated, but, as an added fillip to their morale, Sir Ralph Eure himself was killed. An eye-witness wrote to a friend with a vivid account of the aftermath of the battle. He was a vicar named Ogle and he had been taken prisoner by the Scots. When Arran had sounded his trumpets and withdrawn his men, he summoned the vicar to his presence. He then led Ogle by the hand to where the bodies of the dead lay. Pointing to the corpse of the Warden, he asked if it were indeed Sir Ralph. The vicar replied that it was. 'God have mercy on him,' exclaimed Arran, 'for he was a fell cruel man and over cruel, which many a man and fatherless bairn might rue. And wellaway that ever such slaughter and bloodshedding should be amongst Christian men.' With these words, the vicar reported, 'the tears trickled down on his cheeks.' In a lifetime of inconstancy and self-seeking, Arran was perhaps seldom so sympathetic a man as in that moment of weakness.

The Earl of Angus was made of sterner stuff, however. Arran walked away from the Warden's body 'and by and by met with the Earl of Angus, who asked him if he were merry. The Governor answered him by these words, "My Lord, I am much the merrier for you", and took the said Earl of Angus about the neck and kissed him twenty times, saying "Woe worth him that caused him to have any suspicion or mistrust in the said Earl for England's cause, for he had that day showed a true party and done a great good day's work to Scotland".'[3]

Because his forces were small and his artillery insufficient, Arran decided against following up his victory by invading England. Instead, he rode to Jedburgh, ate for supper the provisions laid in for the English captains, and made merry all night. Next day he rode to Stirling to Mary of Guise, who had retired there again for safety. Mary was delighted with the news of his victory, 'beseeching her God of His grace to increase him [Arran] in maintaining of the defence of Scotland and the common weal thereof'.[4] Pleased with Angus's part in their success, she wrote personally to congratulate him and to urge him to persevere in his 'good and true service towards the Queen's Grace and her realm'.[5] In April she had little difficulty in persuading the lords who assembled at a convention in Edinburgh to reject the English requests that negotiations be reopened on the basis of the Treaties of Greenwich. In a mood of self-congratulation and euphoria, the dissident nobles seemed to be united at last.

Mary was herself too much of a realist to be deceived into thinking that this state of affairs would long continue. She knew perfectly well that she would have to persevere in her role as what one of her advisers termed 'principal mediatrix to labour concord betwixt all lords and great men'[6] and she knew that Henry VIII would be doubly enraged by this Scottish refusal, following as it did on the heels of a Scottish victory. Reports were already filtering through of musters in the north of England and of German, Italian and Spanish mercenaries coming to aid the English cause. It was therefore with mounting impatience that Mary awaited the long-expected French aid promised as a result of a mission by Scottish ambassadors to France.[7]

In May, encouraging news came from Brest. Jacques de Montgomery, Seigneur de Lorges, had been chosen to lead the expedition which would come to her aid. As his name suggests, he was of Scottish descent and he was a captain in the French King's Scots Guard. He himself cheered Mary by sending her a gift of wines in advance of his coming, along with a letter describing how he was all ready with a fine, well-equipped French fleet.[8] He duly set sail, arriving at Dumbarton at the beginning of June. As soon as Mary knew that he was on his way, she summoned Arran and Cardinal Beaton to come to her at Stirling. On his arrival, De Lorges hastened to join them. At the ensuing meetings of the Privy Council, which were attended by Mary, Arran and Beaton, it was agreed that a combined French and Scottish force should invade England.[9]

The immediate outcome of this decision was disappointing. Men were unwilling to come to the army in the middle of the harvest and although Arran did lead a raid into the north of England he returned again at once after setting fire to a few settlements.[10] Despite the happy success of Ancrum Moor and despite the arrival of French help, the Scots had lost the initiative and the coming of autumn brought the dreaded English invasion. The Earl of Hertford led his forces into Scotland once more to continue his 'Rough Wooing' of the little Queen. Entering the fertile valley of the River Tweed, he and his men attacked and burned Kelso Abbey. They burned Melrose Abbey and the town of Melrose. They burned Dryburgh Abbey and set fire to more than a dozen townships in the surrounding area. Arriving at Jedburgh, they burned the abbey there. Hertford reported with pride to Henry VIII that the countryside was fair and fertile, and that so successfully had they burned and razed all the houses and all the crops that not so much damage had been done there for a hundred years.[11]

The usual quarrels and recriminations followed this unhappy sequence of events. When the English had withdrawn once more, the Scots consoled themselves by forfeiting the Earl of Lennox. No doubt Mary of Guise approved of this action, but it became a source of contention between De Lorges and Cardinal Beaton. Both were at Stirling with Mary when a quarrel erupted between them in her presence. De Lorges had known Lennox in France and had liked him. When the conversation turned to his forfeiture, De Lorges felt impelled to defend him. He even went so far as to accuse the Cardinal of luring Lennox to Scotland with false promises of marriage to Mary of Guise. Beaton was always hot-tempered, and he flew into a rage when he heard the accusation. The truth was unpalatable. He lifted his hand as if to strike De Lorges but the Frenchman was quicker and caught him a blow across the cheek. At that point Mary of Guise called upon several bystanders to intervene. Apart from the personal embarrassment of her own involvement in the Lennox affair, she was affronted that any altercation of this kind should take place in her presence. The two men were separated, De Lorges declaring violently that Beaton was a false priest. Highly displeased with the whole episode, Mary ordered Cardinal Beaton to retire to his castle at St Andrews.[12]

Not only was there trouble with Beaton: that summer Mary heard rumours that Arran was once more plotting to marry his son to her daughter, and was trying to win the other lords over to his point of view.[13] Arran's ambitions for his oldest boy had caused Mary a good deal of worry and trouble before, but now she was in a much stronger position. The arrival of the French contingent had strengthened her hand, she was regularly attending the meetings of the Privy Council, and her influence was considerable. By the end of November, Arran was anxiously telling Lord Fleming that he would come to see Mary at Stirling and would do nothing contrary to her advice, 'both anent the affairs of this realm and all other things'. He protested that his enemies had been struggling to sow dissension between Mary and himself, and he even offered to spend Christmas with her if she so desired. Mary's distaste for the Governor had scarcely been mitigated by his recent behaviour, and even Lord Fleming felt it necessary to urge her to be friendly with Arran when the latter did appear.[14]

Not surprisingly, Mary did not press him to spend the festive season with her, so instead Arran went off to St Andrews to stay with Cardinal Beaton. For many months past, Beaton had been holding Arran's eldest son there as a hostage for the Governor's good behaviour, so no doubt Arran was going as much for the boy's sake as for his cousin's company.[15]

The Cardinal was still out of favour, and not only with Mary of Guise. Henry VIII had for years been plotting to have him assassinated or kidnapped, and he had made many enemies in Scotland as well as in England. Many of the noblemen were jealous of his power. There were increasing numbers of Protestants who deplored the very existence of this worldly prelate with his wealth, his numerous offspring and his enthusiasm for burning heretics. Early in March 1546 he sent George Wishart the preacher to the stake, and it was said that he sat in his castle and watched Wishart burn. In the end, however, it was a personal, local feud which ended his career.

Some years previously, he had become involved in a quarrel over land with Norman, son of the Earl of Rothes. He and Norman Leslie knew each other well, for Leslie had been a member of James V's household. On the night of 28 May 1546, Leslie came secretly to St Andrews with his uncle and some other Fife gentlemen. They spent that night in lodgings in the town, and early the following morning they gathered in the Cathedral churchyard, not far from the castle. They then slipped through the quiet streets to the castle gate where, in spite of the earliness of the hour, the drawbridge was down. Beaton had ordered that his castle should be made impregnable by additional fortifications, and as soon as daylight came cartloads of lime and stone were being dragged in for the masons at work on the fortifications. Creeping in unnoticed, the conspirators overpowered a porter who tried to stop them and seized his keys. The man managed to shout out a warning before he was knocked unconscious, whereupon the workmen panicked and came running down from the walls. There were over a hundred of them, and chaos ensued as they jostled to the gate.

Forcing their way into the main building, Leslie and his companions arrived at the room where they knew that the Cardinal slept. Beaton had already been roused by the commotion and, seizing his two-handed sword to defend himself, he ordered his chamber child to barricade the door with chests and furniture.

His efforts were of no avail. Leslie and his friends tried to force the door. It was heavy, and it would not budge. They were not to be dissuaded, however. One of them ran and brought a pailful of coals. 'Fire! Fire!' they shouted, as they prepared to burn down the door or smoke the Cardinal out. Before they could do so, either the Cardinal or his page flung the door open in terror. When he saw the faces of the men outside, Cardinal Beaton knew that the end had come. Sinking down on a chair, he cried desperately, 'I am a priest! I am a priest! You will not slay me!' They did not listen. John Leslie and Peter Carmichael of Balmedie struck him, then James Melville, calling upon him to repent for the death of George Wishart, plunged his sword into the Cardinal's body twice or three times. Beaton fell dying, still protesting weakly, 'I am a priest, I am a priest', then, 'Fie, fie, all is gone'.

By this time, word of the tumult had spread throughout the town. The provost and the townspeople came running up to the castle walls, demanding to see the Cardinal. They saw him. His body was brought out and laid on the east blockhouse head, then his murderers took him down, salted his corpse, placed it in a coffin of lead and threw it into the castle well. After that, they barricaded themselves in the castle. A Protestant preacher named John Knox joined them there.[16]

According to Knox, who describes the Cardinal's death in minute detail, 'the death of this foresaid tyrant was dolorous to the priests, dolorous to the Governor, most dolorous to the Queen Dowager, for in him perished faithfulness to France and the comfort to all gentlewomen, and especially to wanton widows'.[17] This, of course, was one of Knox's more unpleasant innuendoes. There never had been anything improper in Mary's relationship with Beaton and indeed they had scarcely been on the best of terms for many months past. Both might support the French alliance but each wanted power and saw the other as an obstacle to their ambitions. Even so, Mary was shocked by the manner of his death. Not only had the Cardinal been primate of Scotland, he had also been Lord Chancellor. That certain Scots had murdered a churchman and one who held high temporal office was indeed a sorry state of affairs.

Eight days after the Cardinal's death, Mary attended a meeting of the Privy Council in Stirling. It was decided that the Earl of Huntly should succeed Beaton as Chancellor. Four days after that, a further session of the Council agreed that the Earl of Arran should be sent to St Andrews to besiege the murderers.[18] His previous military activities had hardly encouraged confidence in his abilities, but the fact that his son was now held prisoner by Beaton's murderers would surely spur him on to decisive action.

Mary of Guise,
by Corneille de Lyon

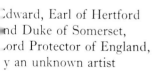

Edward, Earl of Hertford
and Duke of Somerset,
Lord Protector of England,
by an unknown artist

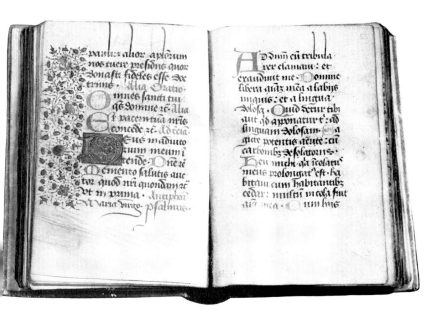

Book of Hours of Mary of Guise; the Book is late fifteenth century and the
fact that the name of St Clare is found in the Litany suggests the possibility
that Mary had received it from her grandmother, Philippa of Gueldres, a
Poor Clare. Mary's own signature is on one of the first pages

Door from Mary of Guise's
house in Leith: the carving
appears to be the work of
French craftsmen

Actually, it merely made the situation more awkward for him. The thought of his own heir behind the castle walls was enough to make him half-hearted in his orders to his men to bombard the fortress. Unable to take the castle himself, he was determined that he would not seek French aid, for he still cherished secret hopes of marrying his son to the little Queen, and the French were liable to make certain that such a marriage would never take place. He did not wish his son to fall into their hands. The result was that the siege dragged on in-effectually throughout the summer, the autumn, the winter and the following spring.[19]

The situation at St Andrews might remain tiresomely static but in other respects there were dramatic changes taking place in the political scene. A matter of weeks after the Cardinal's death, England and France signed a treaty of peace. For the next few months the Scots were much occupied in trying to have a clause inserted in the treaty to the effect that they would be included in the peace. Then in January 1547 Henry VIII died, leaving his young son Prince Edward to succeed to his throne.

If Mary of Guise cherished any hopes that Henry's policies would die with him, she was doomed to disappointment. The man who became Lord Protector of England was none other than the general who had twice led an army of invasion into Scotland, the Earl of Hertford. It was not to be expected that he would suffer a change of heart with regard to the Scots, and the Scottish ambassadors who were admitted to his presence a few days after his appointment found 'as we found at all times' that the English still demanded a marriage treaty. Negotiations continued, but by April Adam Otterburn, one of the Scots, was writing sadly to Mary to tell her, 'I see nothing but as [if] the old king were living and each day I hear of our infelicity'.[20]

To add to the difficulties, the official ambassadors were not the only Scots at the English Court. Three of the men holding St Andrews Castle had managed to escape under cover of artillery from English ships and they had now arrived in London where they were 'well heard'. Then, just four months after the death of Henry VIII, his old rival Francis I of France died. The news of his passing dismayed Mary, but his successor, Henry II, soon sent assurances that he was well disposed towards her and her daughter. In July, he proved that he did mean to help. Twenty-one French galleys under the command of the famous Leon Strozzi arrived in the Firth of Forth and in a short time achieved what Arran had failed to do. They took St Andrews Castle and carried away the men who had held it to imprisonment in France or to enforced labour in their galleys. Arran's son they set free.[21]

This success was cheering, as was the capture of Langholm, on the Borders, but news from the south indicated that yet another invasion was imminent. At the end of August Mary hurried to Edinburgh with Arran to see to the preparations for defence. There they ordered the mustering of men and had the fortifications of Edinburgh strengthened.[22]

On 1 September, word reached Edinburgh that the English were invading by the eastern route. Mary of Guise hastily retreated to the greater safety of Stirling Castle, while Arran prepared to take command of the army. The Earl of Hertford, now with the title of Duke of Somerset, camped near Tranent, to the east of Edinburgh. Arran and his army marched from Edinburgh to Inveresk, near Musselburgh. Perhaps with some presentiment of disaster, perhaps out of natural timidity, Arran made his Will on the battlefield of Pinkie Cleugh, near Inveresk, confiding his family to the care of the King of France.

For three days, the opposing armies faced each other. Some skirmishing took place, then on 10 September 1547, the day to be known in the Scottish chronicles as 'Black Saturday', the English advanced and the battle was joined. At first, the Scots marched forward in good order. The army was now in three main divisions commanded by Arran, Angus and Huntly. Very soon, though, things began to go wrong. Arran ordered Angus to cross the River Esk towards the English. He refused. Arran sent out a herald ordering him to advance on pain of treason, and he moved forward across the river. The English horse then charged but Angus's men were armed with long sharp spears and they resisted effectively. At that moment, however, the English began firing their artillery from a nearby hill and from their ships which were moored just offshore. At the noise, Argyll's Highlanders took fright. They were totally unused to the sound of cannon firing and in a panic they began to throw down their arms. Choking dust was rising in clouds from the stubble fields where the battle raged. This had the effect of obscuring the Highlanders' view of the action and added to their terror.

The English charged forward once more against Angus who, seeing them come at him in great numbers, decided to retreat to seek help from the Earl of Huntly's contingent. As he and his men loomed up out of the dust clouds, Huntly took them for Englishmen. His troops accordingly began to attack their own fellow-countrymen. The English, coming swiftly up behind, killed many more. Lord Fleming, Mary of Guise's faithful friend, fell dying. The eldest sons of Lord Erskine, Lord Livingston, Lord Ogilvie, Lord Methven, Lord Ruthven and many more leading Scotsmen died that day and when Somerset at last sounded his trumpets and the fighting ceased, he numbered among his prisoners the Earl of Huntly, Scotland's Chancellor since the death of Beaton. The Earl of Arran escaped unscathed and rode hard for Stirling.[23]

Mary of Guise, waiting anxiously for news of the battle, was no doubt forewarned of his arrival and of the news he brought. Her distress at the outcome was mingled with a feeling of helpless rage. Many of her own loyal supporters lay dead on the battlefield yet here before her stood the weak and ineffective Lord Governor whose only talent was for self-preservation. It was typical that Arran should have survived the holocaust of Pinkie to bring her the news that her armies had been routed, her Chancellor captured, her friends killed and her daughter placed in greater danger than ever.

Foremost in her mind was the need to find a place of safety for the little Queen. Stirling was strong indeed, but who knew but that the English might not come and besiege it? They had been within six miles of the castle on a previous occasion and they were determined to seize her daughter. Mary decided that she herself would stay on there, but that the child must be moved to a place of increased security. Lord Erskine, one of the little Queen's guardians, had himself been exempted from fighting because of the importance of his task. He had lost his heir and several other members of his family in the battle but, putting personal grief aside, he turned his mind to the urgent problem and suggested that the child be taken to the secluded island of Inchmahone, in the Lake of Menteith, within easy riding distance of Stirling Castle. Members of his own family had been commendators of the priory there for a generation, and they regarded it for all practical purposes as being their own property. Relieved at this sensible solution, Mary accordingly had the little Queen taken to the island.[24]

Her mind somewhat eased of that particular anxiety, she directed her energies towards urging Arran to raise a new army. The English were in Leith again, burning and destroying wherever they went, and alarming news was coming in from the west. The Earl of Lennox had marched north at the head of another English force and was besieging Annan in the south-west of Scotland. Worse was yet to follow, for a small English fleet was sighted at the mouth of the River Tay and it was not long before Broughty Castle on the estuary there was in their hands.[25]

Less than a fortnight after Pinkie, however, the main English armies withdrew from Scotland, leaving a garrison in Broughty Castle. Mary and the Lord Governor could now take stock of their losses. Until Pinkie, Mary had firmly believed that the Scots, given French aid, could inflict a final defeat on the English and that the country could then settle down in peace under what would probably be at first a united rule by herself and Arran, with Mary as the dominant partner and finally as the sole Regent. She would continue to strengthen the French alliance and she would then transform Scotland into a strong, independent, well-organized country, the firm ally of France. They would have a league of mutual protection, and the Scots would be able to invade England should the English armies threaten France.

With Pinkie, she was finally convinced of Arran's complete unsuitability to play any part in her plans. The country was plunged into a greater state of emergency than ever before, and he had shown yet again that he was totally incapable as a military leader. His failure to take St Andrews and his abysmal showing at Pinkie were now to be followed by his failure to win back Broughty Castle. The English were planning further offensives and were still demanding that the little Queen be handed over. The Scottish Borderers in alarm were asking Mary's permission to become 'assured' to the English in order to save themselves until such time as further French help arrived. Sir George Douglas was in England, offering to lead a new invasion of Scotland. No one had any faith in Scotland's survival as an independent nation.

Mary turned anxiously to the French ambassador in Scotland, Monsieur D'Oysel, pleading with him for further aid. The French King, as it happened, had plans of his own for Scotland. His wife Catherine had, to the amazement of all, presented him with a son in January 1544. This son would one day be King of France, and what more suitable bride for him than the little Queen of Scots? Scotland would then be bound forever to France, and England would find herself trapped irrevocably between the French King's realm and his satellite state. He therefore instructed his ambassador to present the marriage in the best possible light to Mary of Guise, promising substantial assistance in return for the little Queen's hand.

Writing in disgruntled tones to the Duke of Somerset, the pro-English Earl of Glencairn declared that the planned negotiations between England and Scotland for peace and marriage had been set at nought when a French gentleman with fair words 'altered the Queen and Governor's purpose'. This no doubt refers to D'Oysel and his proposal, as did the Duchess of Guise's letter to her daughter some four days later, expressing cautious optimism that the French King's new plans would, if they could be effected, seem to be likely to hinder the enterprises of Mary's enemies.[26]

In spite of Mary of Guise's natural reluctance to part with her daughter to anyone, she saw the wisdom of the proposal. Scotland would be firmly tied to the French alliance and, with her daughter safe in friendly hands, Mary could turn her own attention to setting the country in order and carrying out the plans she had long since evolved. Her own position would be considerably strengthened and she would gradually oust Arran and assume the government of the realm. The Lord Governor would go, in any case, whenever Mary, Queen of Scots came of age. The little Queen would one day be Queen of France, and her mother would continue to rule Scotland for her. Of course, the Scots would be no more willing to give their monarch to the King of France than they had been to give her to the King of England, but they were in such a desperate position that they could hardly refuse. They would gradually become accustomed to the idea, they would see the benefits of the augmented alliance, and if they were doubtful, French bribes would ease the way.

Heartened by these new possibilities, Mary hastened to Edinburgh to attend a meeting of the Privy Council which would decide how more money could be raised to finance further resistance against the English. On the first day of the meeting it was proposed that all the Church jewels and treasures be taken for this cause, then on the second day Mary of Guise herself spoke in Council. She announced that, with Arran's advice, she had written urgently to France for more help, but she declared that, should that help not come speedily, they would all do their best to resist the enemy. Shortly afterwards D'Oysel sailed for France to seek the necessary aid.[27]

He set sail in late November. As early as 20 December the English were reporting rumours to the effect that a great force of French galleys would come to Scotland, seize the principal fortresses and take the little Queen to France but in fact it was the English who arrived in Scotland first the following spring.[28] On 21 February Mary was brought the news that Lord Grey of Wilton had entered Scotland at the head of an invading army, by the eastern route, and was marching north. 'I beseech Your Grace to cause my Lord Governor and the nobles to draw together,' the laird of Buccleuch urged her when he wrote to warn her of the approaching armies.[29]

As soon as she received the news, Mary of Guise persuaded Arran to allow her to take her daughter away from Stirling once more, this time to Dumbarton Castle. Dumbarton, on the west coast, was obviously much safer: if the English came near the little Queen could be taken away by sea to France. The move was duly made, and Mary was satisfied. As soon as she managed to persuade the Scots to marry her daughter to the Dauphin, she would arrange for the child to go to the French Court. It was reported that 'The Queen is marvellous glad that she [her daughter] is in yon house [Dumbarton] and out of Scotsmen's hands'.[30]

No sooner had Arran agreed to the move than he began to regret it bitterly. He still entertained hopes of marrying the little Queen to his eldest son, and for her own reasons Mary of Guise had continued to encourage him in these hopes. Knowing full well how easily he would be discouraged from any further military endeavour, she saw that the only way to have him lead Scotland's army against the invaders was to push him along with reminders which would appeal to his own self-interest. If the English were allowed to advance they would surely capture the little Queen and then where would the Governor's plans be? In his own interests he must defeat the English once and for all, otherwise his son would never have the precious bride. Arran perforce bestirred himself, and after lingering at Mary's court for some days, he set off to besiege several English-held houses in East Lothian.

The invading army did not this time spend long in Scotland but as well as causing the usual damage and destruction, they left behind them a dangerous legacy. Not only did their soldiers hold the castle at Broughty Ferry still, but they had captured the town of Haddington, in East Lothian. Haddington was a wealthy burgh strategically placed in a fertile plain. Within easy reach of the Border country and the route south, it was also within striking distance of Edinburgh and it presented a constant source of danger to the Scottish capital.

Throughout the spring, Mary of Guise waited impatiently for news from France. She had done everything she could, but as each day passed the situation grew more desperate and still there was no news. Certainly the French sent constant promises.[31] Henry II himself wrote to reassure her of his good intentions and even her little son, the Duke of Longueville, sent her a careful letter wishing that he were old enough to accompany the army which would come to her rescue.[32] Yet still nothing happened. Mary knew well that the longer she had to wait the more supporters she would lose. Arran himself was displaying a dangerous tendency to send secret messages to the English hinting that he might change sides once more since the promised French help was not forthcoming.

Obviously urgent action was needed to see that he did not carry out this threat. Part of the trouble was that, in return for the promised aid, he had agreed to send his eldest son as a hostage to the French King. Needless to say, he now repented bitterly of his agreement to this and so in an attempt to rally him, Mary persuaded Henry II to offer him a wealthy French bride for his son. On 28 April an official agreement was signed whereby Henry promised that young Hamilton should have the hand of the wealthy Duke of Montpensier's daughter. Arran had already been promised a French duchy for himself if he agreed to the marriage of Mary, Queen of Scots, to the heir to the French throne.

By this time, Mary had received even more ominous news. Lord Grey of Wilton was returning to Haddington with reinforcements. He arrived at Berwick on 23 April and a few days later joined his companions in Haddington itself.[33] Obviously, the English were now planning to use the burgh as a centre of their campaigns in Scotland, and on 3 June, in spite of the presence of Arran at near-by Musselburgh with a small French force, Grey was able to ride out of Haddington, attack Dalkeith Castle and capture it.[34] Four days later the English set fire to Musselburgh itself and to various fisher villages along the sea coast, driving away livestock, destroying the young corn and cutting down trees. Arran and his men then began to besiege Haddington.[35]

It was small wonder that Mary of Guise was reported as being 'ill content' at the French delay.[36] She was waiting in

Edinburgh, anxious for news and almost despairing of the arrival of the promised help. But on 12 June, messengers at last arrived with good news. A French fleet had been sighted off Dunbar, apparently making for Leith. According to some reports there were a hundred and twenty vessels in all, including sixteen galleys, a brigantine and three great ships.[37] On Saturday, 16 June, the French landed at Leith and the commander of the expedition, the Sieur D'Essé, hurried to Edinburgh to consult with Mary of Guise.

Accounts of the numbers of the French army that summer differ. One estimate put the total force at as low as 5000 men, but according to a contemporary English estimate there were 10,000 in the army. Not all of these were Frenchmen: a sizeable proportion were German, Swiss and Dutch mercenaries.[38] Apart from D'Essé himself, the commanders included the celebrated soldier Peter Strozzi, brother of Leon, the 'Count Rhinegrave' who led the Germans, and Monsieur D'Andelot, second in command of the French. Also accompanying Monsieur D'Essé was his friend John de Beaugué who recorded his experiences during the campaign and has left us a valuable record of the general state of Scotland at the time.

Viewing the Scots and their country with a detached but not unkindly eye, Beaugué decided that they were in a sorry state. The English, he noted, had seized their strongholds, had come up to the very gates of Edinburgh upon occasion and generally held the countryside in subjection. This was not, he believed, because the Scots were less warlike than the English but because they were so rent by internal feuds and dissensions that God was annoyed with them, and wished to show them their faults before helping them.[39]

The French, of course, were to be the instruments of God's help, and when Mary interviewed the leaders in Edinburgh she lost no time in urging them to march out and take Haddington. She was now entering a new phase in her career. At thirty-three, she was a mature and energetic woman. From now onwards she would play an active part in military affairs. She could not ride at the head of her country's army but she would no longer remain in the safety of Stirling Castle, far from the actual action. Henceforth she would be found in Edinburgh or even in the military camps of the French and the Scots, urging them on with energy and singleness of purpose. If Arran lacked the necessary initiative to fight the English, Mary most certainly did not. The English ambassador in France had made an interesting observation when he had heard that Peter Strozzi was going with the army to Scotland. Strozzi was expected to do great things there, the ambassador noted, out of regard for the Queen 'in whose exceeding hatred of the English he fully participates'.[40] Many years before Mary might have toyed with the notion of marrying a King of England, but in the 1540s she had seen so much senseless destruction and violence and had endured so many threats to her little daughter that she was now implacable in her opposition to that nation.

Instructed to obey her commands as if they were those of the French King himself, Sieur D'Essé therefore marched out of Edinburgh with his men and to his delight, saw the English withdraw hastily into Haddington. So pleased was he, in fact, that he rode back to Edinburgh to tell Mary of the English retreat and to boast that the English feared the French before they even saw them.[41] Many of his men then lingered in Edinburgh, along with a number of Scots who were gradually drifting away from the army.

This was not what Mary had expected. It was not good enough. The town of Haddington must be taken from the English. The whole enterprise was now placed in jeopardy and those already besieging the town would be in greater danger if they were not reinforced by D'Essé's men. Mary decided that she must take personal action. Summoning the gentlemen of her household and her other menservants, she addressed them, ordering all who could bear arms to go to the Scottish camp outside the walls of Haddington and help with the siege. They were to take with them gifts for the soldiers already fighting there for her cause. Putting the ablest of her gentlemen in charge of the little convoy, she loaded up her servants with bread and wine, barley and meat, and sent with

these supplies a tactfully worded message. Her soldiers were
not to think that these few gifts were payment for what she
hoped they would do. Rather they were a sign that she would
reward the merits of each and every one of them when the
time came, for, she declared, it was not unfitting to urge on
men of courage with promises of recompense: a Prince was the
more dearly loved by his soldiers when he showed appreciation
of their efforts.

Having arranged this part of her plan, Mary mounted her
horse and rode out into the High Street of Edinburgh with
only her ladies for company. Long ago in France, during the
days of her first marriage, she and her ladies had toured the
houses near her residences on errands of mercy, visiting the
sick and helping the poor. On that summer day in Edinburgh
her mission was very different. She rode down the High
Street and she stopped at every house, going inside to seek
out any soldiers who might be relaxing inside. She encountered
several Scots who should have been with the army and she
addressed them in their own language.

'Is it thus, my friends,' she asked them, 'that you support
the French? Is it thus that you set them a good example?
Before God, if I had not seen you with my own eyes and if
anyone had told me that you were like to forget your honour
in this way I would not have believed them. I should have
thought such a thing incredible, having praised you so much
all my life for what I believed and still do believe to be true,
that no nation on earth would equal your courage. I think it
must be that you have come to this town to equip yourselves
with arms and horses rather than in order to escape from
combat with our enemies. All the same, because I believe you
would not wish to fall into some unforgivable fault, I am
warning you that we shall have a battle at Haddington within
two days. I am sure you would not want to live to regret that
you had not been in the right place to wreak vengeance on
those who have injured you in so many ways, to avenge the
deaths of your relatives and friends and to take redress for the
damage to your goods and property.'[42]

Beaugué recorded her words. While there is no need to

suppose that he took them down *verbatim*, there is equally no need to dismiss them as his own invention. What he makes Mary say on that occasion is so much in keeping with her usual methods of dealing with people that it rings absolutely true. As Beaugué himself admiringly remarked, Mary was trying to win the Scots over rather than attempting to force them into doing their duty. Like her father before her, she was an excellent judge of men and she knew better than to try to browbeat her proud, obstinate subjects. Looking at the handsome, dignified Queen and listening to her soft, reasonable words the recalcitrant soldiers felt the full force of her legendary charm and, ashamed of themselves, they set off for Haddington once more. So much for the Scots. With those French soldiers whom she found lurking in Edinburgh, Mary employed a rather different technique. She found far more of them than she had expected and she began to fear that their absence from the siege would have grave consequences. She therefore expressed her astonishment at finding them there, apparently oblivious of the danger to their reputation.

'The English are coming with four or five thousand horsemen in the hope of raising the siege of Haddington,' she told them 'but things have been put in such order that, with the help of God, we should manage to foil their endeavours.' She therefore had only scorn for those who stayed away. 'Even if you do not take their part,' she told her hearers, 'there are enough brave men in the camp to vanquish our enemies. But, in this way, the prowess of the soldiers already there will be plain to see whereas the infamy of the deserters will be published abroad by the whole world. However, regardless of what I say, do as you please . . .' Needless to say, they did as she pleased instead. 'Such prudence is not surprising in a Princess born with all the virtues, who needed no other means to command,' Beaugué observed smugly as he concluded his description of the incident.[43]

Her action had been timely indeed, for, just as she had predicted, a force of some five thousand English horsemen appeared on the hillside above Haddington less than forty-eight hours later. The French, eager to fight, fell upon them and some sharp skirmishing resulted. The English were driven back into the town, leaving several hundred men dead on the field and many others in French hands. Mary was altogether delighted by this minor triumph, and she arrived at the French camp next morning just after dawn. There she went round all the soldiers, speaking to them in a friendly, familiar way, clasping them by the hand and congratulating them. She then made a short speech, praising their valour. 'Since the state of this realm and my service depends only on you,' she told them, 'it is only right that your praise should come from me myself. I have given orders that you will receive certain gifts from me. Take them I pray you, in token not of what I do now but of what I should like to do, hoping that some day I shall have the means of showing you that the greater the dangers, the inconveniences and the hazards of war, the greater will be the wages of victory.'[44]

Thus encouraged, the French spent the first week of July bombarding the town. There were fairly heavy casualties on both sides. The dead among the French were taken to Edinburgh in carts for burial, and Mary was particularly upset by the death of one young French nobleman. His body was brought to Edinburgh in a closed cart at eight in the morning on 1 July, then taken for the funeral service to the Greyfriars'. One observer reported that the dead man was splendidly arrayed and 'had about his neck a great chain manifold and about either arm one: his hose and doublet of crimson satin embroidered with gold very richly. After Mass was done he was interred with no small ceremony, the Queen weeping many tears'.[45]

Mary of Guise was to shed many more tears before the month was out, but for the moment there were important affairs of state to distract her mind from grief. On 5 July she left Edinburgh and rode to Herdmanston, a small village two miles from Haddington. The French were being awkward. They had let it be known that they would not actually take Haddington until a new treaty between France and Scotland had been signed, and the time for that treaty was now ripe. On 6 July Mary arrived in the French camp outside Haddington and on 7 July at the nunnery near by the Scots signed a new marriage treaty for their little Queen. No longer to be the bride of the English King, she would marry the Dauphin instead, the French King 'observing and keeping this realm and lieges thereof in the same freedom, liberties and laws as had been in all Kings of Scotland times bypast, and shall maintain and defend this realm and lieges of the same as he does the realm of France and lieges thereof'.[46] Mary was well content. The old alliance with France had been renewed and greatly strengthened. The French would no longer be half-hearted in their efforts and with French aid it would be possible to drive out the English once and for all. Her daughter's future was safe at last, and she herself could remain in Scotland, governing the country as she had always meant to do.

In order to encourage the soldiers and so hasten on the siege, Mary decided to spend a few days at Haddington touring the French and Scottish camps. Two days after the signing of the treaty, on the Monday evening, she decided to venture as far as St Mary's Church, which lay at the edge of the town. She could climb its tower and from the top survey the whole scene.

The guns from both sides were still firing, but Mary, daughter of a famous soldier, was not afraid to venture so near the area of danger. Accompanied by her usual entourage of ladies and gentlemen she rode up to the back of the church. At that very moment a thunderous explosion filled the air as a cannon from inside the town fired with deadly accuracy. Amid screams, smoke and cries of agony sixteen of her gentlemen as well as other members of her household fell wounded and dying around her. Mary herself fainted from horror and grief.[47]

She was carried to a place of safety, where she recovered, but the loss of so many of her personal friends and servants was a dreadful blow, and she was to mourn them for many months to come. The tragedy served to emphasize the dangers of war, and as soon as she had heard Masses for the dead she left for Dumbarton to make the final arrangements for her daughter's departure. Arran and the other lords went with her to take their leave of the little Queen. Although Mary of Guise had been planning her daughter's removal to the safety of France for many months past, the moment of parting was no less poignant. The child was almost six years old now, a delightful, attractive little girl who in other circumstances would have remained her close companion, a daughter all the more dear because she had been denied the company of her other children. Yet the sacrifice must be made, not only for the child's future but for the future benefit of both Scotland and France.

The French galleys had sailed round the north coast of Scotland and were now lying off Dumbarton. Accompanied by the famous four Maries, the small girls who were to be her companions, by two of her half-brothers and by a retinue of ladies and servants, the little Queen was put on board the royal galley on 29 July. When she had finally parted from her daughter, Mary was tormented by anxiety and grief. 'The old Queen doth lament the young Queen's departure', one English spy reported.[48] It was all very well to decide sensibly that it was best to send the little girl to safety, to concentrate on the fact that the daughter would have a happy upbringing in her own native country with the Guise family, to think of the glorious future in store for her as Queen of France. None of this could compensate for the thought of the loneliness ahead, of the long years with no one of her own beside her and only the occasional letter from her daughter to cheer her.

Because of contrary winds, the galleys lay off Dumbarton for over a week before setting sail. Mary could not bear to remain so close to the little fleet so, in a determined attempt to divert her thoughts, she returned to the east of Scotland. On 7 August, the day that the little Queen finally set sail, Mary of Guise was attending a Council meeting with Arran and the leaders of the French, then she rode along to Leith to find out how the French vessels which had remained in the Forth had fared. She discovered that an English fleet had actually been sighted in the Forth that very week and, fearing a landing, the French had now begun to fortify Leith.[49]

Peter Strozzi offered reassurance but Mary seemed despondent and depressed. Try as she might to think of other things, her mind was taken up with fears for her daughter.

The voyage to France was fraught with danger. At best the little Queen might be lonely, frightened and sea-sick. At worst, the galleys might be intercepted by the English. What might happen then did not bear thinking about. Mary spent a fortnight of wretched anxiety before the longed-for news arrived from France. The little Queen had landed safe and well near Brest. She was now with her grandmother, and they were on their way to the French Court.

8

Return to France

❧

Her daughter safe at last, Mary could concentrate on the business in hand. She was to discover before long that the benefits of the treaty with France were accompanied by at least one disadvantage which she had not fully appreciated. The continuing presence of the French soldiers in Scotland was having a deleterious effect. The perennial feuds and dissensions among the Scots themselves caused Mary trouble enough, but now to her difficulties were added the quarrels between Scots and French. There was trouble over the French lack of enthusiasm for the siege of Haddington, and Arran in particular was finding it hard to agree with his foreign colleagues. As one of Somerset's correspondents put it, the French 'use themselves so ungently towards their partners the Scots that in a manner the Governor repents of all together',[1] while another Englishman summed up the situation even more succinctly: Arran, he said, was 'like one that holds a wolf by the ears, in doubt to hold and in danger to let go'.[2]

Nor was it only the Lord Governor who was displeased. After an abortive attempt to drive England's Spanish mercenaries out of Jedburgh, D'Essé and his men retired to Edinburgh and it was not long before some of his soldiers became involved in a disturbance which was to have serious consequences. One or two of his men had words with some of the townspeople. First of all insults, then blows were exchanged. The Scots tried to arrest the Frenchman who had started all the trouble, but his comrades came to his aid. The Captain of Edinburgh Castle was summoned to put an end to the dispute, and in the ensuing mêlée both French and Scots were killed, the latter numbering among their dead no less a man than the provost of Edinburgh. The original trouble-maker was eventually taken and was hanged later that day, but the ill-feeling against the French was such that Mary had to advise D'Essé to march with his men to Musselburgh and stay there.[3]

The year seemed to be ending gloomily for Mary. Hadding-ton was still besieged, the French were restless, the Scots were resentful and now Arran, who had been persuaded to pay a visit to France, was refusing to go because in his absence Mary would be in charge of the government of the country. Christmas did bring one cheering event, though. Ever since the battle of Pinkie, Scotland's Chancellor the Earl of Huntly had been held prisoner in England. On the pretext of requiring to attend to his Scottish affairs, he persuaded his captors to move him to Morpeth, less than thirty miles from the Scottish Border. This was all part of his plan for a daring escape.

During the Christmas celebrations, he judged that his guards might not have their minds entirely on their duty. He therefore asked one of his friends to bring two good horses secretly to the house where he was held. It was Christmas Eve, and after supper he summoned his keepers and suggested that they might pass the time by playing cards together. Bored as they were with the monotony of their existence, the men agreed and they all sat down at a table. Time passed. After several hours the Earl stood up and declared that he must stretch his legs. He strolled casually over to a window, looked out, and saw through the gloom an indistinct figure making signals to him. Everything was ready. Concealing his nervous impatience, he returned to the card table. A few games later, on some pretext or other, he managed to distract the attention of his guards and he and his servant slipped out at the back door. Leaping on their horses, they rode hard and did not stop until they were safely over the Border. After a brief rest in a friend's house, they continued on their way and the Earl was able to stride dramatically into the midst of the Queen's Christmas celebrations.[4]

While Mary temporarily forgot her worries in the pleasure of seeing Huntly again, the Duke of Somerset was busy with his plans for the conquest of Scotland. In December 1548 he summoned the French ambassador to him and lost no time in pointing out to him 'the King's just title to the sovereignty of Scotland', asserting that he could produce a great number of ancient documents which would prove 'that above six hundred years past and even from the beginning the Scottish Kings have done and sworn homage and fealty to the Kings of England'.[5] The little Queen might have slipped through his hands but Somerset had no intention of abandoning his plans for Scotland.

In spite of these sinister manoeuvres, the new year began quietly enough. The French started to fortify the church at Musselburgh and in February Huntly celebrated his return by leading an expedition to the Borders. In that same month Henry II created Arran Duke of Châtelherault, as a reward for agreeing to the French marriage. It was not until June that the real activity began. Early in the month, an English fleet sailed once more into the River Forth and captured Inchkeith, a small island occupying a strategic position opposite Leith. This event coincided with the arrival in the west of French reinforcements, led by Monsieur De Thermes, who was soon to replace D'Essé. De Thermes had brought with him a hundred armed men, two hundred light horse and a thousand foot soldiers. Mary of Guise therefore decided that with their help Inchkeith could be taken back without delay.

This decision was entirely her own. The French were unenthusiastic, but she could see the dangers of allowing the English to gain a foothold so close to Leith. She therefore sent out Monsieur de la Chapelle de Biron to reconnoitre the island. When he came back with the news that the English were beginning to construct a fort, she summoned the French leaders to an urgent discussion, emphasizing the importance of the expedition she proposed. The French once again demurred. What use could a small, uninhabited outcrop of rock be to them? Mary persisted, but in her usual tactful manner. Far from ordering them to take the island, she merely pointed out that the expedition was so necessary that anyone taking part would be doing her a personal service.

Her charm was as effective as ever. The ordinary soldiers were enthusiastic, their leaders acquiesced, and on the Feast of Corpus Christi they assembled at Leith. Mary went down personally at daybreak, ostensibly to see them off but also to smoothe out any difficulties which might arise over the choice of ships. She took the opportunity of making a stirring speech before they embarked, and once again Monsieur de Beaugué noted down her words.

'My friends!' she began, 'It seems to me that God in His goodness greatly favours your courage by giving you the opportunity of taking part in such an honourable enterprise, and since the greatness of your courage has rendered you invincible just as the unhappiness of the English has made them cowardly, I have no doubt that you will easily enhance your honour at the expense of such feeble adversaries, you, who have been born and brought up in France. For as often as you have attacked the English, you have carried the day by the bravery of your fighting and by your good fortune. Continue in this way, my friends, I pray you. Continue your courageous behaviour and remember that we have a God who has brought you from France to preserve this realm from destruction and from ruin.'[6]

Once again, while no one would pretend that these were Mary's exact words, they no doubt contain the spirit of her message which, Scottish and French chroniclers agree, had a rousing effect on her hearers. As Bishop Lesley was to put it many years after the event, 'as the men of war ascended to enter in the ships, she gave them consolation, partly with her presence, partly with her humanity and gentleness', and with her 'countenance, her gesture, her speech, stirred up their hearts . . .'.[7]

The expedition set off in a mood of optimism, with Mary telling D'Essé just before he embarked that she saw victory already in their hands. 'The outcome of all is in the hands of God,' the commander replied gravely, then he added gallantly, 'but I am very sure that I shall give you the Isle today, or D'Essé will never strike another blow with a sword.' They set sail and he put his words into effect. The French captured the island easily. Noting that it was Corpus Christi Day, Mary declared that henceforth it should be known as 'L'isle Dieu', the Isle of God.[8]

The recapture of Inchkeith improved Scottish morale immensely. True, Broughty Castle and Haddington were still in the hands of the English, but the position of the latter was growing increasingly difficult. The English garrison at Broughty were short of supplies, sick and discontented. 'The air of the country here is cruel and cold,' their leader complained, and too much salt meat had led to the outbreak of illness amongst them.[9] At Haddington, the garrison were in even worse straits, with an outbreak of plague adding to their hardships. In view of these difficulties, they decided eventually to evacuate the town, and so by the end of September Haddington was once more in Scottish hands. Further south, Border raids still continued but the English were now very much taken up with the French attacks on their garrison in Boulogne. Negotiations for peace were opened, and in April 1550 the French and the English signed a treaty in which Scotland was included. This treaty was proclaimed publicly in Edinburgh on 20 April and for the first time since the death of James V the Scots could look forward to a more settled future, undisturbed by invasions from the south.[10]

Mary of Guise welcomed the treaty of peace wholeheartedly. It was exciting and stimulating to address armies, to plan campaigns, but she abhorred the sufferings brought about by war. The country was exhausted. Year after year crops had been destroyed, houses and churches burned down, men killed. Now that peace had come, she could devote her energies to reconstruction, to transforming Scotland into a prosperous, well-governed kingdom. The economic difficulties were daunting, of course, and her own financial situation had become increasingly desperate. She had needed money not only to pay soldiers but to bribe allies. She had the rents from her jointure lands, but Châtelherault, the Lord Governor, still controlled the royal revenues, which he was spending freely. The French King had recently promised him that when he did eventually surrender the governorship he would not have to account for his expenditure, and so he was depleting the crown's resources with greater enthusiasm than ever; pensions for his relatives, clothes for his family; there was no end to it. If Mary was to restore the country's prosperity, she needed money. That money could not be found in Scotland, so she must somehow or other persuade the King of France to augment her finances. Even more important, she must persuade him that the moment had come to remove Châtelherault from the governorship. In time of war it was easy enough for those who opposed this ambition to argue that the country should have a man at its head – even a man as ineffectual as the Duke of Châtelherault. Now that peace had come, there was no reason why he should continue in that office. Once before, Mary had failed to oust him. The situation had changed, however, and if she could convince Henry II that Châtelherault should go, they should between them be able to think of some inducement strong enough to persuade him to relinquish the governorship.

Thinking the matter over carefully, Mary decided that she could best achieve both her objectives by paying a personal visit to France. Private reasons reinforced her decision to make the journey. It was almost two years now since she had seen her little daughter. The Duchess of Guise sent detailed reports of the child's progress, but Mary was anxious for a reunion with her. Moreover, it was twelve years since she had parted from the son of her first marriage. At first Antoinette had given news of him, sending pictures and even a length of cord with his height marked on it so that Mary could see his progress for herself. Then, when he was old enough, young Francis wrote personally to the mother whom he could scarcely have remembered, and Mary kept all his letters carefully. They survive to this day.[11]

Apart from her children, there were so many other relatives she was longing to see. One of the hostages sent to England by the French King after the peace treaty had been Mary's brother Claud, and before long he was given permission to visit his sister in Edinburgh. They had a joyous reunion, and his stories of all the other friends and relations made Mary

eager to see them again. This desire was made all the stronger
when young Claud told her that their father was far from well.
After an outstanding military career, the Duke had retired to
Joinville. He had been restless at first, after the long years at
Court, but he had soon settled down contentedly. During the
past winter, however, he had suffered a lingering illness and
even Antoinette's devoted nursing did not seem to be helping
him. As so often happened upon these occasions, the doctors
spoke darkly of poisoning. There was little they could do, and
they warned Antoinette to expect the worst. Her family was
at that time scattered. Mary and now young Claud were in
Scotland, Louis was in Italy, another brother was in Rome and
two daughters were in convents. The Duke's brother, Cardinal
John, set out for Joinville but died suddenly on the way.
There was more talk of poison. The eldest son, hastily summoned, fell ill and was delayed, but he did arrive in time.
Antoinette, the youngest son René and he were the only
members of the immediate family at his bedside when the
Duke of Guise passed away on 12 April 1550.[12]

The sad news of their father's death put an abrupt end to
young Claud's visit to Scotland, and when he bade Mary
farewell she sent messages promising her mother that she
would come as soon as she could to comfort the Duchess in
person. Of course, she could not make her arrangements in
time to attend her father's funeral. The Duke was buried in
the castle church at Joinville at the end of June, amidst
ceremonies of much splendour. By mid-July, however, her
plans were well advanced. The French King was himself
arranging a safe conduct from the English so that she could
safely sail down the English coast,[13] and Mary was meanwhile
working out every detail with her usual care.

The visit to the French King was vital, and everything must
go well. She gave careful consideration, for instance, to the
matter of her wardrobe. A delicate point of etiquette was
involved, so she wrote to Diane de Poitiers, the French King's
old mistress, to ask her advice. The passage of the years had
brought Diane respectability, and her daughter had recently
married Mary's brother Claud. With her father so recently

dead, should Mary make her entry into France wearing mourning? Diane consulted various friends, and they all agreed. Queens wore mourning only for their husbands, and if she did so for her father, Mary would be lowering her own position. She could wear a black dress if she wished, of course, but any more elaborate evidence of grief would not be consonant with her dignity.[14]

What Mary did decide to take with her to France remains unknown, but a list of dress materials supplied to her early in 1552 consists almost exclusively of black cloth: there is black velvet, black satin and black taffeta, all intended for dresses and for headdresses. There is black velvet for shoes and for detachable sleeves, and even black satin for brassières.[15] In view of this strong preference for black, it is probable that Mary's wardrobe for her French visit consisted of equally sombre garments.

Of much more concern than the clothes she was to take with her were, of course, her travelling companions. She did not intend to make the visit with a handful of French servants. On the contrary, her journey was to be in the nature of a royal progress and so she required a suitable retinue. Moreover, political considerations accorded with those of etiquette. Were she to leave all her lords at home their plottings, feuds and dissensions might lead to open warfare in the absence of her restraining influence. Again, the Duke of Châtelherault would be tempted to take the opportunity of building up a party of his own in opposition to the French alliance, and he could do untold damage. The nobles could not possibly be left to their own devices. Instead, she would take a selected company of them with her, choosing particularly those who favoured England. This would have the double benefit of removing them from the sphere of English influence and of converting them, by subtle use of bribery, to the French point of view. The integration of the two nations would be the more readily achieved if the Scots had spent considerable periods in France and had received gifts of French money. Accompanied by her large retinue of nobles, Mary would therefore return to France not as a faithful French emissary going home for instructions but as Queen Dowager of an independent nation and as future mother-in-law of the Dauphin.

In mid-August Leon Strozzi set sail for Scotland with six galleys to bring back Mary and her suite. His mariners and galley slaves were specially attired for the occasion in white damask. Great preparations were going ahead at the French Court for her reception. She was to be godmother to the recently-born French prince, and the christening had been postponed so that she could attend in person. Her brothers and the leading members of the French nobility were flocking to Dieppe to greet her.[16]

There they awaited her arrival with growing impatience. On 5 September Mary was still in Edinburgh, attending a meeting of the Privy Council. A violent quarrel had suddenly flared up between the Earl of Huntly and the Earl of Cassilis over the arrest of a Highland chief. With some difficulty, Mary managed to compose their differences and, after a good deal of personal persuasion, each man 'has outholden his hand to the Queen's Grace, mother to our sovereign lady, whose Grace took every man's hand thereupon'.[17]

The quarrel delayed Mary's departure, but at last she and her companions were ready to embark at Leith. Both the Earl of Huntly and the Earl of Cassilis were there, climbing aboard the galleys and smiling strained smiles whenever the Queen looked in their direction. The Earl Marischal and the Earl of Sutherland were there, Lord Home, Lord Fleming and Lord Maxwell, the redoubtable Sir George Douglas and a number of prominent churchmen. The Duke of Châtelherault as Governor of the realm remained behind, with Monsieur D'Oysel, the French ambassador acting as Lieutenant General.[18]

Meanwhile, Mary's brothers and friends were growing increasingly anxious. Storms at the end of August led to fears that the Queen might have been driven into the shores of Flanders. The French King decided that his child's baptism could wait no longer and the ceremony went ahead without Mary. Shortly afterwards, however, they were all relieved to hear that she was on her way. On 19 September her little fleet of galleys was sighted off Dieppe and she landed safely. There then ensued a joyous meeting with her brothers.[19] She had been away for twelve years. In the interval they had become grown men, and if she found them changed they must have found her also much altered. In appearance she was little different, although her figure was now matronly rather than elegant. All the same, she was a handsome woman of thirty-four, still young. The real difference was spiritual rather than physical. When she had left for Scotland in 1538 she had been a relatively inexperienced girl for all that she was the mother of children and a cultivated member of the sophisticated French Court. When she returned in 1550, she still had her irresistible charm, she was still warm-hearted, witty and merry but beneath the surface gaiety lay a singleness of purpose which even her friends were to find daunting. Dignified she had always been, but now she was regally imperious as well, and her ambition and determination were not hard to discern.

She was to spend the next twelve months in France. Her brothers escorted her to Paris by way of Rouen, where Henry II and her children were waiting, and on 25 September she made her entry into the town accompanied by 'a large retinue of Scottish gentlemen'.[20] She was received with much honour, and went through the formalities with her usual graciousness of manner, concealing her impatience to see her children. They met at last, the three of them together for the first time. The baby son she had left behind her was now a few weeks short of his fifteenth birthday and her daughter was nearly eight. Delighted with each other's company, they happily attended the pageants and spectacles arranged to celebrate Mary's arrival.

Her reunion with her children was of deep emotional significance to her, but she was not taken up with them to the exclusion of all else. Her visit has sometimes been characterized as in the nature of a holiday as if, having brought her Scottish lords within the sphere of Henry II's influence, she could now relax and enjoy the pleasures of her homeland with a carefree mind. Nothing could be further from the truth. Within a short time of her arrival she was involved in serious talks with the French monarch and his advisers.

The subject under discussion was, of course, Scotland – the domestic affairs as well as her role in the international scene. Foreign policy played its part, of course, and there were long arguments over plans for a Scottish invasion of Ireland, an event which would distract English attention from France itself.[21]

Naturally enough, the future government of Scotland was also a subject for debate. There were those at the French Court who thought that, as the Queen of Scots would so soon become the bride of the French heir, her kingdom should be united to France or at least ruled by a Frenchman in her name. Needless to say, this notion was not received with enthusiasm by the Scots, nor did it accord with Mary of Guise's plans for the future.

Once again there arises the tantalizing question of why she did not take the easy way out. Her life in Scotland had been one long series of difficulties. Her daughter was now safe, with a glittering future before her as Queen of France. The French were willing to rule her northern kingdom for her. Why, then, was Mary not content to leave the government of Scotland to, say, Monsieur D'Oysel, settling herself at the French Court or on her own French estates with her son and daughter for company and the rest of her family close at hand? Those who argue that Mary stayed in Scotland after her husband's death simply to preserve her daughter's kingdom have never given a satisfactory explanation of why she stayed on after 1550. The answer would seem to lie in Mary's own character. She believed implicitly that God had sent her to Scotland to perform a specific task. She had been crowned Queen of Scots. She had lost her Scottish husband and his two sons but the older she grew the more fascinated did she become with the exercise of power. She was determined to rule Scotland herself, not because she wanted power for its own sake but because she wanted to transform the country. The French saw Scotland as a primitive, 'infant' nation which could be transformed into a civilized, sophisticated, well-organized, modern state. Mary wanted to accomplish this transformation and not merely for cold-blooded political reasons. She genuinely cared about the welfare of ordinary people. In her younger days she had devoted much time and care to the men and women on her first husband's estates. In Scotland her concern widened to include all her second husband's subjects. She cared that people suffered the horrors of war. She cared about injustice and poverty and ignorance. This was the woman who, throughout her life, was noted for the assistance she gave ordinary people; the woman who visited the sick, advising on their treatment, and was particularly anxious to help women in childbirth. Her writings and those of her contemporaries show that, just as she exercised an almost maternal role in her own household, so too did she wish to be regarded by her people as 'mother of the commonwealth'. Amidst her political manoeuvrings, her determination to be Regent, her desire to rule, her very real humanity must not be forgotten; she might be the Queen Dowager, involved for long hours in political machinations, but the motives for her singlemindedness were those of an honest, warm-hearted, humane woman and her contemporaries recognized this full well. Throughout her life she was beloved of her friends, her servants and her advisers.

Apart from anything else, she enjoyed the political game, pitting her wits against those of the most devious politicians of the day. She had moments of depression, of melancholy, but basically her energies and her intelligence found an exhilarating outlet in the manoeuvrings and the scheming which had become so much a part of her life. There was no question of her leaving Scotland to live in France. To do so would have been to admit failure. Her task was only now beginning. Real power was once more within her grasp.

In November, the Court moved on to Chartres, and then to Blois, where the King had decided to pass the winter. Mary had by now discussed her ambitions with her brothers and, according to one account, she went to Henry II and 'made plain the cause of her coming, of many causes this to be special, to ask his sentence concerning the government of the realm of Scotland. Further to inquire if it pleased him to commit the governing to her'.[22] Her persuasions were effective. There was no more talk of replacing her by a Frenchman.

Secret discussions continued throughout the winter. The Scots were made much of at Court, and they were bribed generously. The Earl of Huntly received the Order of St Michael. The Earls of Home and Glencairn were given large sums of money and James V's illegitimate sons were nominated to French abbeys.[23] Some of the Scots were allowed to pay visits home in order to attend to their affairs. At the beginning of February, Mary paid a brief visit to her castle at Châteaudun, once her favourite residence, but she was soon back at Court again.[24]

The question of Scotland's internal government settled, the discussions had swung back to foreign policy once more and there was a growing feeling that the French King should renew the war with England. According to the English emissary at Blois, this whole policy had been put forward by Mary of Guise and her brothers, who were highly influential at Court. 'The Scottish Queen,' he wrote bitterly, 'desires as much our subversion, if it lay in her power, as she desires the preservation of herself, whose service in Scotland is so highly taken here as she is in this Court made a goddess. Monsieur de Guise and Monsieur d'Aumale and the Cardinal of Lorraine [her brothers] partly at her egging and partly upon an ambitious desire to make their house great, be no hindrance to her malicious desire.'[25]

This picture of a venomous woman bent on the destruction of the English is scarcely accurate. Mary wanted French men and French money, not so much for the purpose of making war on the English in England but rather in order to drive them out of Scotland and to see that they remained south of the Border. For this reason, she stayed on in France even after Henry II had agreed to her desire for the Regency. In the spring of 1551, however, she began to plan her return to Scotland. She could not stay away too long: there was no knowing what Châtelherault and his friends might do during a prolonged absence.

It was at the end of April, when her preparations were well

in hand,[26] that a horrifying incident caused her to cancel her departure. A plot against her daughter was discovered. An archer of the royal guard had planned to poison the little Queen but luckily the scheme came to light before any damage was done and the man fled to Ireland. When Mary of Guise heard of the plot she was appalled. 'The old Queen is fallen suddenly sick upon the opening of these news unto her' it was reported.[27] For all her strength of mind and determination, Mary was a sensitive and vulnerable woman. The thought that someone should want to poison her beloved daughter, a child of nine years old, was horrible to contemplate. It was hardly surprising that she decided to spend some more time in France with the child.

Sir John Mason, the English ambassador in France, observed her continuing presence with dismay. Convinced that she and her brothers would stir up the French King to make war once more on his own country, he commented spitefully, 'The Dowager of Scotland makes all this Court weary of her, from the high to the low, such an importunate beggar is she for herself and her chosen friends. The King would fain be rid of her and she, as she pretends [claims], would fain be gone.' She was determined to take back with her money, not mere promises.[28]

Mason's waspish remarks apart, there is no direct evidence that Mary was making herself unpopular. Certainly the Court officials may have felt that she had outstayed her welcome and Henry II may have been irritated by her determined demands, but he still treated her as his honoured guest and she moved around the country with him. That summer they visited Tours, Angers and Nantes, then they made a progress through Brittany. While the King moved on to his favourite residence of Fontainebleau, Mary took the opportunity of paying a visit to Joinville. She was accompanied by various members of her Scottish retinue and she must have taken pleasure in showing the elegant castle where she had been brought up, the fine church and the beautiful gardens to such companions as the Earl Marischal, Gavin Hamilton (the Commendator of Kilwinning) and James Ogilvie of Deskford.[29]

Her pride in showing her old home to her Scottish subjects was overshadowed, however, by an attendant melancholy. Reminiscences of the castle as it had been twelve years before called to mind those days when her small brothers and sisters filled the great chambers with noise and laughter, when excited servants prepared for the return from Court of her father the Duke, and when Antoinette was happily occupied with all manner of important concerns. Now there was an air of sadness. Louise, her sister, was dead. The others had grown up and moved away. The Duke himself was dead and Antoinette mourned him ceaselessly. She dressed now in gowns of black and she had placed in the passage leading to the church her own coffin, a perpetual reminder of her mortality.

Mary was delighted at being reunited with her family again and she had often longed to go back to Joinville, yet her stay there could only serve to underline the fact that the carefree days of childhood had gone forever and that this return was a mere interlude in an adult life burdened by affairs of state. The Joinville of fifteen years before no longer existed, nor did the Mary of Guise of fifteen years before.

She stayed at Joinville until the beginning of September, when she could postpone her departure no longer. Taking a sad farewell of her mother, she moved on to Amiens to begin the final preparations for her journey. Her young son Francis travelled with her. It would be interesting to know something of the relationship of these two, mother and son, who had seen so little of each other for so long. Considering that Mary enjoyed a close and loving relationship with her daughter and indeed with all the members of her family, it is safe to assume that her long separation from Francis had now been amply compensated for by more than a year spent with him.

Perhaps she planned to take him back to Scotland with her for a visit. He had often written to her in his childish letters of his desire to be with her in her northern kingdom and as the day for her departure drew near they must have consoled each other with promises of a future if not an immediate visit. Whatever their plans, they were not to be. Francis was suddenly taken ill. With her experience in medical affairs,

Mary nursed him personally. The nature of his illness is not known: probably it was some virulent fever. In the end, Mary could do little to help. Her last surviving son died in her arms.[30]

She bore his loss with fortitude. After his funeral, she hastened her preparations for departure and by 18 October she was in Dieppe, waiting to embark on the return journey. From there she wrote a letter to her mother, thanking her for a message of condolence Antoinette had sent her. It had been, Mary said, a great comfort to her to receive 'this consolation from you, my lady, who have as much need of it as I, but your virtue surmounts all things. God wishes us to think always of eternal life where we shall have perfect rest. I think, my lady, as you wrote to me, that Our Lord must wish me for one of His chosen ones, since He has visited me so often with such sorrow: praised be He for all'. Her mother no longer had any need to preach Christian acceptance to her. She had learned to endure grief without complaint.

From her own loss, she turned in her letter to the practical details of her voyage. 'I leave aside this painful subject,' she went on, 'to tell you that I am about to embark. I think I shall land at Rye, an English port . . .' She explained that she was going home by way of England because the journey would be safer that way than travelling the entire distance by sea. She had heard reports that Flemish ships were abroad and that fact, together with the lateness of the season, had made her choose the short crossing over the Channel instead of the long sea voyage up the coast of England. After all, Scotland and England were now at peace and a visit to the young English King would have a diplomatic purpose as well as satisfying her own curiosity about the country of her enemies.[31]

The decision to visit England was a courageous and imaginative one, and it was Mary's own.[32] Setting sail from Dieppe, she was escorted across the Channel by a small fleet of ten French warships. Storms drove her further west than she had intended, with the result that she landed not at Rye but at Portsmouth. The local gentlemen hurried to greet her and she at once gave orders that messengers be sent to Edward

VI to announce her arrival. He replied congratulating her on her safe journey and making arrangements for her to travel to London.

This she did by easy stages. She left Portsmouth on 23 October to spend two days at the house of a Mr White. Sir Richard Cotton then entertained her, and on 29 October she dined with the Earl of Arundel at Stanstead. After that the gentlemen of Sussex escorted her to Guildford, where Lord William Howard was waiting to greet her. With him, she travelled to Hampton Court. Two and a half miles from the palace itself she found an impressive gathering of notabilities awaiting her. The Marquis of Northampton, the Earl of Wiltshire, now Marquis of Winchester, and many others were there, accompanied by gentlemen, pensioners, men-at-arms and ushers, numbering a hundred and twenty in all. With this dignified company, she advanced towards the palace.

The Marchioness of Northampton and the Countess of Pembroke with sixty others were waiting for her, and they led her to lodgings which had been specially hung with fine tapestries for the occasion, as had all the other principal chambers. That evening and the following day, 'all was spent in dancing and pastime as though it were a Court, and a great presence of gentlemen resorted thither'.

The day after her arrival, Mary was taken on a tour of Hampton Court. Having duly admired its splendours, she watched a deer hunt in the grounds. The moment was now approaching when she would meet for herself the young King of England, Edward VI, and she must have viewed with great interest the prospect of speaking with the boy who might so easily have become her son-in-law.

Accompanied by a flotilla of Thames barges, she travelled by water to London, lodging first at the Bishop of London's palace. The following day she received messengers from the King. He had sent the Duke of Suffolk, the Earl of Huntingdon and others to inquire anxiously if she had everything she needed. At last, on 4 November, she set out in procession for Westminster. Accompanying her were large numbers of noblemen and their wives including Lady Margaret Douglas, wife of the Earl of Lennox. Scotland and France might be the traditional enemies of England, but on this occasion Mary was the Dowager Queen of one country paying a state visit to the monarch of another. Arriving at the Palace of Westminster she was taken into the Great Hall where the King himself was waiting, a thin, pale, grave boy surrounded by his sumptuously dressed lords.

He welcomed her and escorted her to her apartments. That evening they dined together under the same cloth of state, Mary sitting on his left. Edward himself recorded the scene in his diary. 'We were served by two services,' he noted, 'two sewers, cupbearers, carvers and gentlemen. Her Maître d'Hotel [master household] came before her service and my officers before mine. There were two cupboards, one of gold four stages high, another of massy silver, six stages. In her great chamber dined at three boards the ladies only. After dinner when she had heard some music I brought her to the hall and so she went away.'

Edward was undoubtedly precocious, but he recorded the events of that evening with a typical small boy's eye for the detail of a splendid occasion, and he said nothing of Mary herself. She was always fond of children and she probably felt only pity when she looked at the clever, delicate son of her old adversary Henry VIII. Next day, the child sent her presents: two horses and a ring set with a diamond. On 6 November she left Westminster, once more in a stately procession. According to the King's own description, the Duke of Northumberland, Lord Protector since the fall of Somerset, rode with her, accompanied by forty of his retainers in black velvet with white and black sleeves, sixty in cloth liveries. The Earls of Pembroke and Wiltshire were in attendance with their men, and many ladies were present, including the Countess of Lennox. They made their way to Shoreditch, through Cheapside and Cornhill. The gentlemen of Middlesex were ready to take her the next part of the way.[33]

So the journey continued. As she passed through each shire, she was accompanied by the local gentlemen. At last she reached Berwick, where she was welcomed by Lord

Bothwell, Lord Home and others. From there it was a com-
paratively short ride to Edinburgh, where the Duke of
Châtelherault was waiting.[34]

Mary returned in triumph, her standing undoubtedly
enhanced by her state progresses through France and England,
her friendship with the French King strengthened and her
financial situation improved. Yet even now the moment had
not yet come when she could take over the Regency from
Châtelherault. It would not do to be hasty. Henry II had
promised that she should be Regent, but she must still bide
her time. Now that peace with England had been established,
there was the opportunity to turn to domestic problems and
to the persistent difficulties resulting from years of warfare.
Apart from the economic exhaustion, the lack of a firm central
government had brought the inevitable consequence of public
disorder. As ever, there were feuds between the Highland
clans and, worse still, there was murder and there was blood-
shed in the capital itself. Members of the Kerr family fell
upon the laird of Buccleuch and killed him as he walked along
an Edinburgh street. Obviously the enforcement of law and
order was of the utmost urgency, so Mary and Châtelherault
decided that they must have a series of justice ayres, travelling
throughout the country to hold courts.

The summer after her return from France, she and the
Governor set off for the north of Scotland. They went first to
Inverness to deal with wrongdoers, then they moved eastwards,
travelling slowly through Elgin and Banff to Aberdeen before
turning south again to Dundee, Perth and eventually Glasgow.
Those accused of breaking the law were tried, often fined and
sometimes executed. If they did not appear in person, local
magnates were appointed to see that they were brought to
justice.

Mary was not solely interested in the punishment of the
disturbers of the peace. She used the expedition to further her
own cause. According to one later account, a sixteenth-century
translation of Bishop Lesley's History, wherever she and the
Governor went, she 'in that journey was never from him.
Wherever she came, if the nobility of that country made

any resistance to her, to her she allured them, partly with fair promises, partly with cross, threatening and sour words. If to her they consented, with humanity and gentleness she confirmed them, that great was their hope of her to obtain some reward, if the authority of the Governor they would renounce, and grant her the administration of the realm. Neither did she this in public, but quietly, and in secret, and specially now by some friends whom she allured to promote and help forward this matter, her special best friends who, the better they might win all men's favour, the word quietly they caused go through all the land, that if the Queen were admitted in administration of the realm, it were much to the profit of all Scotland and very thankful to the King of France. Wherefore the whole nobility either through hope of good deed or fear of something she had said, all took the Queen's part . . .'.[35]

Bishop Lesley was writing several decades after the event, and no doubt he exaggerated the unanimity of the response to Mary's subtle campaign, but his description of her technique for winning support is entirely accurate and she was indeed gaining considerable ground. So many people were tired of Châtelherault and his ineffectualness that they were willing to set aside their fears of French domination and agree that under the personal rule of Mary of Guise they would be much better off.

On the political front, the peace continued but there were also changes. In the summer of 1553 young Edward VI of England died. He was succeeded briefly by the Protestant Lady Jane Grey, but she was soon replaced by the Catholic Mary Tudor. Naturally, Mary of Guise was pleased with the succession of a Catholic Queen to the English throne, but she was realist enough to be cautious. At first, all did go well. Monsieur de Noailles, the French ambassador in London and her regular correspondent, reported approvingly that the English Queen was doing all she could to re-establish the true religion and justice.[36] Mary Tudor wrote to Mary of Guise welcoming the latter's desire that peace between the two nations should continue.[37] However, there were vague hints of trouble. De Noailles heard from two separate sources that the

Earl of Lennox was once more active. His Countess was the
English Queen's principal favourite and, anxious to take
advantage of this happy circumstance, Lennox was rumoured
to be plotting to seize the government of Scotland for himself.
He planned to send his wife to see her father, the Earl of
Angus, as a preliminary to his scheme, but in the event Mary
Tudor declared that she could not part with the Countess and
kept her at Court.[38]

These intimations of trouble ahead made Mary of Guise
decide that she must now act. The time had come to demand
the Regency for herself. In December she dispatched Monsieur
D'Oysel to the French Court for consultations, no doubt about
this matter. He returned in January, and he and Mary began
in earnest to try to persuade Châtelherault that he must
relinquish his position as Lord Governor. As D'Oysel himself
was to remark, this delicate task was not to be easily accomplished. Châtelherault had no reason to give up the Regency
until Mary, Queen of Scots reached the age of twelve. How
could he be persuaded to withdraw prematurely from his
position of power? D'Oysel and Mary spent many long hours
closeted with him. There were interminable discussions,
exhausting arguments. It seemed as if nothing would move
him, but in the end, when he saw how many of the lords, both
spiritual and temporal, were against him, he gave way.[39]

On 19 February 1554 he capitulated, and on that day he
signed a personal agreement with Mary of Guise. The document reveals clearly the persuasions used by the Queen and by
D'Oysel. Predictably, these were almost entirely financial.
Mary promised that Châtelherault should be granted all sums
of money and taxation owed to the crown since the death of
James V and not yet uplifted by him. He could collect these
when the little Queen came of age, and he could put them to
whatever use he chose. Mary of Guise would also grant him a
free discharge of any of her own goods which had come into
his hands since the death of James V. Grants of property to
various Hamilton relatives, including his illegitimate son
David, would be confirmed and he himself would be given
custody of Dumbarton Castle for nineteen years – Dumbarton

having previously been in the hands of his old enemy the Earl of Lennox. Finally, Châtelherault would replace D'Oysel as Lieutenant General for Scotland, an office which he would be allowed to pass on to his eldest son. In return he would formally and publicly hand over the government of the realm to Mary of Guise and he would give the keeping of Edinburgh Castle to her faithful supporter Lord Erskine.[40]

On Thursday, 12 April 1554, parliament met. That morning, a solemn procession of heralds, lords and prelates rode from the Palace of Holyroodhouse up the Canongate. The officers of state bore the sceptre, the sword and the crown, and immediately behind them rode the Duke of Châtelherault, appearing in public as Lord Governor of Scotland for the last time. To the cheering of the crowds and the firing of cannon they arrived at the Tolbooth. A little later, Mary herself followed, escorted by Monsieur D'Oysel. While the proceedings of the day began, she waited in a private chamber. With an air of depression the Duke of Châtelherault stepped forward and ceremoniously resigned his office. A fanfare sounded, the doors opened, and Mary of Guise made her entrance. Monsieur D'Oysel took the crown of Scotland and placed it on her head, then he handed her the sceptre and the sword of state. Fourteen years before, in the Abbey of Holyroodhouse, she had been crowned Queen as consort of James V. Now, before the assembled estates, she was formally recognized as Queen Regent of Scotland.

The ceremony over, she came out into the Canongate once more, to a tumultuous welcome. Accompanied by her ladies, by the lords and the prelates and the ordinary people, she rode back to Holyrood with the crown, the sword and the sceptre carried before her. Bereft of his former symbols of authority, the Duke of Châtelherault rode with his fellow peers. A new era had begun – or so many people hoped – that day.[41]

9

The Queen Regent

At a personal level, Mary's accession to the Regency was not so much an innovation as a return to the general situation which had existed when her husband was alive. The royal palaces were no longer in the possession of a Lord Governor. She was mistress not just of Stirling and Falkland and Linlithgow but of Edinburgh Castle and Holyrood and Dumbarton. The royal household revolved around her once again, not merely her own household of French and Scottish servants but the official household attendant upon the monarch or the monarch's representative. The royal revenues, diverted no longer to the Hamiltons, flowed directly to her. Once more there was peace with England, although the threat of invasion still remained, and once more Scotland was firmly allied to France, with a marriage in the offing to cement that alliance.

Mary herself realized though, that the resemblances to the situation of before 1542 were purely superficial. Scotland was still an independent kingdom, but a kingdom whose monarch lived abroad and was unlikely ever to return. It seemed inevitable that the country would become a satellite state of France. The French were certainly anxious that it should be so. They did not see this ambition in the terms of one small nation's struggle to maintain its independence: rather, they considered only the international implications. With Scotland as their assured ally, permanently working in their interest, they would be in a much stronger position to resist any threat from England.

Much has been written about the attitude of Mary herself towards Scotland and the Scots. In her own letters of the late 1550s her outlook is perfectly clear. It was desirable for both

France and Scotland that they should unite against England, and her daughter's marriage to the Dauphin would bind the two nations together much more effectively than even her own marriage to James V had done. Scotland could only benefit from such an alliance. French help would be available whenever there was a threat from the south.

As for the Scots themselves, their country was, in the opinion of the French, a young, undeveloped nation with an unruly population, a host of self-seeking, unreliable lords, and a set of impracticable laws. As 'mother of the commonwealth' Mary would give the country justice, peace and order. Scotland would become a well-governed, efficient kingdom, flourishing in perpetual amity with France. Over the years the two nations would grow closer and closer together. The French would hold office in Scotland, the Scots in France. The Scots would learn from the French what it was to be a modern, civilized state.

Mary of Guise knew that this vision of a well-ordered, French-orientated Scotland was far from being a reality, but she was prepared to devote the rest of her life to making it so. Unfortunately, she underestimated the independent nature of the Scots. Over the years she had learned to a large extent how to deal with them. She realized that they were proud and that they were sensitive about their position, and she managed individuals accordingly with considerable success. The trouble was that the Scots remained foreigners to her, people who did not live by the rules she had been brought up to observe; in some ways akin to unruly children whom she had to bring into obedience for their own good. She had tried hard in the early days to win firm friends among them, but such was the self-interest of the nobles that she found it impossible to rely on any of them. Châtelherault, Sir George Douglas, Angus, Bothwell . . . they might be on her side for a few months but consistent loyalty was the last quality she could expect from them.

Accustomed as she was to the machinations of the French Court, Mary was used to the manoeuvrings of great men. Even so, when the French were confronted by their old enemy, England, they could be relied upon to put personal issues to one side for the time being in order to resist a threat from abroad. The Scots did not respond in this way. It seemed pointless to speak to them of those things which French soldiers treasured: glory, honour, reputation. The ordinary Scots came to do their sixty days' military service then went back to their homes. The nobles cared more for money and for self-preservation than for any abstract ideals.

Mary did not understand fully the reasons for this be-haviour. Scotland was a poor, small nation caught between two great powers and consequently in a position of appalling difficulty. Mary would have liked to rouse her subjects with stirring words and send them to drive out the English. The lords, for their part, saw that their best hope of retaining their country's independence and their own property was to play off England against France, France against England. Bribes were useful, of course, but the lords did not wish to commit themselves irrevocably to either of their two influential neighbours. No sooner had they agreed to a binding English alliance in the Treaties of Greenwich than they began to regret it. No sooner had they tied themselves to France than they began to have second thoughts. Alliances were always bought at a price, and the price invariably seemed too high. By marrying their little Queen to a future English King they would lose their independence to the English. Better, then, to turn to France; but now that their Queen was to marry the future King of France they feared that the French would take their independence from them.

People began to say that an alliance with England was preferable, especially now that there was a strong religious element in the problem. The Protestant movement in Scotland was gaining strength as each day passed. Mary of Guise knew this, but she did not know that she was dealing with a move-ment which would change the whole history of Scotland. She saw her Protestant opponents as people motivated by almost exclusively political considerations, and in many cases she was right. It was not as if the Protestants were devout strangers newly come into the country. Rather, those Protestants with whom she had direct dealings were the men she had known personally for years. Some had suddenly embraced the Reforming cause for obvious, non-political reasons. They wanted to keep the Church lands permanently for themselves, or they wanted to gain the support of the Protestant English in order to oppose the French alliance. Some of them had been flirting with Protestantism for almost a decade. How could she believe in the religious integrity of, say, the Duke of Châtelherault, who had favoured the Reforming cause when it suited himself and had abandoned it with alacrity when association with Protestantism became a source of embarrassment to him?

Mary had known these men for years, and she knew just how much reliance to place on their protestations of loyalty to anyone or to anything.

Of course, she was well aware of the strength of the Protestant movement on the Continent, and she knew that there were many abuses in the Church. Had not her husband's old friend Sir David Lindsay written his Satire of the Three Estates condemning these abuses? In the autumn of 1557 she had caused an official letter to be sent from her daughter asking the Pope to send a Cardinal to Scotland with the specific task of reforming the clergy, and that official letter had described the relaxation of ecclesiastical discipline in Scotland, the alienation of Church property by the prelates, the neglect of buildings, the laxity of monks and nuns.[1] To her mind, these were abuses which must be rectified, but which were, for the moment, being exaggerated out of all proportion by those who wished to make trouble for herself and for the French.

She herself was optimistic, possessed of a firm determination to achieve her longstanding ambitions. True, she was desperately short of money still, in spite of French aid. The consequences of the long years of war and the extravagance of Châtelherault were not so easily remedied. The Governor had left her with a deficit of £30,000 and there seemed no possibility that she could pay this off. Her own revenues from France arrived at very irregular intervals, in spite of all her mother's efforts to ensure that they were sent on time, and Mary was forced to borrow continually and to sell off her own valuables. When she had first come to Scotland she had admired the luxurious furnishings of the royal palaces. She had planned great improvements to buildings and to gardens. She had listened to music and she had patronized painters; Peter Quesnel the artist had been an usher in her household in 1543. Now she was forced to sell off plate in order to pay her soldiers. The fine Continental tapestries on the walls of the palaces were becoming threadbare and stretched. The gold and silver threads on the cloths of state were tarnished and dull. The furnishings were worn. Plans for palace extensions had long since been forgotten and there was no time now for musicians and for artists. The more Mary became taken up with affairs of state the more indifferent did she become to her surroundings. All that mattered was the business in hand, the problem of ruling her daughter's turbulent kingdom.

As soon as she became Regent, Mary made new appointments, replacing Châtelherault's men with her own supporters. The Earl of Cassilis became Lord Treasurer, James Makgill was made Clerk Register and the keeping of the Privy Seal was given to the Abbot of Coupar. Similarly, she rewarded her adherents with gifts of lands and of revenues. The property of those who had actively opposed her was seized and given to such men as Lord Erskine and Mr John Spens of Condie, both to be regular recipients of her gifts in the years to come. There were bribes, too, for those liable to waver in their support. Lord Bothwell and Lord Borthwick were encouraged to remain loyal by such means. Nor did Mary ignore those of the Hamilton faction. Instead of leaving them all to assist the Duke of Châtelherault, she set about detaching a variety of lesser members of his family from his cause by a judicious series of gifts.

All this was acceptable enough, but some of those Mary chose to favour did not enjoy general popularity. She had decided to begin her policy of integrating French and Scots without further delay and so she gave the keeping of the King's Seal to one of the French King's councillors, Monsieur de Rubay. Monsieur Villemore, a member of her own household, was given control of the Customs. One Monsieur Bonet became her Bailie of Orkney and in 1557 the Frenchman Jean Roytell was nominated to the post of principal master mason. These appointments were, to say the least, controversial. Indeed, they aroused the immediate hostility of the lords, who regarded all the offices of state as their own perquisites and who resented the appointment of someone of another social class to such places, let alone someone of another nation. There were ominous rumblings of discontent. These Mary accepted philosophically. Given time, the Scots would come round.

Hitherto, she had spent much of her time in Stirling, shunning Edinburgh where Châtelherault held his Court. Now she transferred her own headquarters to the capital and regularly attended Privy Council meetings there. Much of the discussion in Council was devoted to the problem of the Borders. No one could estimate how long Mary Tudor would maintain her attitude of friendship towards the Scots and, as it was, there were continual Border raids by both countries. In public, Mary of Guise expressed a desire for peace in the southern counties, but she privately encouraged the Scots in their incursions into England.

Elsewhere, however, she was genuinely anxious to restore law and order. Disturbances were all too widespread. For so long now had there been war with England that when aggressive energies could not be directed against the enemy they found an outlet in all manner of private feuds. In part, Mary continued the policy of administering justice through intermediaries, appointing the great lords to pacify troubles in their own areas. In August 1554, for example, she ordered the Earl of Argyll to proceed against the rebels of the Western Isles.[2] This policy did not always work, of course, because the very local interests which she was seeking to exploit could militate against her. Later in the same year when she commanded Huntly to take action against wrongdoers in the north he set out but returned without accomplishing anything. He claimed that he had been unable to raise enough men to carry out her commands. Mary was furious. She saw his actions as a flouting of her authority and, for all that he was Lord Chancellor, she imprisoned him in Edinburgh Castle. There he remained until March of the following year when Mary first of all spoke of banishing him to France, then at the last moment relented and agreed that a large fine would satisfy her instead.

These were individual difficulties, of course, requiring special consideration. On a wider scale, Mary was anxious to see introduced legislation which would form a basis for the new stability she hoped to bring to Scotland. Parliament had met in April 1554 but the entire session had been taken up with the formalities of ending Châtelherault's governorship. In June 1555, however, it was arranged that the three estates would assemble once more, and this time there was the opportunity for doing something really constructive.

Mary attended parliament in person that summer, and the diverse laws passed reflect quite strikingly her own aims and methods. After solemnly declaring that the liberties of the Holy Church must be preserved intact, the delegates went on to debate more detailed, practical matters. Much of the legislation was concerned with the administration of justice, or rather with the procedures involved. The correct method of summoning a man before the justices was specified. The proper legal form for the transfer of property was stated. The need for vassals to sign instruments of resignation or at least to have their hand guided at the pen to make some attempt at a signature was recorded. The set number of days' warning to be given to tenants told to leave their lands was laid down. The precise methods of proceeding against murderers and fugitives were prescribed, and it was declared that any man found guilty of perjury was to have his tongue pierced and his goods seized. Less drastically, the qualifications of notaries were to be examined carefully.

Few of these statutes were new. Rather, they reflected the need to end the chaos resulting from years of warfare and the lack of a firm central government. Mary and her advisers were obviously trying to restore law and order, to reintroduce the correct, legal form for all manner of transactions, not merely for the punishment of wrongdoers, and in this desire for correctness and for order we see much of Mary herself. While it would be wrong to imagine that she in any way dictated to parliament what they must enact, it would be equally wrong to suppose that she attended merely as an onlooker. The measures introduced were very much to the point in the context of her own policies.

Similarly, in economic affairs, her desire to restore prosperity and to give stability and peace can be seen in parliament's proceedings. A committee was set up to fix uniform weights and measures. The export of wool and hides to England was expressly forbidden and meat was only to be allowed to leave the country if it was necessary as provisions for those undertaking lengthy voyages. Because of a severe shortage of sheep there was to be no slaughtering of lambs or selling of them at markets for the following three years. Existing game laws were re-enacted in a further attempt to improve the food supply and penalties against those who were caught poaching were extended to include any convicted of stealing bee-hives, damaging fruit trees or peeling bark from other trees. Old laws for protecting trees were repeated and special measures were to be taken to allow the young trees at Falkland Palace to grow unhindered. So much timber had been cut down to provide wood for ships and for military purposes that the country was denuded of its forests.

There was legislation, too, confirming the privileges of the royal burghs. Here again we can see something of Mary's own preoccupations. In her search for money and support she frequently turned to the wealthy townspeople and her desire to cultivate their friendship can also be traced in various gifts and privileges issued under the Privy Seal to the burghs and their inhabitants. Parliament at this time likewise sought to protect workers with precious metals from fraud: goldsmiths were told to use their own mark and that of their town on each article they produced.

As she sat in Parliament each day and saw these measures written down in the records, Mary felt considerable satisfaction.

At last she was making a real start in what she wanted to do. The careful re-enactment of old laws, the deliberate reintroduction of procedures long forgotten in the tumult of war were in many ways a modest beginning, but a beginning they undoubtedly were. She confidently expected that the next time parliament met the work would be consolidated: she was not to know that this was to be her first and only opportunity to see legislation go through in support of her domestic policies.

In fact, in the midst of these plans for peace, there were signs of the troubles which still existed and of the troubles which lay ahead. Parliament had found it necessary to declare null the many bonds of manrent still being made . . . those private agreements between individuals for mutual protection. Even more sinister in its undertones was the act which had to be introduced because 'divers seditious persons have in times bypast raised amongst the common people murmurs and slanders, speaking against the Queen's Grace and sowing evil rumours about the most Christian King of France's subjects . . .'[3]

For the time being, however, Mary was satisfied. Of course there was still anti-French feeling in certain quarters, but it would ebb away with the passing of time. For the present, it was vital that she should help to implement parliament's legislation by doing all she could in the sphere of justice, and so the summer of 1555 found her in Dumfries at the trial of Border thieves. In the following year she was even more active. That summer she held justice ayres throughout the north of Scotland in a repetition of the journey she had made with Châtelherault several years before. She went first to Inverness, travelling in state with a retinue of local gentlemen. She attended the trials of all manner of wrongdoers and, interestingly enough, she informed the clan chiefs that she intended to continue the policy followed by her late husband: as in his time, the chiefs were to be held responsible for the behaviour of their people and if they did not bring malefactors to justice, they themselves would be punished.

According to one account, the Laird of Grant was ordered

in this way to produce a criminal named James Grant and his accomplices. Anxious to avoid any punishment himself, he set off with great enthusiasm. He discovered that he could not take the men alive, and so he killed them and 'caused to be presented their heads to the Queen.'[4]

Mary's reaction to this bloodthirsty gift is not recorded, but all the evidence suggests that if ever such an incident did take place she probably recoiled in dismay. For all her spirit and determination she was a humane woman, always anxious to temper justice with mercy. Whenever possible she pursued a policy of taking pledges for the good behaviour of her subjects, and many offences she punished by fines. She did not want vengeance but she did want money. Even so, her motives were not purely financial. Of course, sixteenth-century ideas of crime and punishment were very different from those of the twentieth century, and Mary's clemency may appear strange to modern eyes. Henry Wynd, a burgess of the small port of Dysart, was convicted of forging coins and was beheaded 'by the Grace of the Queen Dowager'. Normally he would have been strangled at the stake and burned: beheading was a swifter and therefore a more merciful procedure.

William Nasmyth, another forger, was simply banished from the realm by the Queen's command instead of being executed. Adam Sinclair, who broke into a parish church and stole money, chalices and ornaments, was sentenced to be drowned 'by the special grace of the Queen'. Normally drowning was the method of execution allowed for women: Adam asked for this form of death for himself, and Mary granted his request because he was only a youth.[5] Barbarous these punishments were, but it is nonetheless interesting to see that Mary seems to have intervened in a fairly consistent manner to commute the harsh sentences as best she could. Here we see not the cold-blooded, vengeful daughter of the House of Guise as described by John Knox but the real, humane woman with a genuinely sympathetic concern for her subjects.

Her justice ayres in the north were not always concerned with such spectacular cases. In late August she was in Elgin and Forres dealing with the fixing of prices.[6] From there, she moved on to Banff and Aberdeen 'where, with all diligence she made inquisition of crimes and heavy offences. But with such lenience and gentleness she tempered the severity of the law that the guilty she punished not in their head but in a sum of silver'.[7] From Aberdeen she travelled south to Dundee, then across to Perth. She returned finally to Edinburgh with a sense of satisfaction. All was going well. At last she was able to do something constructive about the administration of justice and the maintenance of law and order.

Unfortunately, at that moment there took place an event which was to undermine her authority. Mary, Queen of Scots was taken ill. A short illness would have been worrying enough but this was one of those lingering fevers which would flare up again just as the patient seemed to be recovering. Naturally enough, it was a source of personal anxiety for Mary of Guise but it also had significant public repercussions. Rumour inevitably exaggerated the seriousness of the young Queen's condition, and it was not long before those who disliked the French alliance were stirring up doubts in the minds of their fellow countrymen. What would happen to the nation should the young Queen die? There would be Scotland, tied forever to the French and for no good reason. The King of France would very likely claim the kingdom for his son in spite of all guarantees, and what would happen then to Scotland's dearly prized independence? Discontent grew.

Mary of Guise awaited with great concern the reassuring bulletins which came from her brothers and friends. By January she was able to comment with relief on her daughter's complete recovery, but there was now a new cause for anxiety. The young Dauphin, always a delicate boy, had also contracted a fever. This aroused further murmurings. What if the boy should die? What would then become of Scotland and her young Queen?

Mary found that these personal difficulties were reflected in public affairs. At the beginning of 1557, parliament would meet, but instead of extending the careful measures of 1555, Mary knew that the representatives would have to be persuaded to turn their attention to the raising of money. The French had withdrawn some of their troops from Scotland, much to her annoyance, and there were ugly rumours of renewed hostilities. For all her professions of peace, Mary Tudor was still permitting Border raids. In order to pay for more defensive measures, Mary of Guise decided that she must persuade parliament to introduce new taxes.

She expected the usual grumbling, but when parliament did meet she was unpleasantly surprised at the opposition to her proposals. As she confided to a friend in France, her daughter's illness had caused the Scots to be more obstructive than ever. 'Every day,' she complained, 'I find them more jealous and suspicious, and I think they are following the example of our neighbours the English. Also, whenever it is a question of meting out justice or punishment, they find these things insupportable, thinking always that one wants to give them new laws and change theirs, which in fact have much need of amendment.'[8]

This was a theme which she developed at greater length in a letter she wrote that same day to her brother, the Cardinal of Lorraine.[9] After discussing the worrying prospect of war with England, she explained her reluctance to build new forts. Even if she had the money, she told him, she did not know whether it would be a wise policy, for she had no French troops to garrison them and the Scots had little experience of this type of military service. The great lords had certainly agreed that such forts would be an added defence against the English, but the ordinary people and the lesser lords 'have become so suspicious as to think that it would be a perpetual tax on them. On the other hand, seeing that I am weak, that I am more alienated from them than I first was, the business will take much longer than I had hoped'.

During the last session of parliament various people had told her in no uncertain terms 'that it would be putting the cart before the oxen and deceiving myself if I thought of settling anything before the marriage is accomplished, for they are still doubtful under which lord they shall fall . . . Moreover, my daughter's illness has put many things in doubt and, to keep nothing back from you, men's minds have been so changeable and in such a state of suspense that those from whom I hoped the most I have found more estranged than I have ever seen them, not just since I have ruled them but since I came to Scotland'.

What troubled her more than anything was the lack of progress she was making in her plans to give Scotland a more efficient and more equitable judicial system. When in the past she had acted in a conciliatory manner and discussed urgent matters of peace and war with them, the Scots had done as she had wanted and she 'led them as I wished'. On the question of law and order, however, she found them much less amenable. 'Now that it is a question of my determination to see justice take a straightforward course and they find me a little severe, they will not endure it and say that these are the laws of the French and that their old laws are good (which for the most part are the most unjust in the world, not in themselves but from the way in which they are administered). This is the cause of all our discord which, however, I pass over as gently as I can, preventing things from getting worse, waiting for a better time, and delaying until I see what it may please God to appoint . . . .'.

Even so, in spite of her resolve to be patient, she sometimes despaired of accomplishing the task she had set herself. 'God knows, brother, what a life I lead,' she wrote in a moment of depression. 'It is no small thing to bring a young nation to a state of perfection and to an unwonted subservience to those who wish to see justice reign. Great responsibilities are easily undertaken but not so easily discharged to the satisfaction of God. Happy is he who has least to do with worldly affairs. I can safely say that for twenty years past I have not had one year of rest, and I think that if I were to say not one month I should not be far wrong, for a troubled spirit is the greatest trial of all . . .'

Mary and the Scots were indeed drifting further and further apart. In wartime, she had used all her endeavours to unite them against the English. It had been no easy task but she had enjoyed a measure of success and all the time she had been able to encourage herself with thoughts of what she could do once peace was established, of how she would reorganize this unruly kingdom of hers. Unfortunately, when the direct threat from England had been removed, the Scots were no longer so dependent on her. Instead, they were continually on the watch for any move she might make to transform their country into a satellite state of France. The more she tried to put her plans into effect, the more the Scots would resist. There lay the tragedy of the situation.

As Mary herself had been warned, she could do nothing until her daughter was actually married to the Dauphin. The Scots might fear the consequences of the marriage, but they were determined that it should be accomplished. When parliament met again in March, Mary found its members even more intractable. She decided that she must address them in person. Surely if she spoke to them in rousing terms of the dangers of an English invasion, they would respond. She went in state to parliament and spoke eloquently on the threat from the south. The lords listened to her politely enough, but as she looked round her she could see that they were paying little heed to her words. She had barely sat down when one of them was on his feet, demanding permission to send a deputation to speak to her, and insisting that Monsieur D'Oysel should also be present. At the man's words, there was an immediate feeling of tension, of excitement. All eyes were on her now, as her audience waited for her reply. Fighting down her exasperation, she agreed graciously to their request.

They came to see her. They spoke at length about marriages in general and about the English Queen's recent marriage in particular. They pointed out that Mary Tudor had now become the wife of Philip of Spain. They passed over the political implications of that, and instead declared that the match had drawn their attention to the fact that they themselves lacked a master. In such dangerous times they needed a man at their head. The little Queen must marry the Dauphin at once.

Mary felt her temper rising. They were insulting. How could a young, delicate boy living in a foreign country possibly help them better than she herself could? Catching the eye of

Monsieur D'Oysel, who was shaking his head warningly at her, Mary restrained herself. The future of Scotland was not in question, she said temperately. Her daughter would marry the Dauphin when the time came, and the King of France would never forget to assist the Scots as though they were his own people.

A sullen silence greeted her reply. Monsieur D'Oysel hastily intervened. He made a short, persuasive speech on his own account, confirming what Mary had said. The Scots remained unconvinced. The young Queen must be married at once, one of them burst out, and Mary of Guise must go to France in person to see the ceremony performed. Really, their impertinence was breathtaking. It would have been laughable, had not the situation been so dangerous. Patiently, she explained to the man that, with everything pointing to imminent war, this was hardly the moment for her to set out on a dangerous voyage down the coast of England. Well then, said the Scots, she must send a personal representative instead.[10]

Nothing could be done in the face of such obstinacy. Murmuring vague assurances, Mary indicated that the audience was over. She then retired to her own chamber in a state of considerable annoyance. These men had put her in an awkward position. She was actually as anxious as they were to see her daughter safely married, but she knew that she must tread warily with Henry II. He was, after all, by far the more powerful partner in their alliance and it would not do to press him too hard. However, if she was skilful enough, she could perhaps use the demands of the Scots to hasten the marriage. She might just manage to convince Henry of its urgency, under the cover of deprecating her subjects' demands.

She sat down and composed a tactful letter. She described her recent talk with the deputation, emphasizing that she did so 'only to let you know of everything which comes to my knowledge so that I can govern as you desire . . . for all the power God has given to the mother and to the daughter will never be dedicated other than to what is agreeable to you . . .' She knew what a King of France expected of his correspondents in the way of polite assurances.

Managing the Scots was a rather different matter. As the days passed they were becoming increasingly discontented. All summer she was conscious of undercurrents of trouble, but it was not until autumn that the crisis came, precipitated by a letter from Henry II. He was now at war with Spain. Spain's King was married to Mary Tudor. He therefore required the Scots to divert the attention of his enemies. They must invade England.

His instruction placed Mary in an awkward predicament. Her forces were inadequate. She disliked warfare. She hated the senseless destruction, the human misery involved, yet she knew that Scotland would have to play her part in the Franco-Scottish alliance. If the Scots did not aid the French, how could they expect help in return? There was nothing for it but to go ahead with a military campaign, ill-timed though it might be. With grave doubts, she summoned all able-bodied men between the ages of sixteen and sixty to assemble in Edinburgh.

They came, of course. She could see that they were reluctant, as they had been on similar occasions previously, and the nobles as usual were not slow to make their personal feelings known to her. In an attempt to improve the situation, she rode with them when they left for the Borders. As they neared Kelso their discontent had become so obvious that she decided to address the army herself. Her eloquence might not have had much effect at the parliament of the previous spring, but it had worked on former occasions, at the siege of Haddington and before the taking of Inchkeith. Summoning up all her powers of persuasion, she made a stirring speech on the dangers of an English invasion, on the need to take the initiative. She encouraged them with the news that Monsieur D'Oysel was bringing French soldiers and artillery from the fort at Eyemouth. She urged them to march on, to invade England and to besiege Wark Castle in Northumberland.

Their lack of enthusiasm was depressing but they did march on. Mary herself had decided to wait at Hume Castle. No sooner had the army left her, than bitter arguments broke out between the French and the Scottish contingents. The Scottish lords met together and decided that they had not the slightest desire to invade England at the whim of the King of France. They ordered Monsieur D'Oysel to take himself and his artillery back to Eyemouth, and without more ado they marched home.

For Mary, this was bitter news indeed. The defiance of the lords was an open flouting of her authority, the first time that they had refused outright to obey her. It was a public humiliation for her and it boded ill for the future of the French alliance. Describing the incident in his usual flamboyant language, John Knox decided that this reverse 'kindled such a fire in the Queen Regent's stomach as was not well slaked till her breath failed'.[11]

Mary certainly had a quick temper, and she was a proud woman. Her anger always had flared up at an affront to her dignity and she would rebuke the offender in no uncertain terms, be he husband, lord, subject or servant. Her wrath usually passed quickly, though, and she did not bear malice, but on this occasion she was left with a lingering sense of betrayal, a feeling that here was the final proof that she could never trust the Scots. For years she had wooed them with tact and charm, with genuine friendliness, with promises and with bribes. They had listened to her politely, they had taken her money and they had gone their own way. Now the gulf between them was widening, and as mutual suspicion increased she turned more and more to Monsieur D'Oysel and to her other French advisers.

Something had to be done quickly before her authority was weakened any further, and so she persuaded her brothers to urge the French King to arrange the marriage of his son to her daughter. The Guises were now in an increasingly influential position as a result of their own personal success. In January 1558 the Duke of Guise, Mary's eldest brother, captured Calais from the English and the power and popularity of his family rose to new heights. Eager to reward them, Henry II agreed to go ahead with the marriage plans. Mary of Guise could not risk leaving Scotland in its current state of unrest and so she appointed Antoinette, her mother, to act as her personal representative in the negotiations which followed.

Eight commissioners from Scotland agreed the actual terms of the marriage contract, and on 19 April 1558 the young couple were formally betrothed in the Great Hall of the Louvre, the palace where Mary of Guise had herself been first married. The official marriage contract contained the necessary terms safeguarding Scotland's independence. The young Queen promised to maintain the ancient liberties and privileges of the nation. Mary of Guise was to remain Regent so long as her daughter was out of the country. If no children were born of the marriage the crown of Scotland would revert to the nearest Scottish heir, the Duke of Châtelherault. Henceforth the Dauphin would have the title of King of Scots and when he succeeded eventually to the throne of France the two kingdoms would be united. Scots would become naturalized subjects of France, French of Scotland.

These terms had been accepted by the Scottish commissioners and, although the thought of a union with France was highly unpopular in some quarters, at least the contract was unexceptionable. It did not, however, tell the whole story. Before she signed the official document the young Queen put her name to a secret agreement by which she agreed that, should she die childless, the King of France would inherit Scotland and he would enjoy all the Scottish revenues until such time as he had been repaid for the money he had spent in defence of the northern kingdom. Any future arrangement which ran contrary to these two promises would be null.

For the young Queen, for the French and for Mary of Guise the eventual union of the two kingdoms was an accomplished fact. Mary was satisfied. In the difficult business of governing the unruly Scots she was now assured of the permanent support of her own people. Certainly the Scots themselves would grumble, but even if they did not realize it, the union would be for their own good. Their country and its laws would be immeasurably improved and there would be no more threat of invasion from England. She would now set about preparing the Scots for their new role as subjects of a united Franco-Scottish realm.

On 24 April 1558 Mary, Queen of Scots and the Dauphin were married in the Cathedral of Notre Dame in Paris. The wedding was celebrated with much magnificence and in Edinburgh the cannon at the castle were fired to mark the occasion. Mary of Guise wished that she could have been in Notre Dame that day, but she consoled herself with the thought that all the other Guise relations were there to support her daughter, and with the belief that this wedding would improve her own situation immeasurably. Her optimism was soon to be shaken.

By early autumn, the difficulty of reconciling the Scots to the thought of an eventual union with France had become all too apparent. The Scottish commissioners who had taken part in the marriage negotiations had remained on in France for the lengthy festivities and in September, on the eve of their return, four of them were taken ill and died. There were immediate rumours of poisoning which exacerbated the growing anti-French feeling in Scotland.

That in itself was a more or less isolated incident, tragic though it was. Of greater significance was an event which took place in Edinburgh on 1 September. On that day, the feast of St Giles, an image of the saint was carried in procession from the Church of St Giles through the main streets of the town. As the day approached, there were signs of trouble. There was nothing tangible, though, until one of the Queen's household came hurrying in to her one day in great distress. There were disturbances in the town, he said. A group of Protestants had gone so far as to steal the great image of St Giles from its place in the church. As if that were not bad enough, they had hurled it into the Nor' Loch beneath the castle. Not content with 'drowning' it, they had fished it out and were even now burning it on a bonfire.

Mary was affronted. Senseless destruction always upset her deeply, and this sort of sacrilege was unforgivable. The stealing of images had nothing to do with theological differences. Obviously there were those in the town who wanted to stir up trouble by forcing the authorities to cancel the procession. They must not be allowed that satisfaction. Thinking hard,

Mary gave orders that a smaller statue of the saint should be borrowed from the Church of the Greyfriars. The procession would go ahead as planned, and in order to prevent any outbreak of disorder, she herself would walk at its head.

The first of September came, and the procession set out from the Church of St Giles. Mary, in one of her most dignified gowns, was there with her household. The small statue of St Giles looked pathetically inadequate, but it was better than nothing. It had been fixed to a portable shrine, and various men had been instructed to carry it, holding it aloft as proudly as if it had been the larger image. Behind walked a long line of ecclesiastics. Trumpets sounded, drums were beaten, banners waved, the ordinary people pressed around, the dust rose from the streets. The procession wound its way slowly along the Canongate.

When they reached the house of Sandy Carpenter they stopped; the Queen was to go in and dine there. With a feeling of relief, she went inside. Those who had been carrying the shrine laid it down on the ground. Everything had gone off peacefully until now, but as soon as Mary's back was turned a group of men jostled forward, making as if to help to lift the image. Before anyone realized what was happening, they raised the shrine up and then they began shaking it back and forward, trying to dislodge St Giles from his position. The bearers realized what was happening and rushed to the defence. There was a violent struggle, and the image was pulled to the ground. In a panic, many of the monks and priests fled before the mob. Alarmed by the noise, Mary and her household watched from the windows of Sandy Carpenter's house. There was nothing they could do. They could only wait until the worst of the commotion had died down, then her escort hustled Mary back to the safety of Edinburgh Castle.[12]

She could not but be shaken, but her reading of the situation remained unaltered. The day's riots had been done in the name of Protestantism, but she believed irrevocably that religion was being used as a cloak for political subversion. She knew that there were ordinary men and women who were genuinely convinced Protestants, but she felt that they were being used as pawns in the political game. Had not the English deliberately sent north vernacular Bibles and religious writings for one purpose and for one purpose only, to undermine both Church and state and so conquer Scotland for themselves? They had failed in this purpose, but similar methods were being continued by self-seeking lords who were using religion for their own non-religious reasons, and that was despicable. These preachers who stirred up the mob on St Giles' Day were nothing more than the instruments of men who wished to destroy the French alliance by civil strife, seize the lands of the Church for themselves, then ally themselves with the Protestant English.

She accordingly viewed the series of petitions presented to her by the Protestants in the winter of 1558–9 not as sincere religious pleas from people troubled by corruption in the Church but as demands manufactured by agitators determined to stir up opposition to herself, to the established government and to the established Church.

In November, she received petitions demanding for the Protestants the right to convene publicly or privately for the purpose of hearing prayers in the vernacular. They also asked that any qualified person should be allowed to expound the Scriptures and they declared that not only the baptismal service but the celebration of the Lord's Supper should be conducted in their own tongue and they claimed the right to take Communion in both kinds: that is to say, they wished to take both the bread and the wine, not merely the bread as was the rule in the Catholic Church. They urged that prelates, priests and monks and nuns should be compelled to reform their way of life.[13]

In a second petition they turned their attention to recent heresy trials and asked that all existing acts against heresy should be suspended until the grounds for such trials were thoroughly investigated. They wanted all heresy cases to be tried not by ecclesiastical but by lay courts and they said that the accused must have the right to expound their views.[14] By the beginning of December they were petitioning for freedom of conscience, saying that if any public tumult arose they were not to be held responsible, and that there should be no threat to either their lives or their lands.[15]

Mary of Guise regarded these demands as no more than pretexts, tiresome attempts to challenge her authority. She met them in what she considered to be the appropriate way by having the Archbishop of St Andrews summon another provincial Council to consider their demands, but before that Council could meet there took place an important event which was to alter the whole complexion of international politics. On 17 November 1558 Mary Tudor died.

She was succeeded by her half-sister Elizabeth, and although Elizabeth went cautiously at first, everyone knew that she herself was a Protestant. Initially, however, Mary of Guise felt that things were moving in her favour. She was gradually building up her authority again in spite of the recent challenge to her position. Indeed, when the King of France demanded that the Scottish crown be sent to France for the coronation of the Dauphin, Mary managed to persuade the reluctant Scots to agree. Although in the end the crown never was actually sent, Mary regarded parliament's agreement to her request as something of a personal triumph. Her hand was further strengthened when Spain, England's ally, signed first of all a truce with France and then in the spring of 1559 drew up a peace treaty which included the Scots. The treaty of Cateau-Cambrésis meant that France was no longer in any danger from England and the Scots would not be called upon to invade their southern neighbour. Mary could concentrate on domestic policies. Now was the time for her to assert her authority once and for all over her troublesome subjects.

She had reckoned without the strength of the opposition. In Elizabeth of England, all those Scots who disliked the French alliance or hated the Catholic Church found a powerful source of support. When Mary Tudor was on the throne of England they could not expect any measure of help, but now it was once more worthwhile being an Anglophile and a Protestant. Emboldened by their hopes of English assistance, the Protestants on 1 January 1559 pinned to the doors of the Scottish friaries copies of a document known as 'The Beggars' Summons', warning the friars that they must give up all their property to the poor and infirm not later than the Whitsunday Term – the usual date for entry and removing of tenants.

For the next few weeks there was an uneasy lull, but as the appointed day approached, events began to move with alarming rapidity. On 2 May 1559 John Knox the preacher arrived back in Scotland after the years of exile which had followed his capture at the siege of St Andrews and his period in the French galleys. His friends had urged him to return before, but not until now had he decided that the time was right. He had a burning enthusiasm for the Protestant cause and a way with words. His coming obviously heralded an important new phase in the Protestant campaign. Six days after his arrival Queen Elizabeth aligned herself firmly with the English Protestants when she gave her assent to her parliament's legislation restoring royal supremacy over the Church and authorizing the use of the English Prayer Book.

According to Knox, Mary of Guise had since Easter begun 'to spew forth and disclose the latent venom of her double heart. Then began she to frown, and to look frowardly to all such as she knew did favour the Evangel of Jesus Christ . . . for from that day forward, she appeared altogether altered, insomuch that her countenance and deeds did declare the venom of her heart'. She summoned the preachers to appear before her at Stirling.

In spite of Knox's version of events, Mary had not changed at all. She knew that, as the day appointed by the Beggars' Summons approached, she must take action. She could not allow her authority to be challenged any further. It seemed as though her people would actually rise up against her. Such violence and unrest threatened to disturb the entire realm unless she did something. She decided to outlaw and to banish those agitators who were stirring up sedition. Once they were removed from the scene, their misguided supporters would realize the folly of their recent actions and would return to their obedience to the established authorities. When the Protestants heard that their preachers had been summoned, they flocked to their side, intending to accompany them to

Stirling. This was the last sort of disturbance which Mary wanted, so she sent John Erskine of Dun to persuade them to stay where they were. She then had the preachers outlawed in their absence.

John Knox's reaction to this was to begin a series of inflammatory sermons. He went first to Dundee and then he moved on to Perth. There, on 11 May, he preached in St John's Kirk a sermon which roused his congregation to violent action. A boy threw a stone at a statue, then they were all on their feet, smashing images, tearing down furnishings, trampling on candles and service books. Pushing their way out of the church, they ran along the streets of Perth, gathering excited followers as they went. In a noisy mob they forced their way into the town's friaries, destroying, looting and driving out the terrified occupants.[16]

Mary was appalled when they brought her the news. She felt acute personal distress at the desecration of holy places and at the threat to the monks and nuns. She was greatly angered at the challenge to the authority of both Church and state. She must act at once. She began by summoning the Duke of Châtelherault to come to see her. Her advisers looked doubtful about that. Everyone knew about the Duke's previous Protestant sympathies and there were persistent rumours that he was on the point of declaring himself for the 'Congregation' in Perth. Mary knew him better, though. No one need expect decisive action from him. He would come if she told him to.

To the surprise of many observers he arrived in Stirling. He was shown into Mary's presence, looking more shifty than ever. Seizing the advantage, Mary upbraided him for his inactivity. 'My Lord,' she said with deceptive sweetness, 'I marvel at you, you being second person of Scotland and none between you and the authority but my daughter, who has no succession as yet, and I but a woman that knows not the nature nor falsity of men and baronage of Scotland and I believe they stand in no awe of me because I am but a woman and therefore I marvel at you that you will not help to come at the men that so abuse the common weal and policy of the country in casting down of abbeys and religious places and destroying the liberty of Holy Kirk. I think it should be your duty and your brother's to defend the realm so far as it lies in your power . . .'[17]

She looked at him narrowly as she said this. Surely the flattery, the appeal to his position, the hint that he might yet be King would have the desired effect? He mumbled something about the Reformers, about abuses, about the need for improvement. She spoke to him of the need for peace. She told him that she required his help. She intended to ride out against the rebels in person. She could not do so unless he were at her side. As usual, he was easily convinced; 'by her fair ways and subtle words she brought the Duke to her purpose'. They rode out of Stirling together at the head of a small army.[18]

She had given careful thought about whether or not to accompany her forces. In many ways, it was the last thing she wanted to do. Apart from her distaste for violence, she was far from well and she did not know how she would stand up to the strain of such a demanding journey. On the other hand, the most effective way of asserting her authority was to go in person. When the rebels saw her with her army, they would not dare to take the field against her. They would disperse to their homes, her men could arrest their leaders and order would be restored. Unfortunately, her own invincible courage did not make up for the deficiencies of her army. She had eight or nine hundred French soldiers with her but there were perpetual troubles between them and the Scots. As for the latter, the English were quick to point out that 'many of those with the Queen being of like religion and kindred with the other faction it will likely end without a battle'.[19]

The first night Mary travelled as far as Auchterarder, in Perthshire. There she decided to wait until her artillery could be brought from Edinburgh and Stirling. This was a slow business as always, for local teams of oxen had to be pressed into service to drag the heavy guns across country. She was therefore forced to spend about a week at Auchterarder, during which time the Protestants rallied local sympathizers to their cause and sent to the Earl of Glencairn to bring reinforcements from the west.

At last the artillery arrived, and towards the end of the

month Mary and her army advanced to a position outside Perth. There they soon discovered the weakness of their situation. Spies brought back word that three thousand Protestants were drawn up on the Inch, a flat, grassy area on the edge of the town. Not only were they ready to resist, but news was coming in that Glencairn was arriving with several thousand soldiers of his own.

It was obvious that Mary could not crush the opposition by force. She would have to negotiate. She accordingly appointed her stepson Lord James Stewart to act on her behalf, along with Châtelherault's nephew Argyll. The Protestants named the Earl of Glencairn and Erskine of Dun to act for them. Long discussions followed until, on 29 May 1559, agreement was reached. Both armies were to disband, leaving Mary free to enter the town. None of the inhabitants was to be punished for the recent troubles or on account of support of the Protestant cause and no Frenchman was to enter Perth or indeed to come within three miles of it. When the Queen eventually left, she was not to leave a French garrison behind her. All other causes of dissension were to be referred to parliament.[20]

The day after the agreement was signed, the Congregation, as the Protestants now called themselves, left Perth and Mary made her entrance into the town. The sight of the damage done there rekindled her anger against the Protestants and she was particularly distressed by the destruction done to the monasteries. The worst feature of the whole episode was that the Charterhouse had been damaged. It was the only Carthusian house in Scotland, and it had been founded by James I, who was buried there. She gave immediate orders for repairs to be made wherever possible, then she turned her attention to the re-establishment of royal authority within the town. The provost, Lord Ruthven, was a supporter of the Reformers so she dismissed him, replacing him by one of her own local supporters, the Laird of Kinfauns. Civil order restored once more, she garrisoned the town with Scottish soldiers in French pay, then she withdrew to Falkland.

Some English observers were of the opinion that 'the business between the Dowager and her commons is now pacified',[21] but such was far from being the case. Mary and her advisers were well aware of the gravity of the situation. The agreement at Perth had saved face for them, but nothing had been resolved. As D'Oysel told his friend, the French ambassador in England, their troubles continued on all sides and increased from day to day. The insurgents declared that they had been moved to take action by considerations of religion, but in D'Oysel's opinion 'They have another plan in mind'. These 'new Christians' had now assembled their forces near St Andrews and they had with them Lord James and Argyll, who had changed sides on the pretext that Mary had violated the Perth agreement by leaving French-paid soldiers in Perth. 'In short,' D'Oysel observed wryly, 'you can never know here who is the friend or the enemy, for he who is with us in the morning is with them after dinner.'[22]

It seemed that every day the Protestants were growing in strength. They were continually declaring themselves loyal to Mary, Queen of Scots and Francis, yet each day they were taking up arms against their Queen Regent, pillaging and damaging the abbeys. Mary feared that it was now simply a matter of time until the Duke of Châtelherault deserted her and joined them instead. Her intelligence system was as efficient as ever, and she was receiving reports that the rebels had two new moves in mind. They would seek the support of the English and they would send for Châtelherault's eldest son, who now bore his father's previous title of Earl of Arran.

The boy's upbringing had been unsettled, to say the least. Given as a hostage to Cardinal Beaton for his father's good behaviour, he had been captured by the murderers of Beaton, released, and eventually sent to the King of France – once more as a hostage for Châtelherault's good behaviour. He had made himself popular with Henry II, becoming a leading member of the Scots Guard. Not long before, however, he had suddenly announced his fervent support for Protestantism. His future at the French Court was in doubt, and the Scottish Protestants were quick to see that if he could be brought back to Scotland his presence would have a significant effect. Châtelherault would be won over to the Protestant cause and, if there was the possibility of deposing the existing rulers, in Arran they had a candidate for the throne.²³ Encouraged by these ambitious plans, the Congregation went ahead with the 'reforming' of churches in the St Andrews area, casting down statues, burning the famous Rood of Crail and generally destroying other 'popish' furnishings.²⁴

Waiting in her Palace of Falkland for news of the latest outrage, Mary of Guise knew that the agreement at Perth had resolved nothing. The campaign against the rebels was only beginning and she would have to move against them once more. This time she would send Châtelherault and D'Oysel with her army. She herself was in no condition to accompany them. She had been feeling ill for some weeks now, and after the exhausting march on Perth with its attendant nervous strain she could not hope to take the field in person. She might have all the energy, the courage and the resolution of her father and her brothers but she did not have their physical strength. While her army marched north to meet the rebels, she would rest at Falkland.

Hearing of her military preparations, the Protestants marched west from St Andrews to Cupar, where they drew up their army on the moor. When Châtelherault and D'Oysel arrived with their forces, Lord Lindsay attempted to act as an intermediary. He went first to the Duke, urging him not to take up arms against a force which included Châtelherault's own nephew, Argyll, and he upbraided him for continuing to serve Mary. He then went to D'Oysel and told him that Châtelherault would never willingly fight his own kin when it came to the point, for, as the old Scots saying had it, 'I may well see my friend need but I will not see him bleed'.

Châtelherault seemed to be open to conviction. D'Oysel was more obstinate. However, he was persuaded to climb to the top of the Hill of Tarvit to survey the enemy forces for himself, and when he looked down on Cupar Moor he realized that his men were gravely outnumbered. He agreed to come to terms. By this new agreement the French with their artillery would retire first to Falkland, then to Lothian. Mary of Guise would be free to ride throughout Fife with her retinue as she had always done, but without any French soldiers accompanying her. For her part, she would accord to the Protestants liberty of conscience in worship. They would then disband their army.[25]

With the withdrawal of the French soldiers, Mary knew that she could not safely remain in Fife. She decided to retire to Edinburgh. On 25 June she received word that the Protestants were once more on the move. They were marching to Perth, to eject the provost she had chosen. This time there was no question of her trying to enforce her authority. She knew that she could do nothing. She remained in Edinburgh, receiving frequent reports of what was happening.

Law and order had broken down completely. The Protestants entered Perth. Their followers, quite out of control, poured out of the town to Scone where an ancient abbey stood, the traditional crowning place of the Scottish Kings. The mob looted it and the nearby Palace of Scone, then they set fire to both buildings. After that they marched to Stirling where they seized the town and ejected the friars. Helpless in the face of this tide of violence, Mary felt that even in Edinburgh Castle she was not entirely safe. The stronghold was virtually impregnable but if the town were taken she would be marooned in her fortress, cut off from all communication with France. With a small party of followers she therefore slipped out of Edinburgh and rode for the Castle of Dunbar. Perched on the edge of the North Sea, the castle would be an ideal refuge. She could wait safely there until French aid arrived or, if the peril grew too great, she could make her escape by sea.[26]

She had made her move not a moment too soon. At 3 a.m. on 30 June the forces of the Congregation entered Edinburgh. They pulled down images in friaries and abbeys, burned missals and removed chalices. Even so, Mary remained convinced that their true motives had nothing to do with theology. On 1 July she issued letters declaring that the Congregation had ignored her attempts to pacify the troubles and had plainly shown that it was not a change in religion which they sought but the subversion of her authority and the usurpation of her crown. The same letters ordered proclamations to be made in Edinburgh commanding the Congregation and all other strangers to leave the town within six hours.[27]

D'Oysel's letters from Dunbar to the French ambassador in England underlined his and Mary's attitude to the current troubles. As D'Oysel said, the situation was displeasing. The preachers in Edinburgh were still declaring that they had no design other than the establishment of the Evangelic faith, but he himself was in no doubt that they wished to undermine the royal authority on the pretext of religion and drive out the French. He had heard that they were furious that Mary had retired to Dunbar, knowing that they could not cause her the alarm there that they had done formerly.[28]

Mary could do nothing positive until French help arrived. She was reduced to temporizing once more, exchanging with her opponents a series of demands and counter-demands. In the end, when a message did come from France it did not bring the news she had been expecting. Instead of word of the promised help, she received letters announcing that Henry II had suffered a serious accident. While tilting with his friend Monsieur de Lorges, Captain of the Scots Guard, he had been struck on the face by De Lorges's lance. A splinter had entered his forehead, immediately above the right eye. He had been carried into the palace and the splinter had been removed. His doctors were optimistic in spite of the gravity of the injury. They predicted cheerfully that he would make a speedy recovery, but obviously his life was in some danger. When she heard what had happened, Mary of Guise was greatly saddened and depressed. She had known Henry since their youth: indeed, it had once been rumoured that he was in love with her. She was personally distressed to hear of his injury. Moreover, she had looked to him as a source of strength and assistance. Now it seemed that Henry might die, that her own son-in-law and daughter would become King and Queen of France. In some respects this alteration in circumstances might be advantageous. Her own brothers would be in the ascendant at Court and young Francis would do whatever they wished. What really mattered, though, was the effect that the loss of Mary's powerful and mature ally would have on the Protestants.

As D'Oysel was to tell his friend Monsieur de Noailles, the Congregation were greatly encouraged by the news of Henry's condition.[29] They had already been emboldened by the news that the young Earl of Arran, summoned to the French Court to answer charges against him, had somehow slipped out of the country. By the beginning of July it was rumoured that he had reached the safety of Geneva, and the Protestants in Scotland were convinced that he was on his way home. Once he was with them their position would be immeasurably strengthened. The tide was turning in their favour, and the news of Henry II's injury confirmed their feeling that things would go well with them. Eager for action, on 21 July they seized Scotland's coining irons which had been kept at the mint at Holyroodhouse.

Mary of Guise heard what they had done the following morning, and her anger was aroused. The Protestants were obviously taking advantage of her weakness to try to wrest the royal authority from her completely. She lost no time in summoning Châtelherault, Huntly and her other supporters to a Council meeting and there she announced that she had resolved that they should march on Edinburgh. As D'Oysel made clear, writing within hours of the Council meeting which he had attended, this was her personal decision. The Protestants must be driven from Edinburgh, Mary declared, and she pointed out that Lord Erskine, the keeper of Edinburgh Castle, would probably give her his support. In spite of the objections of her listeners, who protested that their forces were too small to be effective, she managed to persuade them to agree to her plan.[30]

Mary did not ride out from Dunbar with her army: she sent D'Oysel and Châtelherault ahead. They had only about 1700 men with them but they had heard that the Congregation were drifting back to their own homes from Edinburgh and so they planned to march straight into the town.[31] The Protestants, however, got word of their intentions and drew up their forces just outside the town. The French accordingly marched to Leith instead, and took possession. Neither side was anxious for an actual conflict, and so they entered into negotiations once more.

Agreement was reached on Leith Links on 23 July 1559. The Congregation promised to leave Edinburgh early the following day. They would deliver up the coining irons and all the coins in their possession and they would surrender the Palace of Holyroodhouse. They would obey the authority of Mary, Queen of Scots, the Dauphin and the Queen Regent, according to the existing laws of the realm. They said that they would molest neither churches nor churchmen. In return, Mary of Guise's commissioners promised that the people of Edinburgh should be free to choose whichever form of worship they desired, and they undertook that no one would interfere with the Protestant preachers.[32]

Two days later D'Oysel, Châtelherault and Huntly entered Edinburgh, received the coining irons and took possession of Holyroodhouse. When order had been restored, Mary of Guise returned from Dunbar to Edinburgh. The members of the Congregation had indeed dispersed, retiring to their homes, and Mary and her supporters told themselves hopefully that her unruly subjects now showed more appearance of staying peacefully at home than they had done since the beginning of the troubles. Even so, they feared privately that the Protestants were merely taking a rest, harbouring their resources before beginning another offensive. Mary knew that she must prevent further tumults at all costs, preserving a measure of peace until the long-expected reinforcements arrived from France.[33]

10

The Final Struggle

The appearance of peace was indeed no more than an illusion. On 1 August members of the Congregation signed a bond agreeing that none of their number should go to see or speak to the Queen Regent without the consent of the rest and that any message from her should similarly be made public to all. So much did her opponents fear the power of Mary's charm that they could not trust anyone to converse with her in private lest she suborn them. Such suspicion was hardly a sign of future stability, nor did the news that John Knox had gone to meet the English leaders at Holy Island augur well for the weeks ahead. Much to the annoyance of the English themselves, Knox made no attempt to keep his mission secret and Mary soon knew that he was trying to find out whether Queen Elizabeth would be willing to enter into an alliance with the Scottish Protestants.[1]

Mary would have been even more alarmed had she known that Elizabeth was already planning to send a dangerous emissary. On 7 August the English Queen gave instructions to Sir Ralph Sadler to go north, ostensibly to see about the fortifications at Berwick. His public commission was innocuous enough but his private instructions were much more damaging. In a secret memorandum, Elizabeth told Sadler that he was to nourish faction against the French, that he was to urge Châtelherault to abandon Mary of Guise, that he was to persuade the Duke to arrest D'Oysel, and that he was to put pressure on the nobility to have Mary make a treaty of perpetual peace with England.[2]

Mary, for her part, was extremely active. Reports from France about Henry II's condition had become more and more worrying. Instead of making the predicted recovery, he was steadily sinking and a fortnight after his accident he died. Mary did not hear the news until 7 August, when she wrote a letter to Monsieur de Noailles acknowledging his announcement of 'the sad news of the death of the best prince in the world, at which I am greatly saddened, as you may imagine. I do not know where to seek consolation unless with God, who is master of all . . .'.[3]

The realization that her powerful ally had gone and that the rebels would take advantage of this fact inspired Mary to even more energetic preparations than before. She was occupied in trying to assemble all the forces she could, she was arranging to send ordnance to Stirling and she was perpetually trying to win back more of the lords to her cause. She also continued a manner of public dialogue with the Protestants, in the form of various proclamations and counter-proclamations. In these, she made it plain once again that it was the challenge to the royal authority which most nearly concerned her. She complained, for instance, that preachers in their public sermons were speaking irreverently of princes in general and of herself in particular. This, she argued, had nothing to do with religion but told only of sedition and tumult. She urged the Congregation to see that in future the preachers did not meddle so much with civil policy and public government but instead named her and other princes with reverence and honour.[4]

For their part, the Congregation complained bitterly of the French presence in Scotland, of attempts to change Scottish laws and to introduce French-style taxation, of debasing of the coinage and of the appointment of Frenchmen to important offices of state.[5] Reading their replies, Mary was simply confirmed in her opinion that the present difficulties had indeed little to do with religion but much to do with French rule and the authority of the monarchy.

As these communications were exchanged, the Protestant lords had assembled in Glasgow to await the one event which, it seemed to them, would set the whole revolution in motion – the return of the Earl of Arran. Days passed with no word of him, then at last, amidst a cloud of rumour, came definite news. He had been in Antwerp on 25 August and four days later he arrived in London. He was taken secretly to the house of Sir William Cecil in Westminster and there he was concealed while the English interrogated him, assessed him and finally decided that he suited their purpose. On 20 August he had a carefully arranged 'accidental' meeting with Queen Elizabeth of England in the gardens of Hampton Court. What exactly passed between them is not known but she must have promised him her support. It is ironical to think that many years before Henry VIII had tried to bribe Châtelherault by offering him Elizabeth as a wife for Arran.

Immediately after his talk with the Queen, Arran left for Scotland. He travelled incognito, with the Englishman Thomas Randolph as his companion.[6] The day after she had sent Arran north with her encouragement and support, Elizabeth was blandly assuring the French ambassador that the Scottish rebels could hope for nothing from her. Leading Monsieur de Noailles into her Gallery at Hampton Court, she showed him a portrait of Mary of Guise and expatiated at length upon the theme of the Queen Regent's honesty, goodness and virtue.[7]

Meanwhile, Arran and Randolph were riding northwards with all speed. By the morning of 6 September they had reached Alnwick. French, Scots and English were all awaiting news of him with bated breath. Scotland was alive with rumours that he had been sighted, first in one place then in another. His gentleman, a man named Forbes, was seen in Berwick and the news was carried swiftly north. No one waited more anxiously to have confirmation of his coming than did Mary of Guise. She still cherished the hope that his arrival might have good results, that he might wish somehow to pacify the current troubles, though she feared that he had already been so spoiled by those men misled by the 'new opinions' that he would do nothing but harm.[8]

By the time she wrote to Monsieur de Noailles expressing her fears, Arran was already safe in Hamilton Castle with his father.[9] His coming was indeed to have a momentous effect on

Scottish affairs. Now the Scots had an alternative candidate for the Regency, if not for the throne of Scotland. Châtelherault was obviously useless for either position, and so the Protestants had hesitated to move decisively against Mary, even though her step-son Lord James had recently been putting himself forward as an alternative. Because he was illegitimate, his position was weak. Arran was a very different matter though and, unlike his father, he was young, energetic and apparently decisive.

Reunited with the Duke at Hamilton, he spent two days there, during which time Lord James and the Earl of Argyll visited him. Satisfied with his intentions, they carried him off to Stirling to meet the rest of the Congregation. The lords greeted him with delight. Their morale was immediately raised and they felt that their position had been immeasurably strengthened. Châtelherault's half-brother, the Archbishop of St Andrews, came to tell Mary of Guise the details and they agreed that it was all too probable that it was simply a matter of time before the Duke declared himself for the rebels, who would then attempt to put the government of the country into the hands of himself and his son.

Discussing these events anxiously with Monsieur D'Oysel, Mary decided that she would have to take defensive action. The situation was becoming acutely dangerous and if the Congregation marched on Edinburgh again, this time with Châtelherault and Arran at their head, the Queen and her supporters would be in grave peril. It was therefore agreed that Monsieur D'Oysel should fortify Leith, which, in Mary's own words, would then be 'a place of retreat for the French' and for herself and her friends. In a desperate attempt to counter the influence of the Hamiltons, she wrote urgent letters to France, begging young Francis II to sequester the lands and revenues of the duchy of Châtelherault until she saw whether or not the Duke would remain loyal. She also urged that his son David who was in France should be strictly guarded and his servant Captain James Hamilton arrested.[10]

These requests were not the vengeful demands of a merciless tyrant but rather the desperate attempts of a woman in an increasingly dangerous position. Mary knew that she was losing supporters every day. She had already sent for assistance from the French King and although promises came in plenty from her own brothers, as yet no army had materialized. Even as she finished her letter about the Hamiltons, the Archbishop of St Andrews came to her with tears in his eyes to warn her that his family and their friends were preparing to act against her. The soldiers she had were poorly paid, 'our credit decreases daily and our expenses multiply by the hour thanks to the malice of the times and of men . . .' Mary explained sadly as she concluded her letter.[11]

Three days later she wrote again to the French King, and this time her letter contained the bitter confirmation of her earlier fears. 'Sire,' she began, 'this is to tell you that the Duke of Châtelherault has wasted no time after his son's arrival in declaring himself chief and leader of your rebels. For this he had found no better cover than to say that I am fortifying Leith and on this news he and all the said rebels who have assembled in his house of Hamilton have written me a letter of menace and defiance of which I enclose the translation. And they are now leaving to go and gather their men with all diligence for the purpose of interrupting our enterprise, defying me and your men if they can, and at least interfering with us in every way they can by cutting off our supplies and fuel as well as by circulating rumours to win over more and more people and alienate them from you, saying, Sire, that you and the French wish to subvert all their laws and place them in extreme servitude . . . For this reason,' she continued, 'I beg you most humbly, Sire, to have pity on us and help us with good forces and money as quickly as possible, not doubting that the said Duke and his accomplices will do all they can as soon as possible, not forgetting to have dealing with the English.'[12]

After composing this letter, Mary wrote a less formal message to her brothers, equally urgent in tone. 'Our troubles and affairs increase here by the hour . . .' she reported, 'and I am reduced to such need that I shall be forced to retire with all the French to Leith, very poorly furnished with money and with little in the way of food and other supplies . . . As you know, in times of such great change, things are difficult, for it is the greatest in the land who have banded themselves together to authorize (as they put it) the religion which they profess and to advance it by arms, which is the point by which I understand that they want under that pretext to make a King from among themselves . . . It displeases me extremely to see such an unhappy state of affairs here, but one must have patience, do what one can and rely on God and on one's friends.'

For this last reason, she said, she was begging for help, both in the form of men and of money. 'As for myself,' she explained, 'I am very poorly paid as far as the revenues of the Queen and my dowry are concerned, there being, as you know, such disorder among the people here that I do not know where to find wood to make arrows . . .'

Once again her writing was interrupted by a messenger bearing grave news. Châtelherault and his men were assembling and 'we will neither have time to get together supplies nor fortify ourselves properly and they will make a change in the authority of the country, so I beg you to send help soon for I make no doubt that our need is greater than ever. They are secretly helped by the English and they will do all they can to ruin both the Queen and her mother which will, I think, touch your heart, for it is not for my own cause that I suffer so many evils.'[13]

Mary judged correctly that the fortifying of Leith had enraged her opponents, who now accused her of breaking the previous agreement at Leith and of planning to subvert the whole country. With their new-found confidence resulting from the return of Arran, they were eager to seize on any new pretext for moving against the French. In spite of the urgent tone of her letters to France, Mary remained calm and in control of the situation. Not only did she hasten the forti- fication of Leith but she tried hard to win Châtelherault back to her side. She sent Archbishop Hamilton to his half-brother to see if he could be persuaded to abandon his new friends, but the Archbishop found him greatly subdued and subjected by the Congregation and could only warn Mary to 'provide for the worst and to make yourself strong in all sorts'.[14]

Even more than she wanted to win back Châtelherault, Mary wanted to regain the support of her step-son, Lord James. To modern eyes it may seem strange that for so long did she cherish hopes of winning back to her side that determined Protestant known to history as the Earl of Moray, but to Mary he was, first and foremost, her husband's son. She had known him from his childhood and she could not believe that he would ignore her pleas. He was able and he was energetic and she was anxious to have him with her. At the end of September 1559 she sent a special emissary to him, promising him freedom of conscience in religious concerns and emphasizing her own desire for reconciliation.[15]

Her pleas were ignored. The Protestants were moving inexorably towards a confrontation with her. At the beginning of October she issued a proclamation rehearsing recent events and emphasizing once more that the present quarrel was 'no matter of religion but a plain usurpation of authority'.[16] The lords replied by repeating their grievances over the fortification of Leith and the bringing in of the French. They denied that they wished to set up Arran in authority, declaring that they had sought English help simply for God's greater glory. The tone of the reply was intemperate to say the least, stating as it did that princes always break promises to their subjects.[17] Mary was hardly likely to receive the missive with pleasure, and her indignation was increased when her excellent intelligence system reported that Queen Elizabeth was supplying Sadler with sums of money for the purpose of bribing the Scots.[18]

On 6 October the Congregation issued a further manifesto putting forward their grievances in great detail and inveighing against the French. This they followed up a day later by demanding that all French soldiers be removed from Scotland. Mary was still in residence at Holyroodhouse, but she was ready to leave at a moment's notice to take refuge in Leith. She had already sent all her belongings there. Sir Ralph Sadler's spies were reporting that Mary was in great perplexity, very weak and sickly, and 'some think cannot long continue'. Her activities that autumn were astonishing in view of her failing health. Summoning up the amazing energy which characterized her family, she cheered her household when their spirits flagged and she carried on determinedly. 'Some say that she is very sick,' Arran's companion Randolph commented, 'others that the devil cannot kill her.'[19]

She was to need all her courage. On 15 October the Protestants assembled at Stirling and, with Châtelherault at their head, they marched to Edinburgh. They took the town, but they did not find the Queen Regent there. She had slipped away to Leith. With the Protestants threatening daily to besiege the port she renewed her pleas to France, begging the King to send her brother, the Marquis D'Elboeuf, with immediate aid and urging that an even greater force be sent after him.

Her plight was desperate, for her supporters were diminishing daily. She had with her the faithful D'Oysel, Châtelherault's brother the Archbishop, the Archbishop of Glasgow, the Bishop of Dunkeld and Lord Seton.[20] All the other lords of note had either left her or were remaining neutral, and on 21 October the final blow fell. The lords of the Congregation announced that her Regency was suspended. As she would no longer acknowledge them as her subjects, they said, they would no longer acknowledge her as Queen Regent. Her authority was transferred to a Council of Regency under the leadership of Châtelherault.[21]

When Mary received from them the letter announcing this decision she was indignant, but she was far from being intimidated. She sent them a proud reply, refusing to submit to the terms of a message 'which appears to come from a Prince to his subjects rather than from subjects to one that bears authority'.[22] She would not for one moment consider their impertinent orders and in any case she knew that they were much weaker than they would admit. They too lacked money. Their leaders were divided as to whether or not they should besiege Leith. They were far from being the powerful, united force that they would have had her believe.

Proof of this was forthcoming a fortnight later. The Protestants made an assault on the town. D'Oysel marched out with his men, encountered them at Restalrig, between Leith and Edinburgh, and drove them off. So decisive was the action that the Congregation retreated to Edinburgh and held urgent consultations. At midnight on 5–6 November they abandoned the town, marching out to Linlithgow. The following morning at ten o'clock Mary of Guise entered the capital once more.[23]

With her return, she set about undoing the damage done by her opponents. Mass was said once more in the town churches. The buildings themselves were repaired, the ecclesiastical furnishings restored, and the Church of St Giles was reconsecrated. Mary continued to style herself Regent as she had always done. The French continued to fortify Leith while the Congregation remained disconsolately at Linlithgow, arguing about what to do next.

Even so, Mary's triumph was destined to be short-lived, for only a fortnight after she had taken up residence again at Holyrood, she fell so seriously ill that her friends despaired of her life and her enemies broadcast rumours of her death. Hearing these, Sadler observed 'we think this too good to be true, yet she is in great extremity of sickness'.[24]

The nature of her illness is revealed in various contemporary documents. An undated memorandum is entitled 'Advice of the Queen's Doctor'. This is usually assigned to the time of Mary's marriage to James V, but the general context suggests that it would more properly belong to the late autumn of 1559. Reference is made, for instance, to her need to avoid the cares of state which were so bad for her. This is obviously more appropriate advice for the harassed Regent of later years than for the young wife who was frustrated by the very lack of any public activity.

Whatever the date of the memorandum, it is an extremely interesting one. Her symptoms, it records, were severe palpitations, resulting in insomnia, a heaviness of the body, languour, a livid complexion and a general feeling of melancholy. A French doctor whose advice had been sought opined that such a condition was difficult to cure and was caused by 'an abundance of humours spread throughout the body', a diagnosis which may be interpreted as referring to a retention of fluid in the tissues. In order to effect a cure, Mary must avoid all worry and trouble. She should take a little gentle exercise each day, preferably after meals. She should live in a place where the air was pure, clear and healthy, far away from the sea and from crowded places, nor should she stay long in an area which was cold, damp or misty.[25]

There was no doubt that the Queen's malady was as serious as her friends feared it to be. When the symptoms described in the memorandum are considered alongside the other evidence of her illness[26] it seems clear that she was suffering from chronic heart disease, probably of a valvular nature. Such a condition would be caused perhaps by a childhood illness such as rheumatic fever. Very often the effects of the damage on the heart muscle are not felt until the menopause in women, and then the trouble is exacerbated by stress or worry. It is interesting to note that the recommendations made by the French doctor accord very well with the advice given by medical men today for comparable illness: then as now, rest, freedom from worry and mild exercise were recommended. The fact that Mary's doctor suggested that she should avoid a damp climate seems to bear out the theory that she had at some time suffered from rheumatic fever.

The medical advice makes sadly ironical reading. Mary could not avoid the cares of state which were increasing daily. She could not avoid the cold and damp, for the Scottish winter was fast approaching. She could not avoid being near the sea, for Edinburgh stands on the estuary of the River Forth and she might well have to return to Leith itself. It was possibly because of this memorandum that the French began to think seriously of persuading her to come back to Paris to recover her health while her young brother René, the Marquis D'Elboeuf, replaced her as Regent.[27]

Reports of her serious illness continued to circulate throughout November and well into December. On 30 November she was said to be partly convalescent but 'without hope of long life'.[28] Sadler on 5 December was echoing this comment with the remark that Mary languished in great sickness and that her physicians believed that she could not long continue.[29] They reckoned without her extraordinary willpower, however. Three weeks later she was reported as being much improved, and Monsieur de Noailles was able to tell the French King that she had been 'extremely ill' but was now in good health.[30] By sheer determination she had pulled back from the brink of death and it was not without cause that one contemporary who condemned her as 'a haughty Frenchwoman' was nevertheless forced to praise her as 'a woman with a man's courage' who, 'though she was daily deserted by some of her own party, was no ways dismayed'.[31]

On Christmas Eve she was as active as ever she had been, holding a Council meeting with D'Oysel and with two other Frenchmen recently arrived. One was her old friend Jacques de la Brosse, the other the Bishop of Amiens. They had come over from France some weeks before as emissaries of Francis II. As a result of their deliberations, D'Oysel was sent on an expedition to Stirling where he hoped to surprise the leaders of the Congregation. Forewarned, however, they had dispersed before he could come near them.[32] Because of bad weather he stayed on at Stirling for some days, gathering reports that the Protestant forces had moved to Fife. When the bad weather abated, he sent his troops east and drove the rebels back to St Andrews while French soldiers occupied the ports of Kinghorn, Kirkcaldy and Dysart.

The news of this success cheered Mary tremendously and she wrote at once to Monsieur de Noailles to give him details. 'It is good to defeat such men,' she observed, 'who, in place of truth are accustomed to spreading lies: but I am happy that they have only words and we have deeds.' Her other comments show that her intentions were far from bloodthirsty. 'I tell you,' she went on, 'that it is to my very great regret that their infidelity has constrained me to use force, but the best thing that I see is that God has left such a good and great number of men of goodwill far outnumbering the others . . .'[33]

In her letters to Monsieur de Noailles and to other friends,

Mary was much concerned with the attitude of Queen Elizabeth. When she had heard that Elizabeth had succeeded to the throne of England she had remembered the pale, sharp-faced, red-haired young girl she had met on her visit to London and she had not been unduly concerned. Elizabeth, her husband's cousin, was still only twenty-six. Mary was a mature forty-four. She felt that she had nothing to fear from the younger woman. But there was a significant difference between them, age apart. For all her subtlety and dissimulation, Mary's natural instincts were towards honesty and she looked for honesty from other people. This explained her feelings of disillusion both with her husband and with her lords. She had inherited her mother's straightforward outlook and, although she learned to play the game of diplomacy, her letters to her family reveal a woman who had little real patience with deceit. Elizabeth, learning from early childhood that her only means of self-preservation was through a web of deception, had a very different outlook on life. Deviousness came to her naturally by the time she was Queen.

Of course, those who had dealings with Elizabeth realized that she could not be trusted. Monsieur de Noailles listened to her protestations but he decided that she was going to do all she could to help the Scottish rebels, that she would encourage the Scots to have Arran crowned King, and that he would hold his kingdom of her, handing over its strongholds to her.[34]

Apprised of these suspicions, it was with mounting alarm that Mary of Guise listened to the messengers who came hurrying to her presence on 22 January 1560. Agitatedly her spies reported that eight ships had been seen off the coast of Dunbar, sailing northwards. Some thought that they were the long-awaited ships of the Marquis D'Elboeuf bringing French aid, others said they must be English since a boat which sailed out to them was not allowed to go near. On hearing of their presence, Mary instantly dispatched a man to North Berwick to seek further news.[35]

Her worst fears were confirmed on the following day when the ships appeared in the Firth of Forth. They were English. Elizabeth had decided to send north a small fleet under the command of Admiral Winter, with instructions to harry the French and intercept any French aid. They sailed into the road of Leith, capturing two Scottish ships which had been on the point of sailing across to Fife with munitions for the French soldiers there.[36]

Perhaps because of the gravity of the situation, Mary was filled with a new energy. She sent men to garrison Inchkeith. She spoke to all the sergeants who had come to Edinburgh to report on what forces they could muster with a view to attacking the English vessels. 'The Queen forgets nothing,' one of her friends remarked, and it was true.[37] 'The Queen of England's actions truly contradict her words,' she told her friends, 'for she has eight vessels in the Firth which make war openly and attack the subjects of this realm.' She sent out a herald and a messenger to demand the purpose of the visitation. Admiral Winter told them that he had been driven north by bad weather and that, far from being authorized by Elizabeth to help the rebels, he had merely decided to do so of his own accord. 'Such a pretence as this is too easy to discover,' Mary commented scornfully, 'As if a simple subject and officer had the authority or the power to make war without the very express command of his Queen, and as if one could make war at the expense of a Prince without his knowing anything of it!'

She urged Monsieur de Noailles to make immediate protests to Elizabeth. The sending of the ships into the Forth was tantamount to a declaration of war, she said, and war was the last thing she wanted. 'I have known the inconveniences of war for too long,' she confided to Monsieur de Noailles, 'and primarily for the honour of God I desire to avoid it.' She was determined not to make the first move towards hostilities, for, by remaining the innocent party, she would be sure that God was on her side should the worst come to the worst.[38]

Dissatisfied with Winter's attitude, she summoned one of his men to see her in person. When he poured out the same excuses of being driven north by bad weather, she pointed out coldly that the ships had entered the Firth when the wind was against them and had taken up a position never assumed by the English unless in time of war. They had made themselves known only to the rebels, had refused to salute the royal castles, and had captured two Scottish vessels. She had done all she could to avoid hostilities, she said, and she was mightily displeased at this breach of the peace.[39]

Her displeasure, of course, was ignored. Further vessels arrived in the Forth, and there was skirmishing with the French. She continued to supervise the fortification of Leith and she was also making alternative plans for her own safety should another emergency arise. This time she would not risk staying in a town likely to be besieged: instead, she would take her household from Holyroodhouse to Edinburgh Castle, that virtually impregnable fortress.

In the midst of these military preparations she was still trying to strengthen her own party. Even now she had not given up hope of winning back to her side Lord James and William Kirkcaldy of Grange, 'whom she weighs more than a great many of the rest'.[40] Apart from that, her fertile mind was devising a method by which she might separate the Duke of Châtelherault from the Protestants. He was in Glasgow, and in January she knew what she must do. On the 25th of that month she forged a letter purporting to be from the Duke to the King of France, begging to be taken into French protection.

The idea was unscrupulous, but it was effective. Even his intimate friends would not have been surprised to learn that the Duke was playing a double game once more, and it was not the first time that he had thrown himself on the mercy of the French King. Mary justified her action by saying herself that a message of that nature was in keeping with the Duke's character and would be the means of showing everyone his true nature. It would put him under suspicion with the English Queen and it would discredit him with his friends. She also entered into negotiations once more with the Earl of Lennox because, as she herself said, 'he is the person whom the Duke hates most in the whole world'.[41]

These were desperate expedients, but Mary was far from giving way to panic or despair. Her principal emotion was anger, anger at the Protestants and anger at Elizabeth. She was informed that the Congregation were planning another attack on Leith. The Protestants in Fife succeeded now in driving the French out of that county, whereupon Mary's supporters there deserted her cause.[42] She was losing support elsewhere, too. Fearing that Admiral Winter's expedition was the prelude to an invasion by land, she summoned all men between the ages of sixteen and sixty to be ready for war at an hour's notice, and she commanded all her subjects from Edinburgh to the Borders to break their brewing vessels and put away all their victual lest it be used by the English. This scorched earth policy proved highly unpopular. The Scots refused to follow her orders and those who had upheld her cause in the south of the country now began to drift away to support the Protestants.[43]

Mary was also writing vigorous letters of protest to the English themselves. She wrote indignantly about Admiral Winter to the Lieutenant of the North of England, the Duke of Norfolk, and he replied by sending Chester Herald to her with his reply. When he was admitted to her presence, the herald claimed later, she did not even give him time to deliver his credentials but angrily asked him what the English ships were doing in her waters. At first, he reported to Norfolk, they all talked in Scots, the Queen included, but 'the herald not well understanding, he was forced to speak French'. Needless to say, the meeting achieved nothing and at a further audience Mary's protests about Elizabeth's behaviour were ill-received.[44]

There was still no word from France of the promised aid, and at the end of February 1560 Mary's cause sustained a bitter blow. Lord James, Lord Ruthven and several companions from Fife sailed from the little port of Pittenweem on the Forth in an English vessel called *The Hound*. They were bound for Berwick, there to meet the Duke of Norfolk. On 27 February they signed the Treaty of Berwick, agreeing that Queen Elizabeth 'shall accept the said realm of Scotland, the said Duke of Châtelherault being declared by Act of Parliament to be heir apparent to the crown thereof, and the nobility and subjects of the same, into Her Majesty's protection ... Her Majesty shall with all speed send into Scotland a convenient aid of men of war on horse and foot to join with the power of the Scotsmen with artillery, munition and all other instruments of war meet for the purpose, as well by sea as by land, not only to expel the present power of French within that realm oppressing the same but also to stop, as far as conveniently may be, all greater forces of French to enter therein for the like purpose and shall continue Her Majesty's aid to the said realm, nobility and subjects of the same until the French, being enemies to the said realm, be utterly expelled thence'.

In return, the Scottish Protestants promised to support the English forces and to resist any conquest or annexation by France, sending military aid to England themselves should that country be invaded by the French. The treaty terminated with several clauses declaring that none of this altered the Scots' obedience to their Queen and her husband, except of course where subversion and oppression of the just and ancient liberties of the Scots were concerned.[45]

When she read the Articles of Berwick, Mary of Guise declared that she had never seen anything as shameful, both to the honour of God and to the reputation of the King of France. Nothing that had happened in Scotland had given her more torment, she told her brothers.[46] The complete defiance of her own authority combined with her sister Queen's open avowal of help for the rebels was to Mary the ultimate betrayal and it was this which upset her as much as the knowledge that an English invasion would now inevitably follow. More ships had arrived in the Forth and were besieging Inchkeith. The French certainly managed to capture Glasgow but they were in desperate need of money and supplies. Mary was writing daily to her brothers in France, asking for help. Their welfare had always caused her the greatest concern. They seemed oblivious to hers. The Cardinal of Lorraine and the Duke of Guise were much taken up with opposition to their own House and to the Church in France. They wrote her vague, reassuring letters but they did nothing. It was too dangerous for young René, the Marquis D'Elboeuf, to come now, they said, and anyway he had already made one attempt and had been driven back by bad weather. The winds were still not in the right direction.[47]

Mary's few remaining supporters were leaving her daily. The Earl of Huntly had for long refused to commit himself. On 5 March he joined the Congregation.[48] Others followed suit. The Lord James was deaf to her pleas.[49] At the end of the month the army of invasion entered Scotland. Led by Lord Grey, they camped at Halidon Hill on the night of 27 March. According to Sir Henry Percy, there were six thousand foot-soldiers with two thousand more on the way, seven hundred great horse, over a thousand light horse and twenty-four battery pieces. The following night they were at Haddington and on the third day they reached Musselburgh. They camped at Restalrig, just outside Edinburgh.[50]

To all Mary's other troubles now was added immediate personal danger. She could no longer remain in Holyrood-house. It was not safe to go to Leith, so the only place left was Edinburgh Castle. For many weeks she had been trying to enlist the aid of Lord Erskine, Keeper of the Castle. An old friend, his sympathies now lay with the Protestants, who confidently believed that he would hold the castle for them. He did not do so. In the end, either his loyalty to the crown out-weighed all other feelings, or he was simply won over by Mary herself. Perhaps he was persuaded by her charm or moved by pity. When he looked at the careworn face of the Regent, saw her tears, observed her sadly swollen body he knew that there was little time left for her. He opened the gates of the castle to her and on 1 April, accompanied by the Archbishop of St Andrews, by several Bishops and by her own little band of ladies, she went in for the last time.[51]

Once inside, her spirits revived. Although the English were at her gates she would still play for time, holding out until her brother came with help. D'Oysel, the Bishop of Amiens, De la Brosse, the faithful Lord Seton and the French soldiers were now together in Leith. She must keep in communication with them at all costs, and she must prevent the enemy from infiltrating the castle. She therefore made Lord Erskine promise that he would allow no one to enter and that he would speak to those outside only on her express orders. Such precautions were all too necessary in a situation where no one could be trusted.[52]

By now the Scottish Protestants had joined with the English army, and on 2 April their leaders conferred together in a church just outside Musselburgh. Lord Grey explained that he was still awaiting the arrival of his ordnance and munitions, which were coming by sea from Berwick. Once these had landed, he would go ahead and attack Leith. In the meantime, he would send a messenger to Mary of Guise.[53]

The man was escorted through the streets of Edinburgh on 4 April. He was led in by the castle gate and he found Mary standing outside her apartments, near St Margaret's Chapel. His mission was to urge her to negotiate, he said, and he tried to assure her that the English army had not come on any enterprise against the Queen and her subjects. To this Mary replied with some irony that 'it was a strange thing to see the army of one Prince enter in such a hostile manner so far into the land of another, if it had no desire for any enterprise there'.[54]

In fact, the man's arrival had come as something of a relief. If the English wished to negotiate, then negotiate she would, for by so doing she could win valuable days for herself. She would have been dismayed had she realized that out at Preston that very day Lord Grey was writing to the Duke of Norfolk declaring that he was considering changing his mind about besieging Leith. Instead, he thought of attacking Edinburgh Castle. For some reason, he believed that it would be easier to take and it had the added attraction of having the Queen Dowager inside. Most of the Scots lords were agreeable to the plan, he said, except for the relatives of Lord Erskine, so he had not finally decided. He therefore asked for Norfolk's instructions.[55]

Fortunately for Mary, Norfolk replied that an attack on the castle was out of the question. In the opinion of himself and his advisers, Elizabeth would never agree to such an act of aggression against the person of another Queen, and in any case it was not expedient to make an enemy of Lord Erskine.

Plans for negotiations were therefore put in hand. Mary and Lord Grey exchanged a series of messages, discussing the nomination of commissioners. Lord Grey's trumpeter came to Mary to say that the envoys from the English would be Sir James Croftes and Sir George Howard. He asked leave for them to come clad in shirts of mail and accompanied by a dozen men. He was well received, and given ten crowns for his trouble.

Lord Grey was in fact almost as anxious to gain time as was Mary herself. He knew that Leith was well fortified, but his own artillery had not yet come nor had the additional force of 2000 men he was expecting. To make matters worse, his army was diminishing daily as his men deserted, complaining of extreme cold and ill health. Even the horses were growing weak from lack of fodder. He needed help from England just as urgently as Mary did from France.[56]

On 6 April, he moved his men to within a mile of Leith. Next evening, his envoys went up to Edinburgh Castle. It was six o'clock when they arrived, and they were brought to a large tent which had been erected on the castle outworks. Inside the tent, Mary was waiting for them. They sat down together in this dramatic setting, perched high above the town of Edinburgh. The two men took out a paper and they read out their demands. All French soldiers should be sent home immediately and the Protestants should be allowed to present their grievances to Mary, Queen of Scots and her husband.

Mary of Guise listened, read the articles carefully for herself, then laid the scroll on the table. The first demand was out of the question, she explained, because it was quite beyond reason and could not be discussed. The King and Queen would not take orders from any other Prince in the world, much less from their own subjects. She went on to point out that she herself had always conducted the affairs of the realm according to the country's laws and with the advice of the estates.

Howard and Croftes replied that the Articles were simply a basis for negotiation. If she found them unreasonable, then perhaps she could confer with her advisers. The discussion continued. Time passed. Darkness fell and torches were lit. 'Madam,' said Sir James Croftes, who was later to be accused of partiality towards the Queen, 'You have composed so many great differences, I beseech you to bring to the settlement of this one all the means in your power for a true appeasement. Everything lies in your hands.' Mary answered that she had always been inclined towards peace, but when a troop of English cavalry had passed right under her castle walls on the previous day, how was she to think that the English wanted peace, not war? Croftes was persuasive, Mary anxious to prolong the negotiations, and in the end she agreed to put the Articles before Monsieur D'Oysel and her other advisers.[57]

When this had been done, she agreed to a further meeting, this time with representatives of the lords of the Congregation. She had little desire to see them but her brothers were now telling her that the army of assistance would not be ready to sail for Scotland until the end of July. In the meantime, the English were preparing to besiege Leith. Discussions had to go on.

At this further meeting, six commissioners, led by D'Oysel, represented Mary, while six others, including Lord James, represented the Protestants. Once again the Queen's commissioners declared that the French soldiers were still in the country only because of the great disobedience of the Scots, and that, if civil order were restored, then they would be withdrawn. Once more, the Protestants complained of their presence, and haggled over the conditions of the negotiations. In the end, further debate was deferred until the arrival of yet another intermediary, the Bishop of Valence.[58]

The Bishop had been dispatched by the French King at the end of March 1560, with instructions to go first to Elizabeth of England and then to Mary of Guise. To Elizabeth he was to speak of the French King's desire for friendship, and to explain that most of the French troops in Scotland would be withdrawn once peace was restored there. Mary of Guise he was to urge to do all she could to win the rebels back to obedience, promising that the French King would pardon all offences if order were restored.[59]

Complaining loudly all the way about being sent on this mission in his old age, the Bishop duly made his way to London, saw Elizabeth, then set off for the north.[60] When he reached Berwick, his troubles really began. He was afraid of being captured by the Border thieves who recognized the authority of neither Scotland nor England and, worse still, the Duke of Châtelherault refused to give him a safe conduct to travel to Edinburgh. When he heard this piece of news the Bishop was all for returning home to France, but the Duke of Norfolk would not hear of it.

At this point Mary of Guise herself intervened, writing letters of encouragement to the unwilling mediator.[61] As a result of her efforts, the Bishop was at last given a conditional safe conduct and he set out warily for Edinburgh, with Lord Grey as his escort.[62]

He had cause for alarm. The siege of Leith had now begun in earnest and the English were firing on the town all day as well as engaging in frequent skirmishes outside its walls. The greatly augmented English fleet lay off Leith. Nor had the Scottish Protestants abandoned the idea of besieging Edinburgh Castle in spite of Norfolk's prohibition. The latter himself noted that the Scots were eager for a siege, 'for they think the Dowager does more harm than five hundred Frenchmen. She sends continually up and down, which cannot be remedied without a siege'.[63]

Active Mary might be, but she was far from well. The Bishop of Valence was eventually escorted to Edinburgh Castle on 21 April and found her 'in want especially of health and of everything else except greatness of spirit and good understanding, for she is quite undaunted by these troubles, as if she had all the forces in the world'.[64]

They had a long talk. The Bishop explained the nature of his mission and she gave him details of all that had happened, then questioned him anxiously about preparations for her brother's expedition. When they had finished, his English companions escorted him to the tent of the Duke of Châtelherault where he found the English leaders assembled, and negotiations began again. At first, there were polite exchanges. On the second day, however, when the Bishop spoke of English invasions having made the fortification of Leith necessary, there was an outcry. Everyone spoke of French cruelty to the local inhabitants, of men killed and houses burned. The Protestant attitude hardened.

That night, the Bishop was not allowed to go back to his bed in the castle but instead was forced to go to a lodging in the town where thirty or forty armed men guarded him. If he as much as spoke to one of his own little entourage one of the Scottish soldiers would come up and demand to know if he was saying that the Scots were not as good or as brave or as wise as the English. The unfortunate Bishop had to keep assuring the man that he was his friend. Then, in the evening, Lord James arrived with Maitland of Lethington. They demanded to see his commission, and it was only with difficulty that he convinced them that he had given it to Mary of Guise.

After an uneasy night, he was roused to find the Scots telling him to go home to France. Unwilling to leave without achieving anything, he urged that negotiations be continued. He was taken before the lords of the Congregation in Grey's lodgings. They demanded the destruction of the fortifications at Leith and Dunbar. Thinking his position hopeless, the Bishop said that he would leave the country, but this was ill-received too. The Scots now declared that they would negotiate with no one but him. He would be allowed to come and go as he liked to and from the castle.

Sighing with exasperation, the Bishop agreed to talk on. The atmosphere was far from cordial, however. Mary of Guise had by this time sent her own series of demands. Maitland of Lethington, the man who had once been her secretary, declared that some of these were difficult to meet and that others were obscure in language, though the document was in Scots. The Queen's new secretary stood up and said in Scots that the Bishop had no authority anyway to grant or withhold demands.

The Bishop became alarmed at this development, because

he did not understand what was being said, and his alarm grew when the Protestants rose to their feet and declared that they would walk out rather than negotiate with someone who had no powers. Lethington obligingly explained to the Bishop what was being said, whereupon he declared roundly that he did indeed have powers to negotiate. Mollified, they all sat down again and discussed the demolition of the fortress at Dunbar. For a time, it even seemed as though agreement would be reached, but as soon as the Bishop said that the Scots must break their alliance with the English, bitter words were exchanged once more. In the end, the negotiations broke down altogether over the question of the league with England. Both sides refused to discuss anything further. The Bishop of Valence went up to the castle and took his leave of Mary of Guise. On 28 April he set off gladly for home.[65]

11

A Second Judith

Mary was more alone than ever now. To make matters worse, her health was failing rapidly in spite of her assurance to Monsieur D'Oysel that 'My health is better than it was wont to be, but I am still lame and have a leg that assuages not from swelling. If any lay his finger upon it, it goes in as with butter.'[1] Her heart condition had resulted in dropsy. When the heart does not pump strongly enough, the circulation is impaired and fluid leaks from the veins into the tissues. The result is dropsy, which is not a disease in itself but a symptom. It affects the lower limbs first, then gradually spreads to the rest of the body. The sinking in of the flesh which she describes is typical of the condition.

Mary herself realized what her trouble was, remarking ominously to Monsieur D'Oysel, 'You know there are but three days for the dropsy in this country,'[2] and her contemporaries also realized what ailed her. Knox, commenting on her alleged gloating over English corpses at the siege of Leith, declared that 'within few days thereafter . . . began her belly and loathsome legs to swell, and so continued till that God did execute his judgement upon her',[3] while an English observer claimed that only her frequent tears kept her alive by reducing the inflammation. The fact that she was tearful and depressed was hardly surprising, and the melancholy was probably linked with the menopause. Even so, she remained as courageous and determined as ever.

Everyone was warning her that the Protestants would inevitably besiege Edinburgh Castle. In fact, Elizabeth had unexpectedly given her approval to the enterprise. Mary therefore set about strengthening the fortifications and victualling the castle as best she could. She also kept a close watch on the situation in Leith. Apart from continuing their bombardment of the town, the English had begun to dig trenches outside, with the aim of undermining the defences. The French therefore set about countermining, and the skirmishing continued.

All communication between Mary and the Protestants had ceased, and she was finding it increasingly difficult to keep in touch with Monsieur D'Oysel and the others in Leith. Her letters were invariably intercepted and she became aware that even the secret code she used was no longer safe: she had been shown a word for word translation into English of a letter she had received from France some weeks before. Undeterred, she continued to send messages to Leith, using her ingenuity and all her experience of intrigue. She wrote letters to Monsieur D'Oysel asking for ointment and adding her own news in invisible ink. She managed to write another message on a handkerchief. She chose apparently innocent-looking boys to carry her letters. None of her devices succeeded, but she did not give up.[4]

Bad news seemed to come in to her by the hour. The Earl of Morton and Lord Borthwick, two of her remaining Scottish supporters, joined the Congregation. This was a clear indication that few now held out any hope for the French cause. Yet even now the English were not strong enough to take Leith and although they made two breaches in the town's defences, their assault was repulsed.

Worried about the plight of Monsieur D'Oysel, Mary decided to see if she could lessen the pressure on Leith by reopening negotiations. On 9 May she sent the Laird of Findlater and Master John Spens to see the lords of the Congregation and to ask them to appoint some of their number to confer with her representatives. They refused to do so unless she would assure them that the fortifications at Leith would be destroyed and the French sent away. Lord Grey told Findlater and Spens that he was amazed to see them in Mary's service still, for she was oppressing the liberty of their country and had brought the French men of war in to conquer it. Spens replied that the Queen had been made Regent by the estates of the realm and that during her Regency all good Scots were bound to obey her.

The Duke of Châtelherault was there, and he broke in at this point to declare that she had been deposed and was no longer Regent. With dignity Master Spens retorted that she had been appointed at a much fuller meeting of parliament than that which, in a time of dissension and disorder, had sought to depose her. This annoyed the Duke, who retorted sharply that he was lying. However, Lord Grey intervened to say that Spens and Findlater spoke as loyal and faithful servants.[5]

The next day, Châtelherault solemnly confirmed the Articles of Berwick, but Mary remained outwardly unperturbed. She sent Findlater back to the lords, granting their requests on condition that they gave her sureties for their obedience to the King and Queen. The outcome was that on 12 May 1560 Lord James, Lord Ruthven, the Master of Maxwell and the Laird of Lethington made their way up to Edinburgh Castle and were there shown into the Queen's presence. They exchanged civilities, then the Protestants retired to dine with Lord Erskine. When the meal was over, they laid their grievances before the Queen.[6]

It was a familiar story. They complained of taxes, of Frenchmen appointed to Scottish offices, of attempts to change the laws of Scotland. Mary answered them as she had always done. The soldiers had been brought in because of public disorder. Scottish officers had spent the taxes. Any Frenchman had been appointed to a Scottish office with the consent of parliament and, after all, Scots enjoyed the reciprocal privilege of being allowed to hold office in France.

Lord James then brought forward a new complaint. Even before any disturbances had taken place, the French had arranged for Mary to go to France and for her brother to come as viceroy. He would presumably be bringing men and money. Mary replied that she had only intended to pay another visit to France, meaning to treat with the Queen of England on the way. Her brother, she pointed out, would have no wish to come to stay in Scotland permanently. She herself had intended to return soon and she would remain in the country of her adoption for the rest of her life.

On and on they talked, covering the points so often covered before and arriving once again at the principal stumbling-block: the league with England. Nothing would persuade the Protestants to abandon their alliance with Elizabeth. They did, however, manage to agree on one point. Mary said that she was willing to have the fortifications at Leith demolished and that she would send all the French soldiers home except for the garrisons at Dunbar and Inchkeith. Rather than let the negotiations founder, she asked for time to confer with Monsieur D'Oysel and the other leaders in Leith. The Protestants refused her request. The English in particular were convinced that Mary was merely playing for time, and when he heard reports of her frequent tears, the Duke of Norfolk commented that 'her blubbering is not for nothing', declaring at the same time that no one was deceived by 'her bloody sword in a scabbard of peace'.[7]

In spite of her weakening condition, Mary was resolute as ever. The letters she wrote to friends give only an occasional hint of her own illness. When she sent a message to Monsieur D'Oysel, for instance, in the middle of May, she displayed her accustomed grasp of the military situation, noting in great detail the progress made by the English in their attempt to undermine the citadel at Leith and promising him that if he found himself in danger she would do all she could to distract the attention of the English. Only as an aside did she mention that her leg was better. There had been some local infection there, but she had been her own doctor and surgeon and the heat had gone out of it now.[8]

On 24 May she was still carrying on the day to day business of the realm, granting sasine of the lands of Tullibardine to William Murray by personally handing him the symbolic staff and baton.[9] She was up at all hours, receiving the reports which kept coming in from Leith, noting the progress of the mining and countermining, listening to accounts of men being killed in the trenches. From the castle walls she could look out over the countryside towards Leith but she could not see in detail what was happening. Clouds of smoke rising from burning buildings, the distant booming of gunfire – these were the indications of how the siege was going. There was no question of her looking out from the castle to gloat over the casualties laid on the walls of Leith as John Knox alleged. That would have been a physical impossibility for anyone, let alone for Mary in her condition.[10]

She continued to write almost daily to France. She sent exact reports of what was happening, describing minutely the progress of the siege. She did not beg for help. She knew, she said, that her brothers had their own difficulties. With dignity and restraint, she pointed out to them that assistance really must be sent as soon as was humanly possible.[11]

On 27 May her illness took a turn for the worse and that day she wrote her last letters to her brothers and to Monsieur D'Oysel. To her brothers, she gave the usual report, and to Monsieur D'Oysel she wrote urgently for news. 'It is almost three weeks since I have had word from you', she said, and described her own attempts to get messages through. She spoke a little of the undermining beside the citadel, and referred to the departure of Sir James Croftes, who had set off for Berwick. In all this, there is no hint of self-pity or of recrimination at the French delay. 'I have confirmed that our reinforcements will be strong,' she said, 'but that they will not be here before July. The rebels have proclaimed a parliament for the tenth of July. I have sent several dispatches to France by various routes.' Only for a moment did she speak of herself. 'As for my health, since you ask about it, it has been quite good until two days ago when I had a relapse, and for two nights now have had a return of the fever. I do not know what will happen.' Then she turned back to the military situation. That came first. Her own illness was a tiresome interruption, something to be cured if possible but not to be indulged. All her concern was for 'poor Monsieur D'Oysel' his men and her own little household.[12]

By 1 June, her friends knew that her condition was very grave. She could not eat, though she was still up and about.

She found it easier to sit in a chair than to lie down. On 3 June, news came that four hundred more English soldiers had arrived, but by that time she hardly understood what was being said to her. The following day, as the English fired on Leith and brought down the tower of St Anthony's Church, her mind began to wander. She had eaten nothing for the past week, although she had been taking drinks constantly. Lord Erskine, alarmed by her condition, sent his brother to the lords of the Congregation, begging them to allow the Bishop of Amiens to come to her. Except for one notable exception, the Scottish lords agreed. Lord Grey agreed. The other English leaders agreed. Only the Duke of Châtelherault withheld his consent, and Mary was denied the spiritual consolation of the Bishop's presence.[13]

She realized now that there could be no recovery for her, so she sent for the lords. At eight o'clock on the morning of 7 June, they were shown into the chamber where she sat propped up in her chair. The Duke of Châtelherault came in, the facile tears already trickling down his cheeks. Lord James was with him, hard and cold as he always was now. The Earl Marischal followed, with various others. Many of them had talked and joked and argued and struggled with Mary for years: some of them had been in St Andrews Cathedral that June day twenty-two years before when she had married their King. The bitter opposition of recent months slipped away. They all found their thoughts returning to the beginning, to the days when Châtelherault and Mary had played cards together, when he had been the godfather of her short-lived sons, when the future had seemed full of promise.

They gathered round her, coming as close as her anxious ladies would allow. In a weak voice, she complained that her lips, her hands and her legs were very cold; that she was desperately thirsty – again, typical symptoms of someone suffering from terminal heart disease of that kind. Her speech was failing, and her mind was beginning to wander, but she spoke to them at some length. She was most anxious to urge them to maintain the alliance with France and to turn away from the English, who helped them 'not for any other respect than for their own turn and commodity'. She assured them faintly that she herself had always 'favoured the welfare of the realm of Scotland as much as France, considering she had the honour to be Queen and Regent thereof', and she declared that if she had ever done anything displeasing to them it was 'rather for lack of wisdom and judgement than for want of any good will'.

She paused, struggling for breath, and they felt that she would say no more, but she summoned all her resources and urged them to acknowledge their obedience to their young Queen. She pleaded, too, that they would come to a peaceful agreement with Monsieur D'Oysel and the other French people in Leith. It would be for the best, she said, if the English soldiers and the French would all go home to their own countries for, she said, 'she feared greatly . . . lest if the Frenchmen departed, the Englishmen would still remain and subdue the land to their obedience'.

She had almost reached the limit of her strength. Weeping, she asked the lords to forgive her if she had ever offended any of them during her time in Scotland. They hung their heads and mumbled their agreement. She whispered that, for her part, she forgave them for all the offences they had committed against her, then she took each of them by the hand in turn. Many of them were weeping openly as they left her chamber.[14]

Lord James and the Earl Marischal remained behind in the castle, for she had asked that some of them should stay near her until her death. That afternoon, she sent for the young Earl of Arran. He went in with an air of suppressed excitement. Who knew how her death might alter his circumstances? He, too, came out again with a sorrowful countenance. She saw him and his father again the next day.[15] She agreed to see the preacher Willock, sent to her instead of the Bishop of Amiens. On the evening of 8 June, she called for Lord James and the Earl Marischal to come to her. Her mind had cleared a little, and in their presence she dictated her Will. It was a simple document, drawn up in Latin. She asked that the rents and money that were hers should be given to her executors, who should pay the wages of her household servants, her funeral expenses and her debts. She asked that her mother and her brother the Duke of Guise should act as her executors in France. The Earl Marischal and Sir John Campbell agreed to undertake the task in Scotland,[16] although Marischal was to repudiate his undertaking once she was dead.[17]

She lingered on for a little longer. She saw the Earl of Arran for the last time that day, but towards evening her speech failed altogether. She was silent all the next day, her ladies anxiously watching round her. Lord James and the Earl of Argyll were with her when, at about half an hour after midnight on 11 June 1560, she died.[18]

When morning came, her body was embalmed. The doctors who performed the task noted their findings. 'The liver and the heart were found to be without a single drop of blood: the gall very large and swollen, as yellow as saffron, inside and out: the heart rather small and covered with fat; the brain full of fluid'.[19] The condition of the heart shows the fatty degeneration associated with chronic muscular heart disease. The damage to liver and gall bladder may have been associated with the drinking of wine which had been kept in leaden vessels. Whatever the cause, at the age of forty-four, Mary was worn out.

When the doctors had done their work, her body was laid in a black satin bed and covered with a fine white sheet. Her devoted ladies still watched over her day and night although her servants had been told that they could leave the castle in safety. Those Protestants who wished were allowed in. Out of curiosity, Thomas Randolph came. As he and Lady Fleming stood by the black satin bed, he commented on the fact that the ladies had still not received permission to have mourning garments made. ' "Rend your hearts, not your garments" ', quoted Lady Fleming in Latin.[20]

After some days, the dead Queen was laid in a lead coffin which was placed in the little Chapel of St Margaret, the tiny Norman church within the castle walls where she had so often attended services. A pall with a white taffeta cross was laid carefully over the coffin.[21] There it was to remain for many months. The lords of the Congregation would not agree to a burial at Holyrood, fearing a demonstration in favour of the French cause. They would not allow her a Catholic funeral, nor would they agree to send the body back to France as her family wished. Arrangements were delayed again and again. On 6 July the French, the English and the Scots signed a treaty of peace. English and French troops alike would retire from Scotland. On 15 July the English moved away from Leith. The French began to embark for home, and the local people started to dismantle the fortifications.

News of Mary's death had reached France on 21 June, but it was kept from her daughter until a week later. The young Queen wept bitterly for the mother she had loved so dearly in spite of their long separation.[22] In August the Scottish parliament began to negotiate with the French about the dead Queen's funeral.[23] In December the young King of France died. Mary, Queen of Scots decided to return to her kingdom, but it was not until 16 March 1561, at midnight, that her mother's coffin was taken from Edinburgh Castle and put aboard a ship at Leith. Mr Archibald Crawford, the parson of Eaglesham, accompanied the Queen Regent on her last journey. Her body was taken to Fécamp in Normandy, then westwards to Rheims. Her sister was the Abbess of the Convent of St Peter, and it was there that Mary of Guise was buried. The splendid monument erected for her survived until the French Revolution.[24]

A public funeral service was also held in Paris, in the Cathedral of Notre Dame. The entire French Court was there, including Mary, Queen of Scots. The priest who gave the eulogy spoke on the theme, 'Dead is Judith, light of all the world', and it was indeed tempting to draw comparisons between the Apocryphal heroine and the Queen Regent of Scotland.[25] Judith was a beautiful, wealthy and intelligent Hebrew widow who lived in the city of Bethulia. When the Assyrians, under the command of their general, Holofernes, started to besiege the city and cut off its water supply, the governors of Bethulia agreed to surrender in five days' time. There seemed no way out for them.

Judith, however, was appalled at the idea of surrender. If

their city were taken, the whole of Judea would be devastated. She therefore offered to prevent this from happening. Discarding the mourning garments which she had worn ever since her husband's death, she put on 'her garments of gladness' and 'put about her her bracelets and her chains and her rings and her earrings and all her ornaments'. She then went to the camp of the Assyrians and asked to see Holofernes, who was much taken with her. 'Thou art both beautiful in thy countenance and witty in thy words', he told her, and he persuaded her to stay with him. Three days she spent with him, and on the third night, when he had fallen into a drunken sleep, she took out his dagger and she cut off his head. She put it in a bag, then she returned to her own people. Bethulia was saved, Judith was praised by all, and she lived to be a hundred and five, a chaste and respected widow who, though 'many desired her, none knew her all the days of her life'.[26]

Listening to the sonorous words of the priest, the French congregation were well satisfied. Judith and Mary had both been wise, rich and beautiful widows. Both had gone into danger, determined to fight a ferocious enemy. Judith had killed Holofernes. Mary had struggled against the Protestants.

For the French, Mary was a warrior princess fighting for their cause. For John Knox she was a cruel, merciless tyrant. 'God, for his great mercy's sake, rid us from the rest of the Guisian blood. Amen. Amen!' he wrote when he had described her death.[27] He had once sent her a letter and she had joked about it, handing it to the Archbishop of Glasgow with the words, 'Please you, My Lord, to read a lampoon.' Someone had told Knox, and he had never forgiven her.[28]

The Catholic Scots did not, of course, share his view of her. Writing during the reign of her daughter, Bishop Lesley noted that Mary was 'a princess most prudent and very well instructed in sweetness, comely and honest manners and integrity of life . . . Through use and experience, she knew much of our affairs and was very expert, in so far that none was of the nobility and of the common people except very few obscure persons whose engine, mind and manners she knew not perfectly and very well . . . she did justice with all diligence all her days . . . She likewise in virtues and many offices of humanity far overcame many other women for when she had the solicitude and care of all poor honest women, then specially of them who were in their birth or sick of bairn or any way afflicted . . . she herself very often in danger visited them, helping both with her knowledge and her goods . . . therefore she won the hearts of all . . . with wit and wisdom.'[29]

Lesley's account might be dismissed as the result of partiality, but it is interesting to note that the English chronicler Holinshed shared his favourable opinion of the Queen. He wrote, 'She was a wise and very prudent princess, and in her time had learned good experience of the nature and inclination of the nobility and people of Scotland. During the time that she was Regent, she kept good justice and was well obeyed in all parts of the realm, in Orkney and the Western Isles. And if she had to her own experience joined the counsel of the nobles and wise men of the realm of Scotland, without following the advice of strangers, there had been never question nor debate betwixt her and the nobility as some deemed . . .'[30] 'She had the heart of a man of war', said one Englishman, wishing her dead, and her enemies often remarked that she was more dangerous than an army of soldiers.[31]

Yet in truth Mary was no more the warrior princess of the French than she was the vengeful tyrant of Knox: nor was she the bland, insipid widow described by more recent biographers. Perhaps, in the end, the comparison with Judith was the most apt. From her earliest days Mary had endeared herself to her companions by her gaiety, her wit, her compassion and her warmth. It is difficult to define charm, but charm she had in abundance. Even now, at a distance of four hundred years, her letters have the freshness, the directness, the sympathy and the enthusiasm which drew people to her, often in spite of themselves.

Had her first husband lived, she might have spent her life as a French Duchess, bringing up a large family and devoting her formidable energies and intellect to the management of his estates. Her mother had found fulfilment that way, but then

Antoinette had a down-to-earth acceptance of life, a willingness to submit to what God sent her. Mary was like her mother in many ways, but she was also her father's daughter. She needed excitement, intellectual stimulation, power. She was a dignified woman and a proud one. She saw Scotland as a challenge. Judith had made up her mind and had accomplished an unpleasant task. Mary likewise decided that she would set personal feelings aside and go to a foreign people to do what she saw as her duty. She would help to bring Scotland into the modern world. She would transform the infant nation into a well-organized country with equitable laws and proper government.

The odds were against her from the start. She could not have pleased the Scots, no matter how winning her ways. As Queen Consort of James V she would always have found enemies among those courtiers who resented the presence of an able and attractive foreigner, taking up the attention of their King. Again, her position as Regent was doomed to failure. Not only was she a foreigner, but she was also a woman. A crown upon her head, said Knox, was 'as seemly a sight . . . as to put a saddle upon the back of an unruly cow'. Many of his contemporaries would have agreed with him. Had Mary been content to remain a figurehead, allowing one of the nobles to rule the country in her name, they might have tolerated her. As soon as they realized that she had ideas of her own, that she wanted to alter their ways, they were determined to oppose her. They had no desire to be transformed into peace-loving, model subjects. In their own fashion they enjoyed the turbulence, the excitement, the dangerous game of playing one side off against another.

Mary herself enjoyed the game of politics. In spite of all difficulties, she found the business of trying to rule the country both exhilarating and absorbing. The tragedy was that, with all her gifts and good intentions, she became more and more alienated from the Scots. They failed her too often. She turned increasingly to her French advisers. When the Protestants rose up against her, she saw them only as challenging her authority. When the preachers criticized her policies from the pulpit she was more concerned with the disrespectful way they spoke of princes than with the actual complaints they made.

For their part, the Protestants seemed determined to believe that she was merely the agent of France, that she was the French instrument for taking over their kingdom. They forgot how she and they had struggled together against the English, how she had worked for the improvement of their country. Herself a faithful daughter of the Church, she could have tolerated their religious disturbances and reassured them about her own country's intentions had she not been so indignant that they should challenge the civil authority of the monarchy.

Her end was a sad one, yet sick and lonely, waiting for French help which never came, she did not admit defeat. She hated violence, she wept for the tragedies of war, but she believed passionately in what she was doing. In the face of adversity, illness, grief and betrayal, she fought on. She died with her work undone but with her spirit unvanquished. Her life is best summed up in the emblem which she chose for herself. It is a crown, set above a rock which is beaten by winds and by waves but which remains unshaken. Above it are written the words, 'And yet it stands'.[32]

Notes

THE HOUSE OF GUISE

1. René de Bouillé, *Histoire des Ducs de Guise* (Paris 1849, hereafter cited as Bouillé), i, 44–50; H. Forneron, *Les Ducs de Guise et Leur Epoque* (Paris 1877, hereafter cited as Forneron), i, 9 states that René had twelve children; Gabriel de Pimodan, *La Mère des Guises: Antoinette de Bourbon 1494–1583* (Paris 1925, hereafter cited as Pimodan), 16–20.
2. H. Noel Williams, *The Brood of False Lorraine* (London n.d.), 5; Bouillé, i, 50–1.
3. Paris, Bibliothèque Nationale, Portfolio 133 de Gaignières, see Jean Adhémar, 'Les Portraits Dessinés du XVIe siècle au Cabinet des Estampes' in *Gazette des Beaux-Arts* (1973), 12, number 7.
4. Pimodan, 14. The marriage contract is in the Bibliothèque Nationale, f. fr. 4508, f. 102.
5. Bouillé, i, 55–60; Forneron, i, 1–6; Pimodan, 23–4; *Le Journal d'un Bourgeois de Paris*, ed. V.-L. Bourrilly (Paris 1910), 19–23; Pierre de Bourdeille, Seigneur de Brantôme, *Memoires contenant les vies des hommes illustres et grands capitaines français* (London 1739), i, 372; Desmond Seward, *Prince of the Renaissance* (London 1973), 51–9.
6. Noel Williams, op. cit., 6.
7. Pimodan, 25.
8. ibid.
9. ibid., 27–9; Bouillé, i, 41; Micheline de Fontette, *Les Religieuses à l'âge classique du Droit Canon* (Paris 1967), 129–51.
10. Pimodan, 32–6; engraving after an elevation of Joinville drawn in 1747.
11. Bouillé, i, 220–2.
12. Pimodan, 96–8.
13. ibid., 30.
14. Seward, op. cit., 87–113.
15. Bouillé, i, 97n, 110n, 130–3; Forneron, i, 42.
16. Bouillé, i, 54, 222–3.
17. ibid., 61–72; Forneron, i, 23–37; Pimodan, 51; Noel Williams, op. cit., 27–8.
18. C. Merigot, *La Vie de la Serenissime Philippe de Gueldres* (Paris 1627); Pimodan, 28–9.
19. Claud d'Espence, *Oraison Funèbre* (Paris 1561, hereafter cited as *Oraison*), 26–8; see also Hilarion de Coste, *Les Eloges et les Vies des*

Reynes (Paris 1647, hereafter cited as *Eloges*), ii, 535.
20. *Oraison*, 29; *Eloges*, ii, 536.
21. Pimodan, 56–8.
22. Bibliothèque Nationale, supp. franc. 2568, cahier 4, printed in Bouillé, i, 534.
23. Bibliothèque Nationale, supp. franc. 2568, cahiers 1–3 (not printed).
24. Pimodan, 59–60; Agnes Strickland, *Lives of the Queens of Scotland* (Edinburgh 1850, hereafter cited as Strickland), i, 343–4.
25. Pimodan, 60; Strickland, i, 344–5; *The Letters of James V*, ed. Denys Hay (Scottish History Society 1954), 340–1; Paris, Archives Nationales, KK 907, f. 3 (discharge for the third instalment of her dowry, 1537).
26. *Le Journal d'un Bourgeois de Paris*, 357.
27. *Oraison*, 33–7; *Eloges*, ii, 536–7.
28. Strickland, i, 345.
29. Seward, 193–6.
30. Bibliothèque Nationale, f. fr. 5467; Pimodan, 65.
31. *Foreign Correspondence with Marie de Lorraine, Queen of Scotland, from the Originals in the Balcarres Papers*, ed. Marguerite Wood (Scottish History Society 1923–5, hereafter cited as *Balcarres Papers*), i, 5.

THE RELUCTANT BRIDE

1. Gordon Donaldson, *Scottish Kings* (London 1967, hereafter cited as *Scottish Kings*), 139–69.
2. *Letters and Papers Foreign and Domestic of the Reign of Henry VIII* (London 1862–1929, hereafter cited as *LPFD*), ii, 150.
3. ibid., 336–7.
4. ibid., 291–2.
5. ibid., 348.
6. ibid., 421–2.
7. ibid., 449.
8. Antonia Fraser, *Mary Queen of Scots* (London 1969, hereafter cited as Fraser), 7.
9. *LPFD*, ii, 453.
10. Pimodan, 65.
11. *LPFD*, ii, 540–1.
12. *Balcarres Papers*, i, 3–5.
13. *LPFD*, ii, 544.
14. *Papiers d'état, pièces et documents inédits ou peu connus relatifs à l'histoire de l'Ecosse au XVIeme siècle*, ed. A. Teulet (Bannatyne Club, 1852–60, hereafter cited as Teulet, *Papiers*), i, 115.
15. Stefan Zweig, *The Queen of Scots*, translated by C. and E. Paul (London 1935), 1–2. This fascinating letter is something of a mystery and indeed poses something of a problem. It was first published in German by Zweig, who stated that the original was in French. His

book was later translated into English. Neither version gives the source of the letter, and the archives of Zweig's English publisher were largely destroyed during the Blitz. I have therefore been unable to trace the copyright owner or the present location of the letter. So explicit is it of James's attitudes and intentions that there is some reason to doubt its authenticity. The modern flavour of the phraseology may be the result of translation from sixteenth-century French into German, back into French, then into English. Doubts about James's ability to summarize his situation so concisely may lead one to speculate that the actual author of the original, if original there be, was not James himself but Cardinal Beaton.

16. *Inventaire Chronologique des Documents relatifs à l'histoire d'Ecosse*, ed. A. Teulet (Abbotsford Club 1839), 88.
17. Bibliothèque Nationale, f. fr. 5467, f. 66.
18. *Accounts of the Lord High Treasurer of Scotland*, ed. T. Dickson and Sir J. Balfour Paul (Edinburgh 1877–1916, hereafter cited as *Treasurer Accts.*), vii, 56.
19. Pimodan, 66.
20. *Treasurer Accts.*, vii, 59.
21. R. Lindesay of Pitscottie, *The Historie and Cronicles of Scotland* (Scottish Text Society 1899–1911, hereafter cited as Pitscottie, *Historie*), i, 377–8.
22. J. Lesley, *The History of Scotland from the Death of King James I in the Year 1436 to the Year 1561* (Bannatyne Club 1830, hereafter cited as Lesley, *History*), ii, 241; *A Diurnal of Remarkable Occurrents that have passed within the country of Scotland since the death of King James the Fourth till the year 1575* (Bannatyne and Maitland Clubs 1833, hereafter cited as *Diurnal of Occurrents*), 22; Stewart Cruden, *The Cathedral of St Andrews* (Edinburgh 1950; Ministry of Works Official Guide Book); Pitscottie, *Historie*, i, 378–80.
23. Pitscottie, *Historie*, i, 378–80.
24. Pimodan, 67.
25. Pitscottie, *Historie*, i, 381.
26. *Diurnal of Occurrents*, 22.

THE QUEEN OF SCOTS

1. *Balcarres Papers*, i, 5–6.
2. ibid., 17.
3. ibid., 7.
4. ibid., 6.
5. ibid., 13.
6. *Treasurer Accts.*, vii, 107–13.
7. ibid., vii, pp. xxxi–xxxix, xli–xlii, 119, 271–2, 306.
8. ibid., vii, 136–8.

9. *John Knox's History of the Reformation in Scotland*, ed. W. C. Dickinson (Edinburgh 1949, hereafter cited as Knox, *History*), i, 126.
10. *Calendar of the State Papers relating to Scotland 1509–1603*, ed. M. J. Thorpe (London 1858, hereafter cited as *Cal. State Papers*), i, 39.
11. *Treasurer Accts.*, vii, 156.
12. ibid., 123.
13. ibid., 149–50.
14. *Balcarres Papers*, i, 224–5.
15. *Treasurer Accts.*, vii, 204.
16. ibid., 205, 173.
17. ibid., 130–1.
18. ibid., 136–8, 149.
19. *The Works of Sir David Lindsay of the Mount 1490–1555*, ed. Douglas Hamer (Scottish Text Society 1931), 117–22.
20. *Treasurer Accts.*, vii, 184.
21. Edinburgh, National Library of Scotland (hereafter cited as N.L.S.), Balcarres Papers, iv, 45; summarized in *Balcarres Papers*, i, 231.
22. *Balcarres Papers*, i, 38.
23. ibid., 18, 20, 25, 27; *Treasurer Accts.*, vii, 182.
24. *Balcarres Papers*, i, 19, 33, 34.
25. E. Marianne H. McKerlie, *Mary of Guise-Lorraine, Queen of Scotland* (London 1931), 48; *Treasurer Accts.*, vii, 252.
26. *Balcarres Papers*, i, 70.
27. *Treasurer Accts.*, vii, 280, 282, 285–6, 297, 347; *Rentale Sancti Andree*, ed. R. K. Hannay (Scottish History Society 1913), 93; *Accounts of the Masters of Works*, ed. H. M. Paton and others (Edinburgh 1957–), i, 288–9.
28. *Treasurer Accts.*, vii, 277–8; *Diurnal of Occurrents*, 23.
29. *The State Papers and Letters of Sir Ralph Sadler*, ed. Arthur Clifford (Edinburgh 1809, hereafter cited as Sadler), i, 17–39.
30. *Treasurer Accts.*, vii, 299, 300, 304, 307.
31. Lesley, *History*, ii, 243; see also Pitscottie, *Historie*, i, 382; Raphael Holinshed, *Chronicles of England, Scotland and Ireland* (London 1807–8, hereafter cited as Holinshed, *Chronicles*), v, 515.
32. *Treasurer Accts.*, vii, 322.
33. *Diurnal of Occurrents*, 23; Pitscottie, *Historie*, i, 382; Lesley, *History*, ii, 243; Holinshed, *Chronicles*, v, 515.
34. *Treasurer Accts.*, vii, 316, 319–20, 325.
35. ibid., 312, 319–20, 333, 396, 403–4.
36. ibid., 397; Pitscottie, *Historie*, i, 394.
37. *Balcarres Papers*, i, 51–2; *Treasurer Accts.*, vii, 433.
38. Lesley, *History*, ii, 246 and Holinshed, *Chronicles*, v, 515–6 give the child's name as Arthur; Pitscottie, *Historie*, i, 382; *Treasurer Accts.*, vii, 442, 445, 495; *Diurnal of Occurrents*, 24.
39. *Diurnal of Occurrents*, 24; Pitscottie, *Historie*, i, 394; Lesley, *History*, ii,

246; Holinshed, *Chronicles*, v, 515–6.

40. *Treasurer Accts.*, vii, 442; *The Hamilton Papers*, ed. J. Bain (Edinburgh 1890–92, hereafter cited as *Hamilton Papers*), i, 73.
41. *Balcarres Papers*, i, 60–1.

THE DEATH OF THE KING

1. *Hamilton Papers*, i, 74.
2. N.L.S., *Balcarres Papers*, 29.2.1/6. A translation is printed in Strickland, i, 380.
3. ibid., 29.2.1/4; Strickland, i, 397.
4. ibid., 29.2.1/5; Strickland, i, 397.
5. *Balcarres Papers*, i, 69–73.
6. Pimodan, 100–1.
7. Lesley, *History*, ii, 246–7.
8. *Treasurer Accts.*, viii, 34, 75, 76–7.
9. N.L.S., *Balcarres Papers*, 29.2.2/12, summarized in *Balcarres Papers*, i, 228.
10. *Treasurer Accts.*, viii, 116–17, 97.
11. *Balcarres Papers*, i, 78.
12. Lesley, *History*, ii, 254.
13. *Treasurer Accts.*, vii, 137.
14. Gordon Donaldson, *James V to James VII* (Edinburgh 1965), 60; Lesley, *History*, ii, 258–9.
15. *Hamilton Papers*, i, 329.
16. Lesley, *History*, ii, 258–9.
17. *Hamilton Papers*, i, 334–7.
18. Lesley, *History*, ii, 259; *Hamilton Papers*, i, 323–4, 328, 333, 337; Fraser, 12–13.
19. Pitscottie, *Historie*, i, 407–8; *Hamilton Papers*, i, 336–58; *Calendar of Letters, Despatches and State Papers relating to the negotiations between England and Spain*, ed. G. A. Bergenroth and others (London 1862– , hereafter cited as *Spanish Letters*), vi (2), 189–90; Caroline Bingham, *James V* (London 1971), 190–1.
20. *Hamilton Papers*, i, 347–9.
21. Pitscottie, *Historie*, ii, 3.
22. Knox, *History*, i, 40.
23. *Hamilton Papers*, i, 342.
24. Lesley, *History*, ii, 263–4; *Hamilton Papers*, i, 375; Pitscottie, *Historie*, ii, 3; *Spanish Letters*, vi (2), 192–3, 222–3.
25. *Hamilton Papers*, i, 345–6; Pitscottie, *Historie*, ii, 3–4.
26. *Hamilton Papers*, i, 359.
27. *Treasurer Accts.*, viii, 141–5.

THE LORD GOVERNOR

1. *Hamilton Papers*, i, 358.
2. ibid.
3. ibid., 370.
4. ibid., 387–91.
5. *Spanish Letters*, vi (2), 222–3.
6. *Hamilton Papers*, i, 387–91.
7. ibid., 398.
8. ibid., 397–8.
9. Edinburgh, Scottish Record Office, Exchequer Records, E33/3, 4, Depences de la Maison Royal, 1543–4. (Hereafter cited as Depences).
10. ibid.; Roll and number of persons in the service of the Queen, *c.* 1543, E34/23.
11. *Hamilton Papers*, i, 405.
12. ibid., 448.
13. Scottish Record Office, Exchequer Records, E33/3, 4, Depences 1543–4.
14. *Hamilton Papers*, i, 450–3.
15. ibid., 461.
16. ibid., 445.
17. ibid., 468.
18. ibid., 462–7.
19. ibid., 474–8.
20. Sadler, i, 84–8.
21. *Mary of Lorraine Corresp.*, 8–9.
22. Sadler, i, 104–5; Pitscottie, *Historie*, ii, 8; Lesley, *History*, ii, 265–6; *Hamilton Papers*, i, 490–1.
23. Sadler, i, 93.
24. ibid., 104–8.
25. ibid., 110–11.
26. ibid., 111–12.
27. ibid., 113–17.
28. ibid., 136–9.
29. ibid., 145.
30. *Hamilton Papers*, i, 526.
31. Sadler, i, 184–206.
32. Gordon Donaldson, *Scottish Historical Documents* (Edinburgh 1970), 110–11.
33. Sadler, i, 262–4.
34. ibid., 228–9.
35. *Hamilton Papers*, i, 554–94.
36. Scottish Record Office, Exchequer Records, E33/3, 4, Depences, 1543–4; Pitscottie, *Historie*, ii, 13–14; Lesley, *History*, ii, 268–9; *Hamilton Papers*, i, 597.

37. Sadler, i, 262–4.
38. ibid., 249–53.
39. ibid., 270.
40. *Hamilton Papers*, ii, 12–20.
41. Pitscottie, *Historie*, ii, 15.

THE STRUGGLE FOR POWER

1. *Balcarres Papers*, i, 94–5.
2. Sadler, i, 290–4.
3. Pitscottie, *Historie*, ii, 15–16.
4. ibid., 16–18.
5. *Mary of Lorraine Corresp.*, 31.
6. *Hamilton Papers*, ii, 89–90.
7. *Mary of Lorraine Corresp.*, 33–4.
8. Pitscottie, *Historie*, ii, 22–3.
9. *Two Missions of Jacques de la Brosse*, ed. Gladys Dickinson (Scottish History Society 1942, hereafter cited as *Brosse Missions*), 19.
10. ibid., 23.
11. ibid., 23–9.
12. *Mary of Lorraine Corresp.*, 38–40.
13. Jules de la Brosse, *Histoire d'un Capitaine Bourbonnais au XVIe siècle, Jacques de la Brosse, 1485–1562, ses Missions en Ecosse* (Paris 1929), 320–1.
14. *Brosse Missions*, 35–9.
15. *Hamilton Papers*, ii, 137–42.
16. *Registrum Honoris de Morton* (Edinburgh 1853), i, 5; *Hamilton Papers*, ii, 145–51; *Brosse Missions*, 35–7.
17. *Hamilton Papers*, ii, 186–8.
18. *Brosse Missions*, 42–3; *Hamilton Papers*, ii, 220–1; Teulet, *Papiers*, i, 137–42.
19. *Hamilton Papers*, ii, 241; *Diurnal of Occurrents*, 30; Scottish Record Office, Exchequer Records, E33/3, 4, Depences 1543–4.
20. *Brosse Missions*, 46–7.
21. *Hamilton Papers*, ii, 250–1.
22. *Mary of Lorraine Corresp.*, 57–8.
23. *Hamilton Papers*, ii, 276–7.
24. *Calendar of the State Papers Relating to Scotland and to Mary, Queen of Scots 1547–1603*, ed. J. Bain and others (Edinburgh 1898– ; hereafter cited as *C.S.P. Scot.*), i, 46.
25. *Hamilton Papers*, ii, 294; *Treasurer Accts.*, viii, 279–81.
26. *Mary of Lorraine Corresp.*, 67.
27. ibid., 68–70.
28. Pitscottie, *Historie*, ii, 23–5; Lesley, *History*, ii, 274; *Treasurer Accts.*, viii, 278–9; *Hamilton Papers*, ii, 216–17, 323.

29. *Hamilton Papers*, ii, 337; Pitscottie, *Historie*, ii, 25-6.
30. *Hamilton Papers*, ii, 325-7.
31. ibid., 361-6.
32. ibid., 366-9.
33. ibid., 371-2.
34. ibid., 379-80.
35. *Mary of Lorraine Corresp.*, 82-3.
36. ibid., 84-5.
37. *Hamilton Papers*, ii, 409-10.
38. ibid., 410; *Diurnal of Occurrents*, 33.
39. *Mary of Lorraine Corresp.*, 89-92.
40. ibid., 92-3.
41. *Hamilton Papers*, ii, 415.
42. *Treasurer Accts.*, viii, 304.
43. *Mary of Lorraine Corresp.*, 95-7; *Treasurer Accts.*, viii, 301-9.
44. *Hamilton Papers*, ii, 433-5.
45. *Mary of Lorraine Corresp.*, 104-5; *Diurnal of Occurrents*, 35; *Hamilton Papers*, ii, 466.
46. *Mary of Lorraine Corresp.*, 106-8.
47. ibid.
48. *Hamilton Papers*, ii, 486.
49. *Mary of Lorraine Corresp.*, 108-11.
50. ibid., 104.

THE ROUGH WOOING

1. *Hamilton Papers*, ii, 537-8.
2. ibid., 552-3.
3. ibid., 564-5; c.f. Pitscottie, *Historie*, ii, 38-43.
4. ibid., 42-3.
5. *Mary of Lorraine Corresp.*, 129-30.
6. ibid., 132-3.
7. ibid., 134-6.
8. *Balcarres Papers*, i, 111; see also *Mary of Lorraine Corresp.*, 136-8.
9. ibid., 139-40.
10. *Diurnal of Occurrents*, 39-40; *C.S.P. Scot.*, i, 54.
11. ibid., 56-7.
12. Pitscottie, *Historie*, ii, 47-9.
13. *C.S.P. Scot.*, i, 58.
14. *Mary of Lorraine Corresp.*, 151-2.
15. Pitscottie, *Historie*, ii, 49-51.
16. Knox, *History*, i, 74-9; *C.S.P. Scot.*, i, 58; Pitscottie, *Historie*, ii, 84.
17. Knox, *History*, i, 79.
18. *The Register of the Privy Council of Scotland*, edd. J. H. Burton and others (Edinburgh 1877- , hereafter cited as *R.P.C.*), i, 23-30.

19. Gordon Donaldson, *James V to James VII* (Edinburgh 1965), 75.
20. *Mary of Lorraine Corresp.*, 174–81.
21. Knox, *History*, i, 94–7; *Diurnal of Occurrents*, 44; Lesley, *History*, ii, 295–6; Pitscottie, *Historie*, ii, 88–91.
22. *C.S.P. Scot.*, i, 17–18.
23. *Diurnal of Occurrents*, 45; Pitscottie, *Historie*, ii, 96–102; Lesley, *History*, ii, 42, 297–301.
24. Fraser, 28–9.
25. *C.S.P. Scot.*, i, 41–3.
26. ibid., 68; *Balcarres Papers*, i, 172.
27. *C.S.P. Scot.*, i, 41–3.
28. ibid., 107.
29. *Mary of Lorraine Corresp.*, 217–19.
30. *C.S.P. Scot.*, i, 97–8.
31. *Balcarres Papers*, i, 188–97.
32. ibid., 196–7.
33. *C.S.P. Scot.*, i, 85.
34. ibid., 115–16.
35. ibid., 118.
36. ibid., 116–17.
37. ibid., 119.
38. *C.S.P. Scot.*, i, 121–2; Pitscottie, *Historie*, ii, 107; *Diurnal of Occurrents*, 46–7; Lesley, *History*, ii, 307–10.
39. *Histoire de la guerre d'Ecosse; pendant les campagnes 1548 et 1549 par Jean de Beaugué* (Maitland Club 1830, hereafter cited as Beaugué), 11–12.
40. *Calendar of State Papers Foreign Series*, ed. W. B. Turnbull and others (London 1861– , hereafter cited as *C.S.P. Foreign*), 1547–53, 20–1.
41. Beaugué, 13.
42. ibid., 37–8.
43. ibid., 38–9.
44. ibid., 51.
45. *C.S.P. Scot.*, i, 35–6.
46. ibid., 39; *The Acts of the Parliaments of Scotland*, edd. T. Thomson and C. Innes (Edinburgh 1814–75), ii, 481–2; extract printed in Gordon Donaldson, *Scottish Historical Documents* (Edinburgh 1970), 113–14.
47. Teulet, *Papiers*, i, 188.
48. *Hamilton Papers*, ii, 618.
49. *C.S.P. Scot.*, i, 58–9.

RETURN TO FRANCE

1. *Hamilton Papers*, ii, 616–17.
2. *C.S.P. Scot.*, i, 169.
3. Beaugué, 76–7; Lesley, *History*, ii, 315–17.
4. *Diurnal of Occurrents*, 47; Lesley, *History*, ii, 318–21.
5. *C.S.P. Scot.*, i, 170–1.
6. Beaugué, 126–33.
7. ibid., and Lesley, *History*, ii, 327.
8. Beaugué, 127–43.
9. *Mary of Lorraine Corresp.*, 309–11.
10. *R.P.C.*, i, 85–6.
11. *Balcarres Papers*, i, 81–164.
12. Pimodan, 115–38.
13. Teulet, *Papiers*, i, 234.
14. *Analecta Scotica*, ed. J. Maidment (Edinburgh 1834–7), 347–9.
15. N.L.S., Balcarres Papers, 29.2.5, ff. 77–80; c.f. wardrobe of Mary, Queen of Scots, including brassières, in Fraser, 183–4.
16. *C.S.P. Foreign 1547–53*, 53.
17. *R.P.C.*, i, 107.
18. *Diurnal of Occurrents*, 50–1; Lesley, *History*, ii, 333–5.
19. *C.S.P. Foreign 1547–53*, 54–5; Lesley, *History*, ii, 335.
20. *C.S.P. Foreign 1547–53*, 57.
21. ibid., 58.
22. Lesley, *History*, ii, 336–7.
23. Gordon Donaldson, *James V to James VII*, 80; *C.S.P. Foreign 1547–53*, 65; Lesley, *History*, ii, 335.
24. *C.S.P. Foreign 1547–53*, 68; Pimodan, 336.
25. *C.S.P. Foreign 1547–53*, 75.
26. ibid., 90–2.
27. ibid., 93.
28. ibid., 102–3.
29. N.L.S., Balcarres Papers, 29.2.5, ff. 142–51.,
30. ibid., 29.2.1/90; Pimodan, 143.
31. Pimodan, 143.
32. Lesley, *History*, ii, 339–41.
33. *The Journal of King Edward's Reign, written in his own hand* (Clarendon Historical Society 1884), 50–2.
34. Lesley, *History*, ii, 341.
35. ibid., 347–8.
36. L'Abbé de Vertot, *Ambassades de MM. de Noailles en Angleterre* (Leyden 1763, hereafter cited as *Noailles, Ambassades*), ii, 140–1.
37. *C.S.P. Scot.*, i, 103.
38. *Noailles, Ambassades*, ii, 209–12.
39. ibid., 80–1.

40. *Eleventh Report, Appendix Part VI, of the Royal Commission on Historical Manuscripts* (London 1887), The Duke of Hamilton's MSS., 39–41.
41. Noailles, *Ambassades*, iii, 156–60; Lesley, *History*, ii, 349–50; *Diurnal of Occurrents*, 51; Pitscottie, *Historie*, ii, 113–16.

THE QUEEN REGENT

1. *Papal Negotiations with Mary, Queen of Scots 1561–7*, ed. J. H. Pollen (Scottish History Society 1901, hereafter cited as Pollen, *Papal Negotiations*), 4–8.
2. *Mary of Lorraine Corresp.*, 388–9.
3. *A.P.S.*, ii, 492–500.
4. University of St Andrews Library, Letter of Mary of Guise to Monsieur de Noailles, 28 July 1555, MS.DA 784.7; Lesley, *History*, ii, 365–6.
5. *Criminal Trials in Scotland from 1488 to 1624*, ed. R. Pitcairn (Edinburgh 1833), i, I, 393–4.
6. ibid., 389–92.
7. Lesley, *History*, ii, 366–7.
8. Paris, Archives of the Ministry of Foreign Affairs, Angl. Reg., xv (hereafter cited as Angl. Reg. xv), 10–12.
9. Pollen, *Papal Negotiations*, 425–9.
10. Angl. Reg. xv, 12–13.
11. *Diurnal of Occurrents*, 267; Lesley, *History*, ii, 371–2; Pitscottie, *Historie*, ii, 119–20; Knox, *History*, i, 124–5.
12. Knox, *History*, i, 127–9; *C.S.P. Foreign 1558–9*, 79.
13. *C.S.P. Foreign 1558–9*, 78.
14. ibid., 14.
15. ibid., 21.
16. Knox, *History*, i, 161–3; *C.S.P. Scot.*, i, 212–13; *C.S.P. Foreign 1558–9*, 282; Pitscottie, *Historie*, ii, 145–6.
17. Pitscottie, *Historie*, ii, 147–8.
18. ibid.
19. *C.S.P. Scot.*, i, 213.
20. *C.S.P. Foreign 1558–9*, 289; Pitscottie, *Historie*, ii, 148–9.
21. *C.S.P. Scot.*, i, 215.
22. Angl. Reg. xv, 493, printed in Teulet, *Papiers*, i, 310–11.
23. *C.S.P. Scot.*, i, 215.
24. *C.S.P. Foreign 1558–9*, 321; Pitscottie, *Historie*, i, 151.
25. Pitscottie, *Historie*, ii, 152–9; Knox, *History*, i, 182–7.
26. *C.S.P. Foreign 1558–9*, 344; *C.S.P. Scot.*, i, 220–1.
27. *C.S.P. Foreign 1558–9*, 349.
28. Teulet, *Papiers*, i, 316–19.
29. ibid., 331–2.
30. ibid., 325–7.

31. *C.S.P. Scot.*, i, 233.
32. *C.S.P. Foreign 1558-9*, 410.
33. Teulet, *Papiers*, i, 331-2.

THE FINAL STRUGGLE

1. *C.S.P. Scot.*, i, 238-9.
2. ibid., 241-2; *C.S.P. Foreign 1558-9*, 453-4.
3. Teulet, *Papiers*, i, 333.
4. *C.S.P. Foreign 1558-9*, 505.
5. ibid., 509-12.
6. ibid., 509.
7. Teulet, *Papiers*, i, 337-9.
8. Angl. Reg. xv, 36-7.
9. *C.S.P. Scot.*, i, 250; *C.S.P. Foreign 1558-9*, 556-7.
10. Angl. Reg. xv, 37-9.
11. ibid., *C.S.P. Foreign 1558-9*, 548-9.
12. Angl. Reg. xv, 40.
13. ibid., 40-1.
14. *Mary of Lorraine Corresp.*, 424-6.
15. *C.S.P. Foreign 1558-9*, 591.
16. ibid., *1559-60*, 6-7.
17. ibid., 9-12.
18. ibid., 19-25.
19. *C.S.P. Scot.*, i, 254.
20. *Diurnal of Occurrents*, 54.
21. *C.S.P. Scot.*, i, 255; *C.S.P. Foreign 1559-60*, 46-7; Gordon Donaldson, *James V to James VII*, 97.
22. *C.S.P. Foreign 1559-60*, 45.
23. ibid., 99-100.
24. *C.S.P. Scot.*, i, 269.
25. *Balcarres Papers*, 79-80.
26. See p. 254.
27. *C.S.P. Foreign 1559-60*, 146-7.
28. ibid., 152-3.
29. ibid., 163.
30. Teulet, *Papiers*, i, 381-92.
31. *C.S.P. Foreign 1559-60*, 106n.
32. Teulet, *Papiers*, i, 404.
33. ibid., 405-6.
34. ibid., 393-403.
35. *C.S.P. Foreign 1559-60*, 314-15; *Brosse Missions*, 57.
36. *C.S.P. Foreign 1559-60*, 295, 313; *Diurnal of Occurrents*, 55.
37. *C.S.P. Foreign 1559-60*, 324.
38. Teulet, *Papiers*, i, 408-13.

39. *Brosse Missions*, 63-5.
40. *C.S.P. Foreign 1559-60*, 327-8.
41. ibid., 332n; Teulet, *Papiers*, i, 408-13.
42. Pitscottie, *Historie*, ii, 167; *C.S.P. Foreign 1559-60*, 353-5.
43. ibid., 380-1.
44. ibid.
45. Gordon Donaldson, *Scottish Documents*, 119-20.
46. *C.S.P. Foreign 1559-60*, 480-1.
47. ibid., 385-7, 460-1; *C.S.P. Scot.*, i, 135.
48. *C.S.P. Foreign 1559-60*, 430-1, 444; Pitscottie, *Historie*, ii, 167-8.
49. *C.S.P. Foreign 1559-60*, 459.
50. *Report of the Royal Commission on Historical Manuscripts* (London 1900), Montagu of Beaulieu, 8-9.
51. *Brosse Missions*, 89-91; *Diurnal of Occurrents*, 57; Pitscottie, *Historie*, ii, 169.
52. *Brosse Missions*, 93.
53. *C.S.P. Foreign 1559-60*, 499-500.
54. *Brosse Missions,* 95.
55. *C.S.P. Foreign 1559-60*, 501-2.
56. ibid., 502-3.
57. *Brosse Missions*, 101-5.
58. ibid., 111-15.
59. *C.S.P. Foreign 1559-60*, 475-6.
60. ibid., 513-14.
61. Angl. Reg. xv, 82-3.
62. *Brosse Missions*, 121.
63. *C.S.P. Foreign 1559-60*, 560-1.
64. Teulet, *Papiers*, i, 574.
65. *Brosse Missions*, 125-33; Teulet, *Papiers*, i, 571-96; *C.S.P. Foreign 1559-60*, 585-6.

A SECOND JUDITH

1. *C.S.P. Foreign 1559-60*, 604-5.
2. ibid.
3. Knox, *History*, i, 319.
4. *Brosse Missions*, 141-9; Angl. Reg. xv, 106.
5. *Brosse Missions*, 147-9.
6. ibid., 151-9; *C.S.P. Foreign 1560-1*, 56-7.
7. *C.S.P. Foreign 1560-1*, 58-9.
8. ibid., 61-2.
9. *Seventh Report of the Royal Commission on Historical Manuscripts*, (London 1879), Atholl MSS., 714.
10. Knox, *History*, i, 319.
11. Angl. Reg. xv, 86-105.

12. ibid., 105–6.
13. *Brosse Missions*, 171–5.
14. Holinshed, *Chronicles*, v, 601–2; c.f. *Diurnal of Occurrents*, 277; Lesley, *History*, ii, 439–41.
15. Angl. Reg. xv, 113–14.
16. ibid., 112–13.
17. *Third Report of the Royal Commission on Historical Manuscripts* (London 1872), Sir P. Murray MSS., 412.
18. Angl. Reg. xv, 113–14; Pitscottie, *Historie*, ii, 171; Holinshed, *Chronicles*, v, 603; *C.S.P. Foreign 1560–1*, 116–26; *Diurnal of Occurrents*, 59, 277; Lesley, *History*, ii, 439–41.
19. *Brosse Missions*, 178–9.
20. *C.S.P. Foreign 1560–1*, 133.
21. *Treasurer Accts.*, xi, 24.
22. *C.S.P. Foreign 1560–1*, 143–4, 156.
23. Teulet, *Papiers*, i, 615.
24. *Diurnal of Occurrents*, 64; Knox, *History*, i, 359.
25. *Oraison, passim.* Memorandum of arrangements for funeral service, Archives Nationale, Memo 3B, f. 91.
26. *The Books called Apocrypha according to the Authorised Version* (Oxford n.d.), 89–101.
27. Knox, *History*, i, 322.
28. ibid., 122–3.
29. Lesley, *History*, ii, 441–3.
30. Holinshed, *Chronicles*, v, 603.
31. *C.S.P. Foreign 1560–1*, 106.
32. Pimodan, 170.

Index